The Style Thesaurus

LAURENCE KING

First published in Great Britain in 2023 by
Laurence King Student & Professional
An imprint of Quercus Editions Ltd
Carmelite House
50 Victoria Embankment
London EC4Y 0DZ

An Hachette UK company

A CIP catalogue record for this book is available
from the British Library.

HB ISBN 9781529421873
Ebook ISBN 9781529421880

10 9 8 7 6 5 4 3 2 1
Designed by TwoSheds Design
Cover design by Luke Bird and TwoSheds Design
Commissioning editor: Sophie Wise
Editor and project manager: Rosanna Fairhead
Additional research by Anupriya Dutta Gupta and Blazej Palka
Picture research by Angelika Pirkl, Igloo Picture Research

Printed and bound in China

Papers used by Quercus are from well-managed forests and
other responsible sources.

A definitive, gender-neutral guide to the meaning of style and an essential wardrobe companion for all fashion lovers.

The Style Thesaurus

Hannah Kane

Contents

Introduction

What are you wearing today? Take a step back from the mirror. Look down, and back up. Why did you pick this combination of items, arranged in a way that conveys your personality, and is deemed fit for your daily tasks of work and play?

Style has the potential to communicate through the basic processes of selection and combination. The clothes we wear have accrued meaning through history and culture, and function as a language that can, to some extent, be read. They act as a signal and can help the wearer find community with others who have similar interests and lifestyles.

Fashion versus style

Although often used interchangeably, the words 'fashion' and 'style' have separate, nuanced meanings. Fashion is the temporal process by which an idea, here in its most common meaning in relation to clothing, swings in and out of public favour. Style, meanwhile, is the presentation of those ideas as a form of expression.

In this thesaurus 'style' and 'aesthetic' are used almost as synonyms. Aesthetics is the philosophical study of beauty and taste. The eighteenth-century German philosopher Immanuel Kant proposed that taste is by its very nature personal and subjective, while in the twentieth century the French sociologist Pierre Bourdieu countered that individual taste is shaped by the influence of prominent social groups.[1] Having said that, an intricate haute-couture gown has no greater claim over aesthetics than a cheap dress from a fast-fashion brand, and it is not the job of aesthetics to tell anyone which to prefer.

This aesthetic appreciation, at times amounting to pleasure, encompasses everything from the feeling of watching a pastel sunset over the ocean to the human practices of art and design. Consumer trends in fashion are often mirrored in lifestyle areas, such as product design, architecture and interiors. As the contemporary fashion philosopher Lars Svendsen explains, 'We must choose a lifestyle and, as a style, the choice is basically an aesthetic one. Aesthetics, then, becomes a centre for the formation of identity.'[2]

1 Immanuel Kant, *Critique of Judgement*, trans. James Creed Meredith, rev. Nicholas Walker (Oxford: Oxford University Press, 2008); Pierre Bourdieu, *Distinction: A Social Critique of the Judgement of Taste* (London: Routledge, 2015).
2 Lars Svendsen, *Fashion: A Philosophy* (London: Reaktion Books, 2018), pp. 141–2.

Style as self-identity and subculture

The examination of style and its link to identity has its roots in the work
of scholars at the Centre for Contemporary Cultural Studies (CCCS),
established in 1965 at the University of Birmingham in the English Midlands.
One of the most influential texts to come out of this tradition was Dick
Hebdige's *Subculture: The Meaning of Style* (1979), which placed the
counterculture punk, mod, rocker, Teddy Boy and skinhead movements
under the microscope.

Hebdige defines style in four ways. Firstly, as communicative intent:
styles are meant to express something. Second, as bricolage: the innovative
recombination and assembly of readily available signs from material culture.[3]
Third, as homology: habits and preferences, such as the way of dressing
(tidy or unkempt, for example), poses and mannerisms, ideological values,
as well as music and dance choices. Fourth, style is a signifying practice:
the original styling of elements into a look can disrupt existing semiotics
(the understanding of signs) and create new ones.

In the intervening years the work of the CCCS has been carefully
unpicked and criticized, mainly for its assertion that young people are driven
to a style in order to rebel against the system, through subjugation rather
than by free will. There has been a shift in thinking away from the belief in
a fixed self-identity aligned to subcultures, towards one of constant self-
monitoring and revision. The Danish academic Dannie Kjeldgaard observes
that 'the usage of style becomes a matter of searching for and expressing
a personal (imagined) authenticity rather than a subcultural one.'[4]

In the twenty-first century subcultures and countercultures continue to
exist, but their appreciable styles have been opened to the whole of society
and reframed as a menu of available identities. Not every group takes
kindly to finding it is in vogue, however, as in the case of the goth, surfer
and skater cultures.

Style as neo-tribes

A shopping expedition down a high street or to a mall almost anywhere in
the world will confirm that a cacophony of styles is always readily available.

3   Assembling through found objects – 'styling', as it is known in relation to dress – is comparable
    to the bricolage method used by mixed-media artists, such as the twentieth-century American
    sculptor and painter Robert Rauschenberg, who called his work 'combines'. In fashion and style,
    most of the objects combined are bought rather than found.
4   Dannie Kjeldgaard, 'The Meaning of Style? Style Reflexivity among Danish High School Youths',
    Journal of Consumer Behaviour, VIII/2–3 (2009), pp. 71–83.

There is no one trend to rule them all. According to academics, this is thanks to postmodern subcultural theory, which has helped to frame social groups as 'neo-tribes'. Postmodernism, which started in about 1970, saw the dawn of the internet in the 1980s and became a well-defined topic of academic research in the 1990s, brought new self-awareness about style.

The human need for acceptance runs deep, whether as part of the mainstream or in the most alternative community. Neo-tribes are groups centred on shared leisure lifestyles. The sociologist Michel Maffesoli explains that neo-tribes are not as rigid as forms we have already come to accept, but can be seen more as 'a certain ambience, a state of mind'.[5] He observed that, surprisingly – given how ephemeral the neo-tribe's bonds are – they often elicit strong conformity among members. The reason for this was considered by some writers, among them the sociologist and philosopher Zygmunt Bauman, to be the breakdown of such traditional social categories as social class, gender and ethnicity. Bauman explains that postmodern fragmentation has resulted in 'a desperate search for structure', which we can read in fashion terms as a search for community.[6]

Tribal manifestations are fluid not only in their participants but also in their components. The academic Robin Canniford considered that, 'connected to the rapid processes of bricolage, tribes emerge, morph, and disappear again as the combinations of people and resources alter.'[7]

Style as language

Style comes laden with meaning, and with the potential to communicate the most hidden parts of the human psyche to others. Clothing can accrue meaning through combinations of signs. The linguist Ferdinand de Saussure's basic dyadic model of semiotics encompasses the 'signifier', or the form the sign takes, and its 'signified' meaning.[8] Other thinkers built on this purely psychological theory to put forward the 'signifier' as the physical, material form, and the 'signified' as the concept or meaning.[9]

The philosopher Charles Sanders Peirce saw a triadic relationship between the form of the sign, the meaning encoded in it (what it stands for),

5   Michel Maffesoli, trans. Don Smith, *The Time of the Tribes: The Decline of Individualism in Mass Society* (London: SAGE Publications, 1996), p. 98.
6   Zygmunt Bauman, *Intimations of Postmodernity* (London: Routledge, 1992, 2003), p. xv.
7   Robin Canniford, 'How to Manage Consumer Tribes', *Journal of Strategic Marketing*, 19 (2011), pp. 591–606.
8   Ferdinand de Saussure, *Course in General Linguistics*, ed. Charles Bally and Albert Sechehaye, trans. Wade Baskin (New York, Toronto, London: McGraw-Hill, 1966).
9   Notably by the Danish linguist and semiotician Louis Hjelmslev.

and its interpretation.[10] The meaning of the sign is relative to the interpreter; beauty is always in the eye of the beholder. Peirce divided signs into three groups. Firstly, there are icons, which have universally accepted meanings, for example the 'save' icon on a computer program. Second, mental indexes make direct connections between things: smoke usually equals fire, a knock on a door means someone is there, and dark clouds signify rain. Third, there are symbols, in which meaning is contained in an abstract form. Symbols are arbitrary, and rely on meaning accrued by the general understanding of them. Peirce wrote about language, and about the meanings understood of ordinary words, such as 'bird', 'give' and 'marriage'.

In *The Fashion System* (1967), the semiotician Roland Barthes recognized that clothing similarly functioned as symbols, and considered the written language of fashion specifically through the text used in fashion magazines.[11] In *The Style Thesaurus* we consider the accumulated meanings of styles that are widely understood within the fashion industry in their written, verbal and visual forms.[12] We consider the specifics of garments, such as a wide lapel that says '1970s', or a pie-crust collar that says 'neo-Victoriana'. Some details must be seen in context if we are to pinpoint their meaning; lace, for example, could say 'gothic' or 'romantic' depending on its colour (black or blush pink, respectively). As time passes and world events unravel, the meanings of garments and styles may change, in the same way as the meanings of words can be fluid.

It is worth noting that brands also act as what Saussure called signifiers, yet often they are identified by icons, such as the double-C logo for Chanel, or the LV logo for Louis Vuitton.[13] The essence of branding is differentiation from the competition, and brand identities are solidified into products that convey intentional narratives. Conspicuous consumption helps to mark the dividing lines between neo-tribes, and brands can become iconic, signifying a specific lifestyle or set of values.

Style as a good life

The pursuit of a good life means choosing a lifestyle, and style as aesthetics plays a significant part in perceived quality of life. The appreciation of beauty and artistic pursuits elevates the human experience.

10 Charles Sanders Peirce, *A Syllabus of Certain Topics of Logic* (Boston, MA: Alfred Mudge, 1903).
11 Roland Barthes, *The Fashion System* (London: Vintage Books, 2010).
12 Written in magazines, brand copywriting and communications regarding creative direction for photo shoots.
13 Arthur Asa Berger, 'The Branded Self: On the Semiotics of Identity', *American Sociologist*, XLII/2–3 (2011), pp. 232–7.

At the pinnacle of Abraham Maslow's well-known model from 1943, the 'Theory of Human Motivation', was self-actualization, the peak of human flourishing and personal fulfilment.[14] Maslow revised the model in 1970 to add cognitive and aesthetic needs just below self-actualization, and later that year he added transcendence above it, as a kind of nirvana. He referred to these upper tiers of the pyramid as 'growth needs', distinguishing them from the lower four levels, which he called 'deficiency needs'.

There is widespread anecdotal evidence for the transformative power of well-considered clothes. Remember that time you wore a great outfit to a party? You felt great and had a great time. Rarely do those moments happen by pure accident, and at some level there is a requirement for the brain's creative input.

If the brain is fully engaged, for example when getting ready for a big party or wedding, the style is deliberated by the central processing route. The alternative is that the outfit was 'thrown on' almost instinctively, perhaps assembled from whatever was clean at the end of the bed, using the brain's peripheral processing route, which rolls down familiar neural pathways. But even such unconscious decisions are telling. They are a message from the id, our most authentic self, which is driven by instinct and impulse.[15] It is said that good style is a combination of the two approaches: considered during the assemblage, and not given another thought for the rest of the day.

How styles form via trends

In 1962 the theorist and sociologist Everett Rogers published his elegant 'Diffusion of Innovations' (DOI) theory. In it he focused on the characteristics of the individual in relation to trends, and whether they belong to the category of pioneering innovators, fashion-forward early adopters, the on-trend early majority, the conservative late majority, or finally the sceptical laggards who catch the tail end of a new idea only as it fades into obscurity. According to Rogers's model, the diffusion could take months or years.

The DOI theory aligns with the cycle of fashion trends, with its five phases: the introduction of a trend; its acceptance and rise in popularity; the peak, when it's 'hot' and appears to be everywhere; its decline just as quickly into bargain bins and sales; and finally obsolescence, when it is considered

---

14 Abraham H. Maslow, 'A Theory of Human Motivation', *Psychological Review*, ᴜ/4 (1943), pp. 370–96.
15 Sigmund Freud, *The Ego and the Id*, in *The Standard Edition of the Complete Psychological Works of Sigmund Freud*, trans. James Strachey et al., vol. xix (London: Hogarth Press, 1923).

Gareth Pugh Spring/Summer 2009, Paris Fashion Week, 27 September 2008.

'out of fashion' and can't be given away. If the trend is adopted rapidly before dying almost immediately, it was merely a fad.

The more durable of these trends wax and wane without ever fading away. They become classics: among them the Little Black Dress, the beige trench coat, the perfect pair of straight-cut blue denim jeans, and the black leather jacket. These are the foundations of a timeless wardrobe, and fashion stylists believe that such garments are worth investing in. The classics can be more than just specific garments; they can encompass whole styles and looks and become permanent aesthetics, encoded with meaning.

Ideas are prone to being recycled, and designers have been looking to the past for inspiration for the duration of what we recognize as the modern fashion industry. For his collection in 1908 the great Parisian designer Paul Poiret revisited the style of the French Revolution's Directoire period (1875–9), which imagined dresses as flowing columns of fabric, rejecting the corsetry of Poiret's own time. The original Directoire style itself referenced neoclassicism, and through it the ancient Greco-Roman principles of simplicity, virtue and symmetry served as a counterpoint to the extravagance of the Rococo styles that preceded the French Revolution.

There are numerous examples of retrospective fashion with decades referencing other decades, such as the Swinging Sixties' obsession with the hemlines and mood of the Roaring Twenties, and the 1980s' interpretation of the 1940s' silhouette with structured shoulders, belted waists and wide-brimmed hats. In the mid-2000s researchers noticed that the cycle had sped up, thanks to the digital age, with the revival of such 1990s trends as grunge and hip hop. In the 2020s Y2K and mid-2000s trends were already being excavated for meaning. Given enough time, almost everything swings back into fashion – with the possible exception of the Jacobean ruff, which is overdue a comeback.

How trends diffuse across society

When mass-produced clothing first appeared in the West after the Industrial Revolution, as a product of the new capitalism, it was intended to provide consumers with clothing to wear during forthcoming seasons: spring/summer and autumn/winter. The major historic fashion capitals were in the northern hemisphere, so that meant clothing that was suitable for a particular climate. Today's household-name fashion houses have grown from their beginnings in the hands of creative founders into dynasties and megabrands. At the top of the fashion chain is haute couture, the highest artistic level whereby products are custom-made for the client. Brands must be invited by the Fédération de la Haute Couture et de la Mode – the governing body for the French fashion industry – to show at Couture Week in Paris. Below couture is ready-to-wear, also known as 'prêt-à-porter', the off-the-peg options offered by luxury designer brands. These brands may also have diffusion lines that target more price-conscious consumers. Below this is the mid-market, which acts as a bridge to the high street and mass-market fashion at the base of the chain.

The classic trickle-down theory postulates that since Western industrialization fashion trends have been created by the upper classes, or on high-fashion catwalks, before descending to mass-market brands and value retailers. The newer trickle-up theory of subcultures and countercultures suggests that some trends are born on the street, noticed by designers and crystallized into ideas on the editorially attended runways. In reality, the path of trend diffusion is rarely linear any more, as customers engage with one another and with brands across many touchpoints.

In the digital age, consumers are no longer divided by geographical distance. Trends are diffused across society at the speed of light through fibre-optic cables. Smartphones hold the world in a palm, and on social media microtrends bubble and pop before the season changes. In the mid-2020s some 1.81 trillion photographs are taken worldwide annually. By 2030 that number is predicted to grow to 2.3 trillion.[16] Billions of hours of video content are shared across such platforms as Instagram and TikTok/ Douyin. Engagement through likes, shares and follows eases the feeling of postmodern loneliness. Our image communicated via still or moving images matters.

The rise of artificial intelligence will have an impact on every sector. In the fashion industry there are companies that analyse millions of images shared on social media every day, to give quantitative data on the evolution of consumers' preferences. Heuritech, for example, created in 2013 by two doctors of machine learning, analyses three million images daily and can recognize more than 2,000 apparel details.[17] The data is sold back to retailers, whose design teams and buyers may make the trend-forecast clothes a reality. The garments are purchased and snapped for the consumer's social media, and the images fed back into the machine as the ghost of a trend.

16 Matic Broz, 'Number of Photos (2023): Statistics, Facts and Predictions', Phototutorial, 21 February 2023, www.phototutorial.com/photos-statistics.
17 Data from Heuritech, 2023; www.heuritech.com.

Style and sustainability

Ethically conscious fashion devotees across the world debate whether the agent of over-consumption is the capitalist, money-hungry fashion brand as the producer, or the consumer who buys the product. Clearly, there should be ethical consideration at all stages of a product's life cycle, from design and ideation, to manufacture and distribution, to retail, purchase, wear and end-of-life recycling.

The problem is not people wanting to change their looks, but the fact that they buy new clothes each time that happens. Fashion brands are weapons of mass consumption: an inordinate number of garments are produced each year across the world, of which 92 million tonnes end up in landfill. If the trend continues, the waste output is expected to reach 134 million tonnes a year by 2030.[18]

Style could be an answer. If meaning is encoded through the assembly of products, there is nothing to say that the products assembled must be new. Research by Dr Carolyn Mair, a cognitive psychologist working in the fashion industry, and published by Oxfam shows that it is indeed possible for consumers to find newness through the rearranging of second-hand goods.[19] Furthermore, the thrill of buying new clothing fades after around four wears, but 25 per cent of participants in Mair's research said the sense of newness lasted longer when buying second-hand. This is hardly ground-breaking for many, and according to Thredup, a leading online retailer of second-hand and consignment clothes, the worldwide second-hand and resale market is set to grow from $96 billion in 2021 to $218 billion in 2026.[20] By 2030, the Ellen MacArthur Foundation estimates, it could reach $700 billion.[21]

The good news is that once the stylist or wearer understands the communicative intent of a style, they can create a myriad of styles from a modest selection of garments and accessories. *The Style Thesaurus* is a guide to enclothed meaning.

18 Martina Igini, '10 Concerning Fast Fashion Waste Statistics', Earth.org, 2 August 2022, www.earth.org/statistics-about-fast-fashion-waste.
19 Carolyn Mair, 'Does the Thrill of Buying a New Item of Clothing Last Longer When You Buy Second Hand?', Oxfam blog, 16 August 2022, www.oxfam.org.uk/oxfam-in-action/oxfam-blog/does-the-thrill-of-buying-a-new-item-of-clothing-last-longer-when-you-buy-second-hand.
20 Thredup, *Resale Report*, 2022, www.thredup.com/resale.
21 'Rethinking Business Models for a Thriving Fashion Industry', Ellen MacArthur Foundation, www.ellenmacarthurfoundation.org/fashion-business-models/overview (accessed 28 February 2023).

How to Use the Thesaurus

The styles described in this book are intended to inform all types of styling. They can provide inspiration for personal styling and communicating identity. They can be used as a reference for stylists, to aid story-telling for photo shoots, style other people, and create magazine editorials, as well as costumes for film and television. The book is also intended for influencers and bloggers, as self-led communicators of an image – in finding both their own style and the words to describe it – as well as for fashion journalists and marketers.

The first section, Time, describes clothing shaped by the political, economic, social, environmental, technological and legal factors of an epoch, whether real or imagined, past, present or future. To an extent, all fashion can be situated in time. The second section, Utility, looks at how clothing was elevated from the basic need for protection from extremes of temperature and precipitation as we walked, rode, drove and sailed to the four corners of the Earth, then took to the air and ventured into space beyond. The third section, Music & Dance, looks at styles that have evolved through their symbiotic relationships with musical genres and dance styles. The fourth section, Play, opens the dressing-up box and pulls out styles that represent our true selves, authentic, spontaneous and light-hearted. The fifth section, Conformists, understands the need for security of employment and acceptance within social groups, while the sixth, Subcultures & Countercultures, explores rebels and those who dare to oppose the status quo. The seventh, Statement, looks at styles that to a greater or lesser extent communicate ideas and philosophies. The final section, Sex & Gender, explores the function of style in love and belonging, sexual intimacy and attracting a mate.

Key

Each style begins with a header. The first line, with the symbol ◐, references what the style is also known as, giving near synonyms. The next line, with the symbol ◑, identifies those styles described in the entry that have their own entry elsewhere in the thesaurus. In some cases, styles are discussed in relation to their near antonyms, so this list can include opposing styles. Styles that are involved in the formation or dissemination of the style under discussion are also referenced here.

The line that follows, with the symbol ●, names common pairings with other styles in the book. For the sake of clarity, named styles appear here or in the previous line, but never in both. As time passes, many styles pair authentically with those that immediately preceded or followed them chronologically. The styles can of course be used in any combination, and the pairings are merely suggestions; they are not intended to be prescriptive. Indeed, the art of good styling is to include many references in an outfit.

The main text for each style delves into its history and its later expression on catwalks or in popular culture. When a style from elsewhere in the thesaurus is mentioned in the entry, it is underlined and cross-referenced. We explore garments or details that are key to symbolizing the style, and discuss the wider context and world events that shaped it. Terms that appear in the glossary are given a wavy underline.

At the end of each entry is a box containing an overview of key signifiers of the style. 'Colours and patterns' shows the key palette associated with the style, including commonly occurring prints. 'Fabrics' gives a nod to some of the textiles seen in the style. The two exceptions in the thesaurus are digital fashion (which is an anomaly and does not have specific fabrics or design details) and heritage (the patterns and textiles of which vary according to origin). Where these lines are absent, it is intentional.

'Garments and accessories' lists the key products associated with the style. 'Details' gives the flourishes: the length of hemlines, the cut of the pattern, and types of embellishment. It is impossible for such a list to be exhaustive, but the intention is to allow the reader to understand key components of the styles. Finally, where relevant, 'Hair and Make-Up' describes the styling features commonly adopted by those who wear the style.

Author's Note

Style is culture.

Wherever I travel, I am captivated by what people are wearing and how they present their image to others. The clues that people give to their personality through dress are telling, and sometimes they can be read like a book. Style is a powerful tool for self-expression, helping us to connect with like-minded people. It can be adapted for different environments, to fit in or stand out.

In the many years I have worked in fashion as a journalist, lecturer and consultant, I have been involved with hundreds, perhaps thousands of fashion photo shoots, whether as art director or producer, or selecting the pictures at the editing stage. The entries in *The Style Thesaurus* cover some of the most durable aesthetics that reappear time and again on the catwalk and on the street, and through the lenses of magazine editorials. I have analysed the same trends at catwalk shows and in street-style photography at fashion weeks. In my experience, these styles are widely understood within the fashion industry as meaning a specific arrangement of garments, fabrics, textures and colours.

I should add a caveat. Although it is not my intention to be reductionist, by necessity, styles as they have become distilled into the general consciousness will be prone to stereotyping. There is also the possibility that the list of styles in this book could be considered heavy on 'Western' influences, although – as I explained in the introduction – social media in the digital age means that to some extent trends have been homogenized across the globe. My aim throughout is to celebrate the diversity of human expression.

No style exists in a vacuum. While writing this book I have been constantly struck by the extent to which all styles are connected, forming threads in time that weave their way back to the present. We are all stylists, assembling meaning to find our tribes. I hope you will use this thesaurus to read the world.

Time

Fashion is a zeitgeist, the spirit of its time. As any marketing graduate will explain, it is shaped by 'STEEPLE' factors: Sociocultural, Technological, Environmental, Economic, Political, Legal and Ethical. This is why hemlines rose with the emancipation of women, and why daywear became infinitely more casual during the Covid-19 pandemic.

Some styles, such as the flapper, are inherently connected to a moment in time. Some, such as cyberpunk, are a vision of a time yet to come. This section highlights styles that bear a sense of either past or future (or both, as in the case of retrofuturism).

Fashion is cyclical by nature, and for decades designers have been looking to the past for inspiration. The great Parisian couturier Paul Poiret is widely considered to be the first modern fashion designer in his approach to fashion as an art form. For his collection published in the illustrated work *Les Robes de Paul Poiret* in 1908, he was influenced by the Directoire style of the late eighteenth century, presenting dresses as unstructured columns of fabric that shunned the rigid corsetry of France's belle époque or the Victorian era in Britain. The Directoire style itself referenced neoclassicism, and ancient Greco-Roman principles of simplicity, virtue and symmetry were mined nostalgically during Napoleon Bonaparte's reign, as a counterpoint to the extravagance of the Baroque and Rococo styles that preceded the French Revolution. While women embraced versions of the draped

1.

ancient Greek chiton, men did not follow suit and revert to tunics and togas. They did cut their hair short as a statement against Louis XVI's flowing locks, and to this day short hair remains the prevailing style for men.

Latent for periods of time, garments and aesthetics reappear with unfailing certainty. Even the corset – banished by Poiret – made a comeback courtesy of Vivienne Westwood, in her Autumn/Winter 1990 'Portrait' collection, as a feminist reappropriation of sexuality. The early 2020s zeitgeist for all things 90s, including Westwood, and the popularity of the Regency-core Netflix show *Bridgerton*, led to the return of the corset once more.

Aesthetics that reference a future that may or may not come to pass represent another approach to the perception of time. They constitute an arena for stylists and designers to have fun with fashion, and have had a strong mutual influence with film and popular culture. For aesthetics influenced by the popular music styles of particular decades, see section 3, <u>Music & Dance</u> (p.108).

Retro

◑ VINTAGE, REVIVALIST
→ NEO-VICTORIANA, FLAPPER, ATHLEISURE, PUNK, PREPPY,
   BOURGEOISIE, SLOANE, BCBG, SKINHEAD, DANDY
⊕ ROCKABILLY, TEDDY BOYS & TEDDY GIRLS, FUNK, DISCO,
   HIPPY, MOD

Retro styles are those that are knowingly derivative of the past.
They are different from 'vintage' clothing, which refers to authentic
items from a bygone era; 'retro' describes the old-world aesthetic
of a garment, whether it be newly made or an original piece.
It is curiously hard to perceive the stylistic impact of a decade
while it happens. Only through the lens of time can many of the
peculiarities of microtrends be distinguished.

   Silhouettes shifted dramatically during the twentieth century,
especially for women. The 1920s were famous for the newly boyish
silhouette of the Flapper style (p.30), but hemlines dropped to the
floor again in the 1930s as the glamour of golden-age Hollywood
took hold. Rationing in the 1940s ushered in simple, utilitarian
garments, with hems just below the knee and nipped-in waists.
Two years after the end of the war Christian Dior unveiled his New
Look, resplendent with full skirts and fluted sleeves (although fabric
rationing continued until the end of the decade). The hourglass
figure Dior popularized continued into the 1950s, parallel to an
equally modish trend for streamlined sheath dresses and boxy
jackets. Music-loving teens of the 1950s were influenced by the
leather and denim of Rock & Roll (p.110), while in Britain Teddy
Boys & Teddy Girls (p.115) made a case for reinventing the tailored
style of the Edwardian Dandy (p.247). The Space Race of the
1960s and a Futuristic zeitgeist (p.33) ushered in the clean lines of
modernism (see Mod, p.228), with slim-cut suits and a new sexual
liberation signposted by the miniskirt, which tumbled into the
flowing Bohemian (p.217) style of the 1970s and the continuing
influence of the free-spirited Hippy (p.223) movement.

   For men, up to this point, lapel widths and trouser legs ebbed
and flowed (see also Tailoring, p.195). The palette was by and large

sombre until the peacock revolution of
the 1960s, spearheaded by such icons
as the Beatles, James Brown (see Funk,
p.137), Mick Jagger (see Classic Rock,
p.118), John Travolta and David Bowie
(see Glam Rock, p.122).

Both the Skinhead (p.237) and
Punk (p.125) movements rejected the
loving nature (and long hair) of hippy
counterculture, but in different ways.
The former were militantly working
class in beanie hats, braces (suspenders)
and monkey boots, while the latter
rejected all social conventions entirely,
destroying garments before fixing them
back together with studs and safety pins.

Club culture saw languid Disco
(p.139) styles reign on the dance floor,
but by the 1980s disco was extinguished
to make way for Hip Hop (now referred

Gucci Spring/Summer 2016, Milan Fashion Week, 23 September 2015.

to as 'old-school hip hop') with its casual, Athleisure (p.60) and
Preppy (p.191) aesthetic. At the same time, the increasingly
wealthy middle-class Bourgeoisie (p.202) – specifically the achingly
posh London Sloane (p.205) and its Parisian equivalent, BCBG
(p.207) – roamed some of the world's most desirable postcodes
wearing cashmere knits and silk scarves.

Not every trend of yesteryear conjures the mental picture of
a retro style. Grunge (p.134) in the 1990s and the reboot of Y2K
styles in the 2020s are referred to by fashion writers as 'nostalgic'
rather than retro, and this tends to be the case the first time a trend
cycles back within living memory. That is not to say, either, that any
old style is automatically retro, since styles more than 100 years old
gravitate towards historical. For example, the corsets, crinolines and
bustles of the Victorian age (see Neo-Victoriana, p.26) are rarely
referred to as retro, while the mid-century styles from the 1950s to
the 1970s very much are. A general rule is that anything between
10 and 30 years old is merely nostalgic, while over 30 years old
is retro, becoming historical once it is 100 years old or more. The
table overleaf describes the broad trends of the twentieth century.

Retro cont.

	HEMLINE	LAPELS	WAIST	TROUSERS	COLOURS/PATTERNS/DETAILS
1910s	maxi, tubular silhouette	standard	corseted (F); high (M)	tapered, cuffed at the ankle, with creases	jewel colours, black, grey, old rose, check, hobble skirt, three-piece lounge suit, showing the ankle
1920s	above the knee, calf-length, asymmetric	peak	dropped (F); natural (M)	wide/baggy	navy, brown, gold, hunter green, burgundy, violet, black, florals, polka dots, geometric patterns, stripes, ribbons, boat necklines, beading, embroidery, large brooches, strings of pearls, cloche hat
1930s	mid- to low calf	wide	high, belted	wide, turned up at the hem, with creases	raspberry, brown, mauve, pink, ditsy prints, small dots, thin stripes, florals, bows, ruffles, pleats, satin evening gown, low back, first use of nylon and zips
1940s	midi, below the knee	wide	natural and fitted	wide, pleated	primary colours, stripes, abstract prints, florals, check, sharp shoulders, pocket square
1950s	knee-length, A-line	slim	high/ hourglass (F); loose (M)	straight, cropped, loose-fitting	black and white, yellow, red, pink, teal, polka dots, large florals, polo shirt, tweed suit and jacket
1960s	mini	narrow; later wide	straight	slim	white, pale blue, yellow, orange, brown, paisley, tropical prints, Pucci prints, gingham, babydoll dress, pinafore
1970s	micro, mini, maxi	wide	high	flared, wide, bell bottoms	earth colours, batik, tie-dye, Indian prints, frayed denim, platform shoes, kaftan, bell sleeves, floppy hat
1980s	below the knee	notched; peak	high	peg; also tights, joggers and sweatpants	black, red, white, neon yellow, geometric patterns, graphic prints, embellishments, pleats, skirt suit, double-breasted jacket, braces (suspenders), leotard, oversized sweatshirt, baggy top with wide belt
1990s	mini	peak	low	baggy	jewel colours, animal prints, bleached/ dark denim, slip dress, aviator glasses, sweatshirt, bucket hat
2000s	asymmetric	narrow or wide	low, very low	bootcut	white, pale pink, purple, iridescent, animal prints, logos, blue denim, UGG boots, crop top

Heritage

◉ CULTURAL
◑ PUNK, DANDY
⬤ CLASSIC

Trends become homogenized as they are diffused across
traditional and social media, and with an increasingly connected
world comes the danger of a shift towards a global monoculture.
To prevent this, the United Nations Educational, Scientific and
Cultural Organization (UNESCO) protects local crafts, traditions
and techniques through its 2003 Convention for the Safeguarding
of the Intangible Cultural Heritage.

Fashion is an important symbolic metaphor of the relationship
between individuals and the cultural systems in which they
operate, and it can be a subtle yet powerful way of expressing
and reinforcing values, relationships and meaning. Humans have
constructed a variety of elaborate meanings to textile making
and dress, from the women's brightly coloured and patterned
silk headscarves known as kelaghayi, made in the Republic of
Azerbaijan, to the painstaking technique of point d'Alençon
needle-lacemaking, practised in the town of Alençon in Normandy
(each square centimetre takes seven hours to complete), the
ancient craft of barkcloth making by the people of the Buganda
kingdom in southern Uganda, and the Japanese ways of producing
handwoven, tie-dyed vegetable ramie fabric, known as Ojiya-
chijimi and Echigo-jofu, in Niigata Prefecture.

Even within the commercial fashion industry, some traditional
fabrics are protected, such as luxurious Harris tweed from
northwestern Scotland, which is covered by its own Act of
Parliament and must be 'handwoven by the islanders at their
homes in the Outer Hebrides, finished in the Outer Hebrides, and
made from pure virgin wool dyed and spun in the Outer Hebrides'.
Vivienne Westwood is said to have described the fabric as 'the
royalty of the cloth world', and in fact her iconic logo incorporates
the Harris tweed orb, surrounded by Saturn's rings. Even the art of
making suits is protected by the Savile Row Bespoke Association,

founded in 2004 to promote the heritage of custom tailoring practised on this famous London street (see Dandy, p.247).

Fashion as the perpetual carousel of newness is balanced with a desire among consumers for tradition, and the search for timeless style can be referred to as 'anti-fashion' (see Classic, p.209). Branding experts have established that heritage and authenticity are drivers of fashion consumption, and storytelling around brand heritage continues to add value to companies. Antiquity alone is not enough to confer heritage status upon a brand, however, and there must also be an emphasis on the historical content of the brand's identity.

Dressing in a 'heritage' style treads a fine line between celebration and cultural appropriation. No one could have a problem with a Chinese customer wearing the quintessentially British Burberry check, a design introduced in the 1920s. Similarly, a Western customer wearing a modern Shanghai Tang cheongsam dress or Tang jacket is deemed acceptable, despite Shanghai and Hong Kong both adopting the UNESCO Convention to curate their own lists of cultural practices, including details of the proper fabrication of the Shanghai qipao and the Hong Kong cheongsam.

Where is the line between cultural appreciation and cultural appropriation drawn, then, and who gets to choose? It is still a topic of discussion for fashion academics why a kilt is deemed permissible by most Scots, but a Native American headdress at Coachella is always offensive. Celebrating one's own cultural heritage is always acceptable. Appreciating another's depends on on the frame of reference, and the wearer should respect the culture enough to educate themselves on the meaning of specific garments and fabrics. There are some items that will always be off limits, such as those bearing religious, spiritual or sensitive historical context, and tribal symbolism.

Neo-Victoriana

≈ OLD-WORLD, PRIM AND PROPER
→ <u>EQUESTRIAN</u>, <u>RURAL</u>, <u>BOHEMIAN</u>, <u>LA SAPE</u>, <u>ROMANTIC</u>, <u>FETISH</u>
⊕ <u>STEAMPUNK</u>, <u>PRAIRIE</u>, <u>COTTAGECORE</u>, <u>LOLITA</u>, <u>GOTH</u>

We cannot understand Neo-Victoriana without understanding the Victorian aesthetic itself. Named after the era-defining British queen Victoria, who reigned from 1837 until her death in 1901, the period itself ran from about 1820 until roughly 1914. While Charles Darwin was unravelling the mysteries of evolutionary biology and Charles Dickens was an unprecedented publishing sensation, the mass-manufacturing processes that had been ushered in by the Industrial Revolution meant greater affordability and variety of garments. Many clothmakers saw the potential of an increasingly wealthy middle class and moved to open department stores. Arguably the first of those was Le Bon Marché in Paris, founded in 1838. Harrods in London opened its doors in 1849, and in 1852 came Chicago's Marshall Field's, where an illustrious partner called Harry Gordon Selfridge later cut his teeth in retail before bringing the glamour of the US department store to London under his own name in 1909.

As the engine of consumerism fired up, the working class moved in droves to the cities, which had not caught up with running water and proper sewage disposal to support the burgeoning population. Typhoid, tuberculosis and cholera were rife. The smog from coal-fuelled power stations turned the houses black, and urban-dwelling Victorians favoured black clothes that didn't show the soot.

A reaction to the advances of industry came with a nostalgia for the past and a sense of the <u>Romantic</u> (see p.263), with a revival of medievalism and its ideals of chivalry and virtue. The textile designer William Morris was inspired by the naturalistic designs of medieval and Gothic tapestries. He belonged to the group known as the Pre-Raphaelites, a 'brotherhood' of young English artists and art critics who were against the rigid promotion of the Renaissance master Raphael by the esteemed Royal Academy. The group's

Joseph Abboud Autumn/Winter 2016 Menswear, New York Fashion Week, 2 February 2016.

Neo-Victoriana cont.

founding artists Dante Gabriel Rossetti, William Holman Hunt and John Everett Millais brought a new realism to painting, influenced by the legend of King Arthur, the work of Shakespeare and Chaucer, and tales of medieval romance and chivalry. Victorian dresses are often pictured in paintings by the Pre-Raphaelites with the fluted sleeves, square necks and flowing skirts of medieval dress.

In tandem, the autotelic idea of 'art for art's sake', which is credited in its original form to the nineteenth-century French poet Théophile Gautier, would become the maxim of free-spirited Bohemians (p.217). Rebelling against conservative Victorian values, followers of the Aesthetic Movement – among them the colourful Irish poet Oscar Wilde – dressed to shock. The bespoke bronze-and-black coat cut in the shape of a cello that he is said to have worn to an opening-night party at the Grosvenor Gallery in London is in some ways reminiscent of the work of the Italian Futurists (p.33).

It is clear that not all representations of Victorian-style dress have the same meaning. Colonial expansion during the era resulted in bloodshed in many countries. The Herero people of Namibia underwent the first major genocide of the twentieth century at the hands of German missionaries, with much of the violence directed towards the women. Those ladies were initially forced to adopt Victorian-style dresses, but today these garments are celebrated as an integral part of their heritage and identity, serving as a reminder of the past. The brightly coloured, elegantly subversive gowns can contain up to 10 m (33 ft) of fabric, and a girl's first handmade dress is a rite of passage into womanhood. The Herero dress known as *ohorokova* is styled with a horn-shaped *otjikaiva* hat that references the importance of cattle as a status symbol within the community. (For more on Europe's colonial past and its impact on global styles, see La Sape, p.240.)

However, it is the great optimism and ingenuity of the Victorian era with its advancements in science and medicine that feed into Neo-Victoriana and the associated retrofuturistic style of Steampunk (p.42). Neo-Victoriana also lends its overtly feminine ruffles to the girlish Lolita style (p.177), and its roots in Gothic literature are a key reference point in Goth style (p.220).

Neo-Victoriana appeared as a Hipster subculture in the 2000s (p.226), represented in popular culture in such movies as Guy Ritchie's *Sherlock Holmes* (2009). Since then it has been a perennial trend on the catwalk, inspiring the rural-loving Cottagecore (p.161), among other styles. Horse riding adds such details as leather harnesses and riding boots to Neo-Victoriana (see Equestrian, p.70), and Fetish (p.293) lends it a BDSM edge.

Queen Victoria herself set some enduring trends. She chose a white dress for her wedding to Prince Albert (at the time a bold choice, now de rigueur for many brides). After the death of her beloved husband, she wore black every day until her own passing 40 years later, setting the standard for mourners for decades to follow.

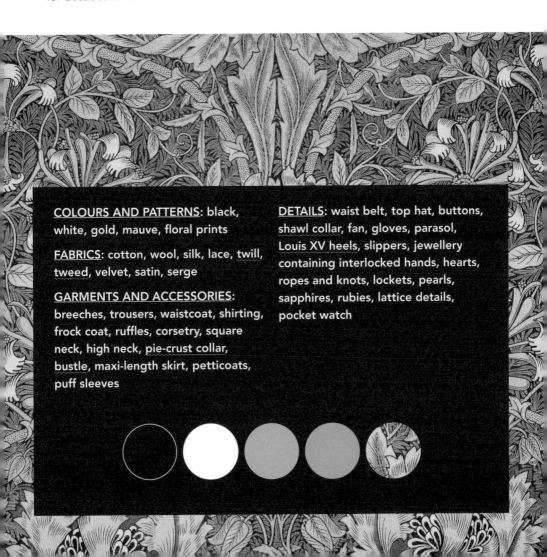

COLOURS AND PATTERNS: black, white, gold, mauve, floral prints

FABRICS: cotton, wool, silk, lace, twill, tweed, velvet, satin, serge

GARMENTS AND ACCESSORIES: breeches, trousers, waistcoat, shirting, frock coat, ruffles, corsetry, square neck, high neck, pie-crust collar, bustle, maxi-length skirt, petticoats, puff sleeves

DETAILS: waist belt, top hat, buttons, shawl collar, fan, gloves, parasol, Louis XV heels, slippers, jewellery containing interlocked hands, hearts, ropes and knots, lockets, pearls, sapphires, rubies, lattice details, pocket watch

Flapper

⊜ JAZZ BABY, EDDY
➡ RETRO, CAMP
⊕ ANDROGYNOUS, GARÇONNE, MODEST

The flapper is immortalized in popular culture as the iconic image
of the sleek bob-haired girl in a short, fringed dress, dancing the
Charleston with cocktail in one hand and cigarette in the other. But
by focusing on the visual aesthetic only, this stereotype undermines
the significant influence the flapper had on societal attitudes
towards gender and indeed on our very sense of modernity.

Young people in the 1920s could be forgiven for wanting to
have some fun. World War I left nearly 20 million soldiers and
civilians dead worldwide, and another 21 million injured, and was
punctuated at its end by the so-called Spanish influenza pandemic
of 1918–19, which killed another 50 million or so as it swept across
the globe. It was a frightening time, made worse by the pandemic's
unusual characteristic of a high mortality rate in those who were
young and otherwise healthy.

Women had taken up the jobs of men during the war, proving
their capability as more than housewives and mothers. In August
1920, in the United States, the 19th Amendment to the Constitution
was ratified, granting women the right to vote. While the suffrage
movement was strong in the United Kingdom, spearheaded
by such advocates as Emmeline Pankhurst, it wasn't until the
Representation of the People (Equal Franchise) Act of 1928 that
men and women were for the first time granted equal voting rights.

In the background was the Art Deco movement, which
flourished after World War I. It celebrated the decorative arts,
such as furniture, sumptuous textiles, fashion and jewellery, and
technology (with such exciting new inventions as radios, vacuum
cleaners, cars and glamorous ocean liners). A new era of luxury,
consumerism and glamour came sailing in. Aesthetically it had its
roots in the abstracted, geometric lines of Cubism and the bright,
impressionistic colour palette of Fauvism, both movements that
had arisen in France at the beginning of the century. Travel opened

Louise Brooks, c. 1926.

people's eyes to the wonders of the East, which led to what would now be considered colonial 'Orientalism', while the discovery of Tutankhamun's tomb in Egypt in 1922 inspired a fascination with adventure in the desert.

The corset had fallen out of favour in 1908 with the designs of Paul Poiret, but the war effort killed it off entirely as women took to wearing brassieres and unstructured lingerie, to allow them to work more easily in the factories. Women wanted the freedom that men had, figuratively and literally, and in defiance they cut their hair short; some even bound their chests for a flatter silhouette, in a dramatic move away from the unnatural 'S' curve of the Edwardian era. Gabrielle 'Coco' Chanel borrowed design details from menswear, popularizing trousers and boxy <u>blazers</u> for the first time. The androgynous <u>Garçonne</u> look (p.273) was born. By 1925

Flapper cont.

women's hemlines were at the knee, arguably the shortest they'd been in recorded history. (In the Early Dynastic Period in Egypt, about 3150–2613 BCE, upper-class women wore floor-length dresses, while humbler men and women wore simple knee-length kilts; interestingly, bare breasts were not a problem in ancient Egypt for women of any station. See Modest, p.284.)

As women became emancipated, shifting gender norms allowed young men to express their more feminine side, too. A flapper was a 'Sheba' and her male counterpart a 'Sheik', after the dashing silent-movie idol Rudolph Valentino, who starred in *The Sheik* (1921), based on the popular desert romance novel of the same name by E.M. Hull. And so it was that the Italian immigrant actor formally known Rodolfo Alfonso Raffaello Pierre Filibert Guglielmi di Valentina d'Antonguolla popularized the 'Latin Lover' look, with rakish, slicked-back hair, what looked suspiciously like eyeliner, and face powder. He was a trendsetter and bona fide heart-throb, although not all of society was ready to see men embrace their femininity (see Camp, p.275).

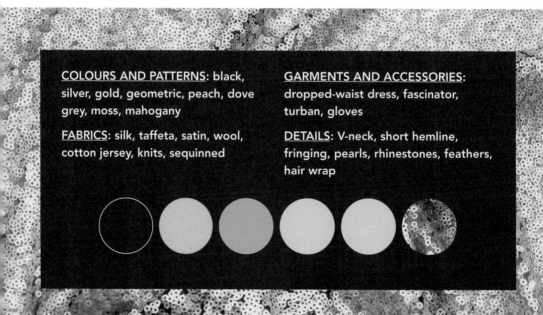

COLOURS AND PATTERNS: black, silver, gold, geometric, peach, dove grey, moss, mahogany

FABRICS: silk, taffeta, satin, wool, cotton jersey, knits, sequinned

GARMENTS AND ACCESSORIES: dropped-waist dress, fascinator, turban, gloves

DETAILS: V-neck, short hemline, fringing, pearls, rhinestones, feathers, hair wrap

Futurism

⊖ FUTURISTIC
➡ MOD
⊕ AVANT-GARDE

What does a futurist look like? In the aesthetic sense, Futurism started with the modernist art movement that arose in 1908–9, when the Italian poet and editor Filippo Tommaso Marinetti published his *Manifesto of Futurism*. Futurism celebrated velocity, industry, urbanism and technology. The roaring motor car was deemed more beautiful than a work of art in the Louvre, and the Italian artists who led the movement – among them Umberto Boccioni, Carlo Carrà and Luigi Russolo – wanted to break free from their country's past, which they considered to be mired in classicism.

The *Manifesto* glorifies war as a signifier of change, renounces museums, libraries and academics, and is often cited as anti-feminist (although Marinetti clarified later that his 'contempt of woman' referred to the idealized versions of 'woman' as an institutional homemaker, femme fatale and muse). In fact, the movement went on to welcome female artists as a break from tradition, and such Futurist painters as Marinetti's wife, Benedetta Cappa, helped to pave the way for first-wave feminism. The Futurists' artworks were united in their dynamism and use of colour, capturing the essence of speed in a manner that has its roots in the rapidly distilled painting styles of the post-Impressionists and Cubists.

The Futurists were not just artists and political agitators; they also had plans to revolutionize gastronomy, performance, architecture

Courrèges Spring/Summer 2022, Paris Fashion Week, 29 September 2021.

Futurism cont.

and fashion. Giacomo Balla described their new style in his *Futurist Manifesto of Men's Clothing* (1914), which includes a description of fast fashion: 'WE MUST INVENT FUTURIST CLOTHES, hap-hap-hap-hap-happy clothes, daring clothes with brilliant colours and dynamic lines. They must be simple, and above all they must be made to last for a short time only in order to encourage industrial activity and to provide constant and novel enjoyment for our bodies. USE materials with forceful MUSCULAR colours – the reddest of reds, the most purple of purples, the greenest of greens, intense yellows, orange, vermilion – and SKELETON tones of white, grey and black. And we must invent dynamic designs to go with them and express them in equally dynamic shapes: triangles, cones, spirals, ellipses, circles, etc. The cut must incorporate dynamic and asymmetrical lines, with the left-hand sleeve and left side of a jacket in circles and the right in squares.'

A notable development in garment types was the invention of the jumpsuit, credited to the Futurist designer Ernesto Michahelles, who went by the name Thayaht. Designed in 1920 to be unisex, utilitarian and inexpensive to make, the all-in-one was called a *tuta*, from the Italian *tutta*, 'all'.

Chronologically, the next visual representation of the future style came when the literary genre of science fiction began to be made into movies. First came the towering cityscapes and metal humanoid robot, 'Maria', of the silent film *Metropolis* (1927), directed by the German Expressionist Fritz Lang, and in 1936 came an adaptation of H.G. Wells's *Things to Come*, which introduced minimal silhouettes, short hemlines, sculptural shoulder details, round collars, long capes and white fabrics as signifiers of the style. *Flash Gordon* (also 1936) added metal accents, more flesh on show, more round necklines and collars, and more capes, as well as an unfortunately xenophobic portrayal of an East Asian villain in Ming the Merciless.

The term 'futurology' – the study of current trends to predict future scenarios – was coined by the German professor Ossip K. Flechtheim in the 1940s. Along with mid-century modernism and the atomic-age optimism of the 1950s, this forward-looking sensibility inspired the designers André Courrèges, Pierre Cardin and Paco Rabanne (see also Mod, p.228) to create their now iconic 'space-age' designs of the 1960s. The house of Paco Rabanne, known for the designer's debut couture collection, '12 Unwearable Dresses in Contemporary Materials' (1966), took the concept of 'unwearable' a step further in 2023 with a collection of twelve conceptual NFT dresses (see <u>Digital Fashion</u>, p.54).

In 66 years humanity advanced from the first Wright Brothers' flight to landing a man on the moon. The Space Race gave futurism and futuristic clothes new touchpoints, which designers interpreted as the liberating trapeze silhouette (similar to A-line, with narrow shoulders but a wider hem), flat-soled mid-calf boots, helmets and goggles in the style of astronauts, oversized glasses, reflective silver fabrics, bodysuits, cut-outs, and a palette of clinical white offset with bold primary colours. Echoing the dynamism of the original Futurists, Courrèges and Cardin knew that women didn't walk through life any more; they ran, they danced, they drove cars, and their clothes must be able to move too. Popular culture absorbed these catwalk trends, only to project them back via the costume designs of such TV shows as *Star Trek* and *Lost in Space* in the 1960s.

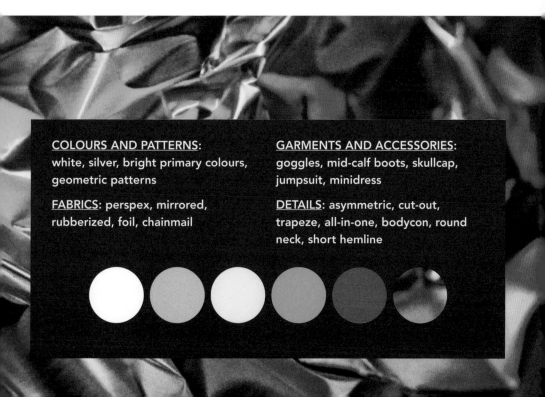

COLOURS AND PATTERNS:
white, silver, bright primary colours, geometric patterns

FABRICS: perspex, mirrored, rubberized, foil, chainmail

GARMENTS AND ACCESSORIES:
goggles, mid-calf boots, skullcap, jumpsuit, minidress

DETAILS: asymmetric, cut-out, trapeze, all-in-one, bodycon, round neck, short hemline

Retrofuturism

◉ RETROFUTURISTIC
➔ RETRO, NEO-VICTORIANA
⊕ CYBERPUNK, STEAMPUNK, DIESELPUNK, AFROFUTURISM

The 1970s gave us the gloriously over-the-top style of Glam Rock (p.122), and David Bowie's Ziggy Stardust character, who ticked all the boxes for futuristic costume: boldly striped all-in-one, plastic boots, oversized shoulders, and make-up with planetary symbolism. While Ziggy was always forward-looking, other creatives of the time began to reassess past visions of the future, giving rise to retrofuturism.

From a fashion perspective, retrofuturism has a couple of meanings. Firstly, it is immortalized in the 'youthquake' ideology of 1960s space-age designs, an optimistic view of the future as seen from the past. Second, it transposes Retro styles (p.20), such as Neo-Victoriana (p.26) and early Cowboy (p.79), to an alternative time somewhere between past, present and future, as in the subgenre Steampunk (p.42), or Dieselpunk's (p.45) fusion of World War I and II uniforms (see Military, p.91) and roaring internal-combustion engines.

COLOURS AND PATTERNS: silver, black, white

FABRICS: plastic, perspex, chainmail, aluminium

GARMENTS AND ACCESSORIES: miniskirt, knee-high boots, jumpsuit

DETAILS: mandarin collar, sculptural details

Jane Fonda in the film *Barbarella*, 1968.

Cyberpunk

● MATRIX
● STEAMPUNK, DIESELPUNK, DIGITAL FASHION, PUNK
● COMBAT, RAVE, GOTH, FETISH

Somewhere in a dystopian near future, in a neon-hued cityscape, we meet cyberpunk. It emerged in its proto form as a literary genre from the minds of such New Wave science-fiction writers as Roger Zelazny, J.G. Ballard, Philip José Farmer and Harlan Ellison, crystallizing in the 1980s into the style we now recognize. The term 'cyberspace', meaning 'widespread, interconnected digital technology', is credited to William Gibson in his short story 'Burning Chrome' (1982), two years before his acclaimed debut novel *Neuromancer* (see also Digital Fashion, p.54).

As a recurring theme, cyberpunk offers a nihilistic view of an advanced capitalist society imploding, with themes of crime, drugs and sex, as well as transhumanism through technology, robotics and artificial intelligence. It is a 'high-tech, low-life' aesthetic.

Cyberpunk was the first of the Retrofuturistic styles (p.36) to be described, and is at the root of the other 'punk' derivatives, such as Steampunk (p.42) and Dieselpunk (p.45). Whether or not it is truly Retro (p.20) is up for debate. It does, however, align with highly stylized film-noir tropes of the 1940s: the lone crime-fighting protagonist, the dark urban scenery, and the fusion of grit and glamour.

Through silver-screen incarnations, cyberpunk has collected elements of retro dress from the 1940s, 80s and 90s. It is heavily influenced by science-fiction films, among them *Blade Runner* (1982), based on the novel *Do Androids Dream of Electric Sheep* (1968) by Philip K. Dick. It is set in an imaginary 2019 in Los Angeles, where replicant humans are engineered by a powerful corporation to work on space colonies. In the 1980s there was a return to the nipped-in waists and shoulder pads of Dior's 'New Look', and *Blade Runner*'s costume designer, Charles Knode, makes direct visual references to that silhouette for the beautiful replicant Rachael, played by Sean Young. The protagonist, retired

Carrie-Anne Moss as Trinity in the film *The Matrix Reloaded*, 2003.

Cyberpunk cont.

detective-turned-replicant hunter Rick Deckard (played by Harrison Ford), wears an oversized trench coat – a classic film-noir garment – styled with graphic patterned shirt and tie to add a Futuristic element (p.33). (It is said that Ford – fresh from filming *Raiders of the Lost Ark* – refused to wear a fedora in *Blade Runner* to complete the film-noir trope, because he had already become known for his hat as Indiana Jones.) The leader of the replicants is dressed in a floor-sweeping black leather trench coat, which becomes a recurring item of dress.

The iconic anime *Akira* (1988) by the Japanese manga artist Katsuhiro Otomo – also set in an imaginary 2019 – offers an Eastern take on the style. Its iconography of the decaying metropolis has echoes of Tokyo or of Hong Kong's now demolished Kowloon Walled City, which had become a notoriously lawless place run by triad gangs. The Japanese influence on cyberpunk is sometimes interpreted as a cute Kawaii style (p.170). Another anime masterpiece, the cult film *Ghost in the Shell* (1995), continues the black-and-chrome colour palette and reinforces hacker culture and cybernetics as a theme, as seen also in the film *Johnny Mnemonic* of the same year, based on another story by Gibson.

There is disagreement over whether cyberpunk is truly 'Punk' (p.125). 'Punk' was originally a Shakespearean-era term for a prostitute, and later it came to mean any outsider or hoodlum. In this sense, the noir crime fighter at odds with society fits the description loosely. By the 1970s 'punk' had acquired its meaning of counterculture rebellion, which materializes in the long leather trench coats of *The Matrix* (1999), along with elements of techwear and what the internet likes to call 'warcore': hardcore Military details (p.91), such as combat boots and trousers, buckles and straps. There is also an element of DIY fashion, with distressed edges; textiles are deliberately unnatural and designed to shock, with slick black latex and PVC taking elements from Fetish style (p.293). Contemporary designers, such as Rick Owens, Gareth Pugh and Yohji Yamamoto, have added to the narrative.

Within cyberpunk lies the subculture cybergoth, which fuses elements of Rave (p.146) and Goth (p.220). The disaffected youth will see in the apocalypse, dancing to industrial techno in sheer, body-conscious clubwear and Y2K faux-fur shrugs. Artificial dreadlocks, circuit-board tattoos, alien heads, equalizer motifs and body modifications, such as horns and subdermal piercings, are signifiers of the look. It should be noted that artificial cyberlocks can cause offence and constitute cultural appropriation, as the American designer Marc Jacobs found after styling his (predominantly white) models with a spectrum of rainbow-coloured dreads for his Spring/Summer 2017 show.

    As we hurtle towards the metaverse, cyberpunk starts to feel more like the present and less like the future.

COLOURS AND PATTERNS: black, chrome, neon pink, neon blue, neon purple, acid yellow

FABRICS: leather, PVC, fishnet, spandex

GARMENTS AND ACCESSORIES: trench coat, combat boots, ripped knitwear, rimless micro sunglasses

DETAILS: 1940s styles, body-con, buckles and straps, DIY and distressed, robotics

Steampunk

⊛ VICTORIAN FUTURISM, CLOCKPUNK, RETRO TECH
➡ <u>COWBOY</u>
⊕ <u>NEO-VICTORIANA</u>, <u>COSPLAY</u>

Inspired by such nineteenth-century writers as H.G. Wells and Jules Verne, and playing on the technology and ideas of that time (steam engines, airships, clockwork, alchemy), steampunk was the second derivative retrofuturistic style to be described. The term itself was coined only in 1987, allegedly by the writer K.W. Jeter, author of *Morlock Night* (1979), in a letter to the science-fiction magazine *Locus*: 'Personally, I think Victorian fantasies are going to be the next big thing, as long as we can come up with a fitting collective term for [Tim] Powers, [James] Blaylock and myself. Something based on the appropriate technology of the era; like "steam-punks", perhaps.' The look had manifested much earlier in Japanese manga and anime of the 1950s, such as *Nextworld* (1951), written and illustrated by Osamu Tezuka; and into the 1970s, as in the female-focused *Rose of Versailles* (1972).

Steampunk's dapper scientists in their British Edwardian, French Napoleonic <u>Dandy</u> finery (p.247) or <u>Neo-Victoriana</u> (p.26) seem at odds with our understanding of <u>Punk</u> (p.125), but elements of punk's DIY aesthetic can be seen in steampunk's celebration of ingenuity. There are some who call themselves steampunks who do engage with the political aspects of punk, addressing such nineteenth-century issues as colonialism, imperialism and class divides, and their aftermath.

As a form of speculative fiction, steampunk can also be transplanted to the American Wild West (see <u>Cowboy</u>, p.79) or take on fantastical elements. Cinema has plundered the steampunk aesthetic in myriad films, from the reworking in 2002 of H.G. Wells's *The Time Machine* (1960), to *Wild Wild West* (1999), *Sky Captain and the World of Tomorrow* (2004), Guy Ritchie's *Sherlock Holmes* (2009) and *Fantastic Beasts and Where to Find Them* (2016).

MGPIN Collection show by Maogeping Image Design Art School at the Mercedes-Benz China Fashion Week, Beijing, 27 March 2013.

Steampunk cont.

Fashion has a soft spot for steampunk, with its dramatic juxtaposition of sharply cut suits, corsets, voluminous bustle skirts and sculptural metal hardware, and its penchant for an overload of accessories. As a trend, it remains on a long orbit, latent for extended periods outside its popularity in Cosplay (p.158) and other fancy dress. It cropped up on the runways of Ann Demeulemeester Autumn/Winter 2009, Dior Autumn/Winter 2010 and Prada Autumn/Winter 2012 menswear, among others, and is an ongoing reference at Alexander McQueen in the punky structured leather and metal dresses, coats and trousers.

COLOURS AND PATTERNS: brown, copper, grey, black, beige, tan, white, dark green, burgundy

FABRICS: leather, hemp, jute, cotton, linen, velvet, lace

GARMENTS AND ACCESSORIES: tailcoat, breeches, corsetry, bustle skirt, suit and tailoring, waistcoat, top hat, bowler hat, pocket watch, goggles, parasol

DETAILS: shirting, frogging, cogs, screws, pipes, DIY and distressed

Dieselpunk

⊜ BIO SHOCK
➔ RETRO
⊕ BIKER, COSPLAY

The horrors of World War II spawned ideas of terrifying alternative futures for writers of speculative fiction, such as Len Deighton and Philip K. Dick, whose respective counterfactual novels *SS-GB* (1978) and *The Man in the High Castle* (1962) consider the consequences had the Nazis won. These proto-dieselpunk works influenced later writers and filmmakers.

Dieselpunk literature imagines a future reliant on gas-guzzling fossil fuels, as seen in the *Mad Max* franchise. Often post-apocalyptic, this comes with the semiotics of an imagined return to humans' roots in tribal societies with ragged clothes, dirty skin and rune-like tattoos.

With cyberpunk as their genesis, further retrofuturistic styles have been disseminated. Among them are biopunk (cyberpunk, but using biotechnology), solarpunk (an optimistic view of the future based on renewable energy and low tech), lunarpunk (a similar eco-based future with space themes, planets, dark florals and sorcery), medievalpunk (from the Middle Ages), bronzepunk (from the Bronze Age), silkpunk (like steampunk, but based on Eastern aesthetics and philosophy) and atompunk (the 1950s atomic era, concerned with nuclear power). The genre of retrofuturism continues to evolve.

Left to right: Charlize Theron, Zoë Kravitz, Courtney Eaton, Riley Keough, Tom Hardy and Nicholas Hoult in the film *Mad Max: Fury Road*, 2015.

<u>**COLOURS AND PATTERNS**</u>: black, pewter, gunmetal, sand, blood red

<u>**FABRICS**</u>: leather, cotton, hemp

<u>**GARMENTS AND ACCESSORIES**</u>: flight suit, aviator jacket, biker jacket, overalls, goggles, gas mask, pillbox hat, <u>fedora</u>

<u>**DETAILS**</u>: 1950s styles, military details

Afrofuturism

◉ AFRODIASPORIC CULTURAL MOVEMENT
◓ FUTURISM, PUNK
✛ CYBERPUNK, GLAM ROCK, FUNK

Earlier forms of Futurism (p.33) promised the stars; however, they did not adequately represent the Black diaspora. For many there was a deeper metaphor to be found in the narrative of the white man invading unknown worlds, and kidnapping people via alien abduction.

The Afrofuturism movement liberates Blackness from the prevailing narrative of historical events, presenting an alternative and optimistic future of a Black utopia, which reconnects with lost tribal heritage. The term 'Afrofuturism' was coined in 1994 by the cultural critic and writer Mark Dery in the essay 'Black to the Future', published in his book *Flame Wars*. He explained, 'The notion of Afrofuturism gives rise to a troubling antinomy: Can a community whose past has been deliberately rubbed out, and whose energies have subsequently been consumed by the search for legible traces of its history, imagine possible futures?'

The cultural movement emerged in the 1920s from the science-fiction writing of W.E.B. Du Bois in his short story 'The Comet', via Octavia E. Butler and the avant-garde free jazz of the 1950s and 60s. Such artists as Sun Ra (who claimed to be from Saturn) and his big band Arkestra defined the genre with their album *Space Is the Place* (1972), as well as John Coltrane and the blues artist Jimi Hendrix, who was an avid science-fiction fan.

The 1960s obsession with futuristic themes is seen in such television shows as *Star Trek*, where Nichelle Nichols broke new ground with her authoritarian role as communications chief Lieutenant Nyota Uhura, sharing television's first interracial on-screen kiss with William Shatner's Captain Kirk in 1968. Despite the public controversy, Nichols was persuaded to stay on the show by Dr Martin Luther King Jr, who recognized the importance to the general public of seeing Black astronauts, doctors and professors represented on television.

Lupita Nyong'o (left) and Letitia Wright in the film *Black Panther*, 2018.

In the 1970s and 80s, artists such as George Clinton and Bootsy
Collins (both of Parliament-Funkadelic) and Prince infused futurism
indelibly with Funk (p.137), and Grace Jones added a New Wave
'glam-punk' edge (see Glam Rock, p.122, and Punk, p.125).
During his short but prolific career, the artist Jean-Michel Basquiat
expressed Afrofuturist themes of abstracted heads resembling
robots or African masks in his works. In the 1990s the duo Outkast
(see Hip Hop, p.142) and the R&B star Erykah Badu continued
the look, and such artists as Janelle Monáe, Kendrick Lamar,
Thundercat, Childish Gambino and Solange Knowles are taking
the Afrofuturism baton forward.

The Afrofuturism look fuses futuristic motifs, such as technology
and sustainable materials, with African crafts and mysticism.

Afrofuturism cont.

In contemporary popular culture it appears in the Cyberpunk (p.38) armour of the millennium-era vampire-hunting trilogy *Blade*, starring Wesley Snipes, and notably in the film *Black Panther* (2018), with costumes by Ruth E. Carter, who won the Academy Award for Best Costume Design. Carter incorporated several elements from African peoples, including the neck rings of the Ndebele of South Africa, cloth inspired by the scarified body modifications of Nuba women and the Dinka people of Sudan, and the red cloth of the Maasai of Kenya.

On the catwalk, the British designer Priya Ahluwalia, who has Indian and Nigerian heritage, the streetwear blog-turned-fashion label Daily Paper, and many other Black designers and music artists continue to channel this relevant retrofuturistic style.

COLOURS AND PATTERNS: gold, silver, red, blue, orange, bright green, yellow, black leopard print, giraffe print, zebra print, snake print, Ankara prints, isi-agu (lion-head) print

FABRICS: leather, cotton, velvet, kente cloth, *aso-oke*, *ukara*, *adire*, *bogolan*, wood

GARMENTS AND ACCESSORIES: cloak, flares, bodysuit, technical wear, armour, dashiki/kitenge tunic, isicholo

DETAILS: stars and moons, beads, sequins, armour details, visor, wood, necklaces, anklets, Egyptology

HAIR: Bantu knots, Fulani braids, flat top

E-Boy & E-Girl

◉ ELECTRONIC BOY, ELECTRONIC GIRL, ELECTRONIC EMO
◉ COSPLAY, DECORA, ACADEMIA, PREPPY
⊕ EMO, GRUNGE, KAWAII, GOTH, SKATE, ANDROGYNOUS

The Electronic Boy and Electronic Girl are Gen-Z digital natives who live their lives online, often gamers with a presence on the streaming platforms Twitch or Discord. Emerging around 2018 on the social-media platform TikTok, this style borrows many of its signifiers from previous approaches. The internet-fuelled melting pot of style fuses the sadness of Emo (p.129) with the palette of Goth (p.220), the angst of Grunge (p.134), the countercultural philosophy of Skate (p.231), the provocative nature of BDSM (see Fetish, p.293), the school uniform and intellectualism of Academia (p.188), the innocence of Kawaii (p.170), and the eclecticism and self-expression of Decora (p.173), adding cartoonish elements of Cosplay (p.158) and the gender-fluid beauty of K-pop.

As is common when defining subcultures, 'E-girl' was originally a derogatory term, used against females who entered the gaming sphere. It has now morphed into a word to describe an attractive, alternative girl with an online presence. The perception of E-girls as sirens using their looks online for attention and/or money springs in some part from the TikTok craze for the hyper-sexualized *ahegao* pose, commonly seen in Japanese *hentai* (animated porn): eyes rolled back in ecstasy, face flushed, heart symbols in the eyes, mouth open, tongue lolling. Some E-girls also adopt doll-like dresses similar to those of the Lolita style (p.177). However, like most trends for Gen-Z – a demographic raised on memes – there is an underlying irony to the look. It has its roots in the original Tumblr Girl look from the mid-2000s, where girls would produce planned yet candid ('plandid') shots of themselves 'waking up' with a full face of make-up and artfully dishevelled hair.

E-boy and E-girl are gender-fluid terms, and make-up plays a large part in the look, often referencing the cartoonish colours of Japanese anime. E-boys are characterized by their flowing hair, use of blusher and black nail polish – 'soft-boy' elements used by the

E-Boy & E-Girl cont.

actor Timothée Chalamet and the musician Yungblud at the start of the trend. A Soft Girl or Soft Boy revels in their beta status, choosing intellect over brawn (see also <u>Academia</u>, p.188, and <u>Preppy</u>, p.191), and often has a predilection for pastels. Some proponents of the look focus on such themes as mental health and addiction, as well as a general sense of malaise, calling themselves 'sadboys' and 'sadgirls'.

The look bubbled up to the catwalk via the designer Hedi Slimane for the Spring/Summer 2021 Celine menswear show, which provided a checklist of E-boy garments: tailored trousers, pleated skirt, flannel shirt, silver chains, beanie and skate shoes.

Yungblud performs at the Tabernacle in Atlanta, Georgia, 28 January 2022.

The electronic emo was firmly on the luxury fashion radar.

In contrast to the E-girl is the VSCO girl, named after the photo-editing app VSCO, which allows users more control when editing their pictures and places less emphasis on the number of 'likes' a picture receives. VSCO girls are defined by a narrow segment: the all-American Californian Surf aesthetic (p.234) with clean, natural make-up, cut-off denim shorts, oversized tee and baseball cap: healthy, wholesome, and noticeably white and suburban.

Social media continues to spawn new aesthetics that diffuse quickly around the world. The ubiquitous Instagram look known as 'Baddie' is worn by strong, sexually confident women and characterized by a tight-fitting Body-Conscious silhouette (p.287), often with cropped tees and sweatpants and never without a full face of make-up, lashes and nails for the run to the drugstore. Kim Kardashian has a lot to answer for.

COLOURS AND PATTERNS: black, white, pastel pink, pastel blue, pastel purple, pastel green, black-and-white stripes, black-and-white checks, stars and moons, hearts, checks and tartan, leopard print

FABRICS: cotton, denim, sweatshirt jersey, fishnet

GARMENTS AND ACCESSORIES: white and black dress shirt, cropped tee, oversized tee, long-sleeve tee, skater and band tee, pleated miniskirt, kilt, polo neck

DETAILS: layers over layers, hoody, chain belts, skater shoes, chunky boots, brothel-creeper shoes, chains, tattoos and piercings (especially septum), beanie hat, safety pins, stockings, hair clips, round spectacles, animal-ear headbands, headphones

HAIR: long hair, two-tone hair, pigtails, space buns, curtains

Digital Fashion

- AVATARS, WEB 3.0, METAVERSE STYLE
- AFROFUTURISM
- FUTURISM, CYBERPUNK, STEAMPUNK

Humans will in the future spend more and more time inhabiting an extended reality comprising augmented-, virtual- and merged-reality experiences. In 1992, in his influential Cyberpunk (p.38) novel *Snow Crash*, the writer Neal Stephenson coined the term 'metaverse' to describe 'a world beyond the physical realm in which we find ourselves'. The book connected William Gibson's *Neuromancer* (1984) with Ernest Cline's novel *Ready Player One* (2011), which was made into a film by Steven Spielberg in 2018.

Simply put, the metaverse is the internet in three dimensions: a place where we find ourselves shopping, socializing, learning and working in increasingly immersive digital environments, supported by technology such as headsets, earpieces and motion-detecting gloves that allow us to use natural gestures as we navigate the space. In its relative infancy in the 2020s (comparable to the internet of the 1990s), the metaverse appears as a fragmented collection of separate worlds, among them Decentraland, Roblox, the Sandbox and Bloktopia, although interoperability is the vision. Most of these worlds – where virtual land can be bought and sold, NFTs (non-fungible tokens) traded, and other users interacted with socially – are powered by a specific blockchain, such as the decentralized open-source blockchain Ethereum. Ether is its native cryptocurrency, like bitcoin or dogecoin, but the metadata on its blockchain also records who is holding and trading the digital asset. It provides irrefutable proof of provenance and can be attached to both tangible and intangible assets. These 'smart contracts' are automated, self-executing and irreversible.

In this parallel computer-generated existence, we still wear clothes, a fact that presents infinite opportunities for brands to market their products. In 2021 Nike, ahead of the curve, acquired the digital sneaker and collectibles pioneer RTFKT (pronounced 'artefact') for a figure rumoured to be close to $1 billion. The

Leomie Anderson wearing the Institute of Digital Fashion's accessory on the red carpet of the Fashion Awards at the Royal Albert Hall, London, 29 November 2021.

Digital Fashion cont.

same year Facebook rebranded to Meta, staking out its three-dimensional intentions, and the American investment multinational Morgan Stanley predicts that the metaverse and NFTs will comprise 10 per cent of the luxury-goods market by 2030, an opportunity worth $50 billion.

Digital fashion wearables are often sold as non-fungible tokens. Whereas fungible tokens are divisible and non-unique ($1 in Washington is the same as $1 in London, and 1 bitcoin is the same everywhere), NFTs are unique. You could swap an Hermès Birkin for another Hermès Birkin, but it wouldn't be the same bag. The digital item can be 'worn' within a specific metaverse platform, or brought to life through augmented reality, projecting its image into your space using a smartphone or tablet. Some NFTs come with both real and digital versions of the garment, as well as access to exclusive customer experiences – the ultimate in loyalty programmes.

In 2022 the alternative music artist Grimes closed the inaugural Metaverse Fashion Week as part of a show on the Decentraland platform, wearing a CGI bodysuit designed by the digitally native 'luxury' house Auroboros. According to the designers, the bodysuit was inspired by the shape-shifting *X-Men* character Mystique, and Ruth E. Carter's Academy Award-winning futuristic costumes for *Black Panther* (2018; see Afrofuturism, p.48).

Digital fashion can also be worn using augmented-reality lenses in the social-media platforms Snapchat, Instagram and TikTok, making it a promising solution to social media's insatiable appetite for new content on the one hand and the problem of disposable fast fashion on the other. At the Fashion Awards in London in 2021, the Institute of Digital Fashion invited guests on the red carpet to try on an otherworldly digital accessory resembling a body harness of metallic feathers via augmented reality, built to be inclusive of all bodies, abilities and genders. It was later minted as an NFT on the digital fashion platform The Dematerialised, where it sold out in 24 minutes.

There is a rapidly evolving trend for brands to use virtual influencers in marketing communications. Miquela Sousa, a permanently 19-year-old Brazilian-Spanish CGI 'robot' who 'lives' in Los Angeles, has modelled for such brands as Prada and Calvin Klein. In reality, Sousa is neither a robot nor powered by artificial intelligence (AI), but merely a digital puppet operated by a savvy marketing team at the tech company Brud and brought to life through digital imagery. Prada also revealed its own digital spokesperson, Candy, who has fronted a perfume campaign. Virtual humans powered by AI will eventually become commonplace, replacing chat bots for customer service and able to interact seamlessly with humans. Shudu, proclaimed the 'world's first digital supermodel' by her creator, Cameron-James Wilson, can only put on clothes originally designed in 3D, or must wear real-world clothes through a composite image of a human model photographed as the 'muse' wearing the look, laid over Wilson's image of Shudu.

Hardcore gamers have inhabited virtual spaces for years and are familiar with purchasing in-game 'skins', cosmetic add-ons that customize the look of a character. Collaborations between fashion brands and video-game creators started in 2012 with *Final Fantasy* x Prada; in 2015 there was a pop-culture moment with *Super Mario* x Moschino, followed in 2020 by *Animal Crossing* collaborations with a host of brands, from Net-a-Porter to Valentino, and Autumn/ Winter 2021's *Fortnite* x Balenciaga collaboration. Fashion brands, keen to engage on an experiential marketing level with Gen-Z, have developed 'advergames': stand-alone games developed to advertise a brand's product or collection. Balenciaga's *Afterworld: The Age of Tomorrow*, for instance, was used to promote the fashion house's Autumn/Winter 2021 range.

In virtual spaces it is common for people to design their avatar to resemble their real-world form (a phenomenon known as the Proteus effect). Some design a similar but 'improved' version of themselves, while others are happy to detach from the real world completely and self-identify as an alien or mythical creature. This opens an exciting realm of creativity for fashion designers. Balenciaga for your dragon avatar is surely only a few seasons away.

Digital NFT fashion sites:
  The Dematerialised, www.thedematerialised.com
  The Fabricant, www.thefabricant.com
  OpenSea, www.opensea.io
  Known Origin, www.knownorigin.io
  RTFKT, www.rtfkt.com

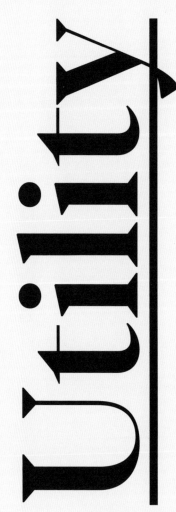

Utility

Clothing is fundamental to humans' physiological need for protection from the elements. With our frail flesh we are ill equipped, compared with other mammals, to deal with extremes of temperature and exposure. This section explores styles that have evolved from the need to shield ourselves, to move to the best of our ability, and to go into battle.

Military clothing worn by members of armies, navies and air forces merged the functionality required for physical exertion with the pomp of rank. Warfare moved from hand-to-hand combat to the use of long-range weapons, and with that came the need for stealth and camouflage. The armed forces remain among the most enduring influences on fashion trends, reappearing unfailingly from year to year.

For five thousand years humans' equine companions were the fastest mode of transport available, allies in war and peace until just over 100 years ago, when their humble one horsepower was usurped by the internal-combustion engine. Our shared history is hidden in plain sight today in the details of suit jackets. Manufacturers of strong, pliable leather harnesses and saddlery, such as Hermès and Gucci, extended their product ranges to become purveyors of luxury accessories, and from there made the jump into ready-to-wear.

Cowboys rode horses to round up livestock, and in the process stamped the enduring image of the Wild West on Americana like

2.

a brand on a bull. With them came the frontier spirit of daily life on the prairie. South of the border, the cattle-herding lifestyle was mirrored by the gauchos and their uniquely woven textiles, touched by Spanish design influences.

Humans like to go fast, by road, sea or air. While motorbikes were initially a gentleman's ride in the 1920s and 30s, by the 1950s they were an accessible option for World War II veterans and rebels with or without a cause. Biker culture's tough black-leather-clad aesthetic collided with rock and roll and never left it.

In more recent times, sports, artificial technical fabrics and the increasing casualization of dress have instigated a shift towards athleisure clothing as the norm everywhere from street to catwalk. Urban professionals espouse the merits of expedition-worthy gear, even if merely venturing to the local bodega. Utilitarian style generally prioritizes function over form, and for that we can be thankful. Clothe yourself for the environment and you will never be overdressed.

Athleisure

● ACTIVEWEAR, CASUAL, LOUNGEWEAR
● POLO
⊕ HIP HOP, NORMCORE

The apocryphal tale of athleisure is that the Canadian retail
magnate Dennis J. 'Chip' Wilson, who founded Lululemon in 1998,
made the wearing of yoga pants from mat to brunch, boardroom
and bar a global trend. Although Wilson made a significant
contribution, 'athleisure', a portmanteau of 'athletic' and 'leisure',
meaning wearing activewear in everyday life, has been around
at least since the tennis and Polo (p.76) players of the 1920s.
That said, it developed considerably after the invention of such
technical fabrics as spandex (known also by its brand name, Lycra)
in the 1950s, and subsequent innovations such as Dri-Fit polyester,
which wicks moisture away from the skin, and 3D knits.

Athleisure was born on the track and grew up on the streets.
Tracksuits, first worn by athletes to warm up before and warm
down after training in the 1930s, became a trend away from the
track in the 1970s, and when the Hip Hop scene (p.142) blazed in
in the 1980s, Run-DMC made the Adidas signature three-stripe
tracksuit an iconic look. In the 1980s and 90s the tracksuit became
a countercultural emblem worn by disaffected youth around the
world. This group garnered various derogatory terms, among them
'chav' in the UK, where they were associated with the hooliganism
of football terraces; *racaille* in the suburbs of France; and *gopnik*
in Russia, Ukraine and Belarus, where they were influenced by
Adidas's Soviet Union team uniforms for the Moscow Olympics
in 1980, as well as the 1980–81 strip of the football club Spartak
Moscow. Some of the hottest fashion designers of the twenty-first
century – including the Russian Gosha Rubchinskiy and Georgian
Demna Gvasalia (first as the founder of Vetements in 2014 with his
brother Guram, and from 2015 as creative director of Balenciaga)
– firmly reference this post-Cold War youth-led aesthetic.

As might be expected, American fashion brands spearheaded
the casual revolution, among them Original Penguin (established

American hip-hop band Run-DMC, c. 1985.

1955), Nike (1964), Calvin Klein (1968), Perry Ellis (1976) and
Tommy Hilfiger (1985). On the catwalk, athleisure first started
to make an appearance around 2010, when Alexander Wang
interpreted it via an American football aesthetic, and his
collaboration with H&M in 2014 was a hit from San Francisco to
Shanghai. The designer admitted to living in sportswear, despite
not being an athlete. The late, great Virgil Abloh (founder of
Off-White in 2012), during his tenure as the first African-American
Men's Artistic Director of Louis Vuitton from 2018 until his passing
in 2021, democratized what could be perceived as luxury with an
emphasis on streetwear. The house had previously made inroads
into athleisure under Nicolas Ghesquière, who in 2016 echoed
the sentiment that we now all live in our sports clothes.

Several international music artists have built athleisure empires
via collaborations with major activewear and mass-market retailers.
Among these Kanye West is notable with his Yeezy franchise, which
collaborated first with Nike (2009–14), then with Adidas (2015), and
later had a three-way collaboration with Demna Gvasalia and the

Athleisure cont.

American Normcore (p.199) stalwart Gap in 2022. Beyoncé's Ivy
Park venture launched with the high-street brand Topshop in 2015
and relaunched with Adidas at the beginning of 2020. Rihanna's
Fenty partnership with Puma, which ran from 2016 until 2018,
was critically well received, and the now billionaire businesswoman
sells leggings and loungewear through her joint-venture Savage x
Fenty label.

Comfort eating and comfort dressing during the Covid-19
pandemic gave athleisure an extra push, firmly establishing it as an
enduring style. Despite Karl Lagerfeld's notorious mistrust of
tracksuits – he considered them a sign of defeat – leggings and
cycling shorts received the Chanel seal of approval on the Spring/
Summer 2019 ready-to-wear runway in the designer's penultimate
show for the house before his passing. Elasticated waistbands had
never looked so good.

COLOURS AND PATTERNS:
primary colours, black, white, stripes

FABRICS: spandex, nylon, polyester,
sweatshirt jersey, velour

GARMENTS AND ACCESSORIES:
leggings, trainers, crop top,
tracksuit, sports bra, cycling shorts,
baseball cap

DETAILS: zips, snap fastenings,
hood, pockets

Aviator

◑ AIR FORCE, PILOT
◑ FUTURISM, BIKER, PREPPY, VARSITY
⊕ COMBAT, HIP HOP

In the early days of flight, following Orville and Wilbur Wright's first
successful attempt in 1903, aviators were travelling far slower than the
average motor car of the day, with airspeeds of up to 65 km/h (40 mph)
and altitudes below a couple of thousand metres. A gentleman's tweed
coat, scarf and cap offered adequate protection. When the French
engineer and inventor Louis Blériot made the 37-minute crossing of
the English Channel in July 1909, he was wearing a tweed suit, a blue
cotton boiler suit, a wool-lined khaki jacket, sheepskin-lined boots,
goggles and a skullcap with ear flaps. As the number of pilots
grew, such stores as Burberry's and Dunhill's produced specialized
items, including fleece-lined leather overcoats, gauntlets and
fleece-lined all-in-one twill overalls. A white silk scarf was used to
plug any gaps around the neck, to act as a mask in case of dust
or fumes, and to serve as a cloth to clean goggles and apparatus.
The pale colour was functional; it meant the pilot could see where
they had used the cloth, and avoid smearing dirt back on later.
　　As planes ascended to more than 6,000 metres (20,000 ft) and
airspeeds increased, pilots were at the mercy of the cold and wind
in their open cockpits. The one-piece flight suit was cemented
as the garment of choice during World War I, in the winter of
1916, when Sidney Cotton, a pilot for the Royal Naval Air Service
(a precursor to the Royal Air Force, which was formed in 1918),
had to scramble into his plane while making repairs, wearing his
grease-stained boiler suit. On landing, he observed that his fellow
pilots were shivering while he was unaffected by the cold. He had
the London outfitters Robinson & Cleaver make him a double-
breasted, three-layer suit with an outer layer of Burberry fabric,
an interlining of windproof silk, and a fur lining and collar; this
was registered as the 'Sidcot Suit' in honour of its inventor. The
suit went into production in 1917, with a few modifications,
and remained the Allied pilot's uniform until World War II, when

Burberry Prorsum Autumn/Winter 2010 Womenswear during London Fashion Week at the Parade Ground, Chelsea College of Art, London, 23 February 2010.

cockpits became enclosed and cabin heating was introduced. The slanted wrap-over breast feature remains a feature of aviator jackets and inspired the early design of motorbike jackets in the 1920s (see Biker, p.67).

Early flight suits served as prototype jumpsuits for military paratroopers, and this modern shape, along with Futurism (p.33), started to inspire fashion designers, such as Elsa Schiaparelli, in the 1930s.

The classic sheepskin-lined flight jacket was invented in 1926 by the American Leslie Irvin, aviator, stuntman and inventor of the ripcord parachute, who set up business in the United Kingdom and supplied the RAF for most of World War II. The jacket featured a vertical front zip closure, a wrap chest, and zips up the sleeves so that gauntlets could be worn. There is often confusion between this and a bomber jacket, which owes its genesis to the Type A-1 of the US Army Air Corps. It was introduced in the same year as the Irvin jacket as a summer-weight flying jacket made from horsehide leather, cotton-lined, with large cargo pockets, and knitted woollen cuffs and waistband. While the A-1 was buttoned down the front, the type A-2 (1931) closed with a zip. A similar style of flight jacket with a fur collar, the M-422, was developed by the US Navy in the 1930s and evolved into the World War II G-1 jacket of US Naval Aviators. It was popularized by Tom Cruise in the film *Top Gun* (1986) and remains standard-issue for US naval pilots on active flying duty. Pilots would decorate their jackets with embroidery and patches detailing the missions they had flown.

By 1943 the US Army Air Forces had decided that leather was a luxury, and introduced the sage-green B-10 cotton flight jacket (still with fur collar). The advent of the jet age in the 1950s meant increasingly climate-controlled cockpits, so that the pilots required less from their jackets than had previously been the case. The MA-1 jacket was introduced in nylon with pared-back knit collar and an orange lining that made the jacket reversible in an emergency. This bomber style was one of the first to cross over from military to general civilian use, and its utilitarian pattern continues to inspire designers of both fashion and costumes. It also forms the basis of the letterman jacket (see Varsity, p.193), and may remind some people of the Harrington jacket (see Preppy, p.191).

Aviator cont.

    Before World War II parachutes were made from silk (mainly imported from Japan), but after successful testing by the pilot, stuntwoman and parachutist Adeline Gray in 1942, nylon was introduced. Billowing clouds of silk or nylon gathered with ripcord have been seen on many catwalks, among them John Galliano for Dior Autumn/Winter 1999 couture; Brioni, Jil Sander and Z Zegna for Spring/Summer 2016; Thierry Mugler Spring/Summer 2019 ready-to-wear; and Holzweiler Spring/Summer 2023. Parachute-inspired styling details, such as loose-fitting trousers, drawstring waists and tied cuffs, take on a Combat (p.95) or Hip Hop (p.142) edge in streetwear.

COLOURS AND PATTERNS:
RAF and Commonwealth Air Force blue #00308F, US Air Force #00308F, sage green, chestnut brown, camel, white

FABRICS: leather, sheepskin, silk, nylon

GARMENTS AND ACCESSORIES:
jumpsuit, boiler suit, flight jacket, bomber jacket, combat boots, wristwatch, goggles, helmet, aviator glasses, white scarf

DETAILS: parachute cord, large pockets, badges

Biker

● GREASER
◐ <u>AVIATOR</u>, <u>EQUESTRIAN</u>, <u>ROCKABILLY</u>, <u>DISCO</u>
⊕ <u>ROCK & ROLL</u>, <u>PUNK</u>, <u>INDIE</u>, <u>GRUNGE</u>

The keystone of the biker aesthetic is the biker jacket, a perennial
style classic that will never go out of fashion. The iconic shape was
originally designed and produced in 1928 by brothers Irving and
Jack Schott, sons of Russian immigrants living on the Lower East
Side of Manhattan, New York. They were inspired by World War I
flight jackets (see <u>Aviator</u>, p.63), and the pattern features the same
wrap-over chest detail and diagonal zip. It was the first civilian
jacket to feature this modern fastening. Irving named the jacket
'Perfecto', after his favourite cigar brand, and they were sold for
a princely $5.50 at a Long Island Harley-Davidson distributor. The
motorcycle brand, established in 1903, was already the biggest
in the world at the time, and its machines were capable of speeds
over 160 km/h (100 mph).

The Schott jacket accelerated into the public eye when Marlon
Brando wore one in the silver-screen hit *The Wild One* (1953), and
James Dean, a speed enthusiast and budding racing driver, was
pictured in publicity stills wearing one shortly before he was killed
tragically in a road accident in 1955 at just 24. The mid-century
American greaser subculture channelled its eternally rebellious
teen spirit with one part engine grease to one part <u>Rock & Roll</u>
(p.110) and <u>Rockabilly</u> (p.113) slicked, quiffed hair. The look was
immortalized on screen in the movie *Grease* (1978), where Olivia
Newton-John confirms her transition to 'bad Sandy' with a glossy
black biker jacket, skintight <u>Disco</u> pants (p.139) and cigarette.

The hardwearing leather construction of the Schott jacket offered
riders excellent protection in the case of a fall; however, it was less
practical in the rain-soaked climate of the UK. Two major competitors
filled the space there. Barbour, the traditional hunting, shooting and
fishing brand founded by John Barbour in 1894 and popular with
the aristo pack, diversified into motorcycle jackets in the 1930s. In
1924 in Stoke-on-Trent, Staffordshire, Eli Belovitch and his son-in-law

Biker cont.

Marlon Brando in the film *The Wild One*, 1953.

Harry Grosberg founded Belstaff (a hybrid of Belovitch and the county name) and started making jackets out of waterproof, breathable waxed cotton. Introduced in 1948, the company's Trialmaster style, with its four utility pockets and belted waist, is still available today. The style was an instant classic and has been worn by such legends as the Argentine revolutionary Che Guevara, and the 'King of Cool' Steve McQueen in the wartime movie *The Great Escape* (1963). McQueen was an authentic bike enthusiast who competed in many off-road bike races and is credited with collecting 210 motorcycles, 55 cars and 5 aircraft. He also owned and rode in Barbour jackets, and both brands lay claim to the star's heritage.

The Punk movement (p.125) of the 1970s, first with the Ramones in New York, then with the Sex Pistols in London, appropriated the Schott biker jacket as a symbol of countercultural insubordination, and added such do-it-yourself embellishments as studs, spikes and hand-painted slogans. Blondie and Patti Smith in the 1970s, and Joan Jett and Madonna in the 1980s, proved the garment wasn't just for the boys. By the mid-1980s, Japanese bikes, such as the Kawasaki Ninja, were gaining popularity, bringing with them a sportier and altogether more modern aesthetic characterized by bold primary colours, lime and neon hues, white accents, stripes and graphic patterns, sponsor logos and a streamlined silhouette for MotoGP and Superbike racing.

Biker style incorporates a few key accessories, such as the biker boot, which harks back to the 1930s 'engineer' boot, originally designed to protect the fireman (whose job it was to stoke the engine) from hot coals tumbling out of the firebox of a steam train. It features a simple pull-on stovepipe design made from black leather, modelled on earlier English-style horse-riding boots (see Equestrian, p.70), to protect the wearer from the heat given off by the engine block and offer stability on the pedals. Bikers also favour pocket chains, a practical approach to the risk of losing your house keys on the open road (later adopted by punks), as well as leather gloves and gauntlets. The biker style remains an in-demand route to utilitarian dress, laced with sex appeal and a hint of danger.

COLOURS AND PATTERNS:
black, chrome

FABRICS: leather, denim, waxed cotton

GARMENTS AND ACCESSORIES:
biker jacket, leather waistcoat, helmet, engineer (biker) boots, leather trousers

DETAILS: padded shoulders and sleeves, zips, chains, skulls, buckles

Equestrian

◉ CHEVALIER
● NEO-VICTORIANA, TAILORING, ROCOCO, ANDROGYNOUS
⊕ MILITARY, PREPPY, CLASSIC, FETISH

The noble horse, over the course of its 5,500-year evolution alongside humans, has provided transport and military strength, and partnered with us in sport and leisure. The domestication of wild horses started on the vast plains of the Eurasian steppes, and it's no coincidence that the earliest designs of trousers emerged around the same time, among the nomadic horsemen of western China (try riding a horse with a bare undercarriage and you'll understand why). Horses became both cherished companions and status symbols, and their bones have been found in the tombs of rulers and warriors. Noteworthy among those is the tomb of Duke Jing of Qi (reigned 547–490 BCE), in which the bones of approximately 600 horses were found.

Many present-day clothes contain traces of our equestrian past. The split vent on the back of any business suit (see Tailoring, p.195) originated as a feature of the nineteenth-century morning coat, designed to fall more easily over the back of the saddle and divert rain away from the rider. The 'morning' coat itself, which is now mainly found at Western weddings as part of a suit, was named after a well-to-do gentlemen's early riding exercise. It has a tapered, cut-away front skirt, while the more formal 'dress' coat is cut open and falls squarely. The Regency-era dress coat was a popular day coat until about 1830, when it was overtaken by the frock coats of the 1840s; those in turn were usurped by the more casual morning coats associated with the Victorian era (see Neo-Victoriana, p.26). The dress coat is now reserved for white-tie events and orchestral conductors.

Both are types of tailcoat, which developed from an earlier style of a British riding coat. Riders undertaking long journeys on horseback were at the mercy of the elements, so in the early 1700s the British developed a warm double-breasted, full-skirted 'riding coat' to protect the rider's legs from the weather. It was adopted in

John Galliano for Christian Dior Autumn/Winter 2010–11 Ready-to-Wear, Jardin des Tuileries, Paris, 5 March 2010.

Equestrian cont.

France, where it was Gallicized as a loanword into *redingote*. The utilitarian garment was then adapted for ladies to ride side-saddle, presenting a masculine top half balanced by full, feminine skirts underneath, and styled with an androgynous cotton shirt – making it an early example of menswear-inspired fashion (see Androgynous, p.270). Historically, a 'frock' was the term for a loose-fitting skirted garment, giving the coat its alternative name, 'frock coat'. The French still call a knee-length frock coat a *redingote*, and a tailcoat a *frac*.

As Anglomania swept across French society in the 1780s, Marie Antoinette (see also Rococo, p.257) was a follower of the riding-coat trend, although she was also known to wear breeches to ride astride. This shocked members of the court, since women riding astride in trousers did not become socially acceptable until the turn of the twentieth century, in part owing to the designs of Coco Chanel, who was a keen horsewoman and rode alongside her string of polo-playing lovers, including the cavalry officer, aristocrat and racehorse owner Étienne Balsan, and the dashing Boy Capel.

The presence of scarlet riding jackets, breeches and highly polished leather boots on the catwalk is a throwback to both Military dress (p.91) and fox hunting. However, most equestrians today have unbridled themselves from the hunting connection. Riders competing in showjumping and the art of dressage follow a strict dress code of tailored jackets, shirts, boots, breeches, ties and stocks. The discipline has resisted the influx of spandex experienced by other Olympic sports, and Grand Prix dressage riders still wear top hats and tailcoats after the style of the Spanish Riding School of Vienna, which was recommended in 1572 by the Habsburg monarchy as the best place for royalty to learn equestrianism.

With a historically affluent customer base that values premium leather craftsmanship and timeless design, it is unsurprising that several of the world's biggest luxury houses have an equestrian heritage. Thierry Hermès founded his eponymous harness shop in Paris in 1837 to supply tack to noblemen, and the brand continues to operate as a respected saddler. In 1953 Gucci introduced its now iconic horse-bit hardware into its accessories range (a single-jointed eggbutt snaffle, to those in the know), which pleased the house's aristocratic European and wealthy Hollywood patrons.

Humankind's equine friends remain a key reference point for many brands, and memorably, for Autumn/Winter 2021, Chanel sent Monaco royal Charlotte Casiraghi cantering down the catwalk on her beloved horse Kuskus, wearing a tweed jacket that was the epitome of Classic style (p.209). Horse racing also occasionally influences equestrian trends via the brightly patterned, light-as-a-feather silk shirts, known as 'silks', that are worn by jockeys, as seen on the Gucci catwalk that same season.

Owing to the predominance of leather straps and harnesses, whips and spurs in equestrianism, the style is sometimes subverted by fashion designers to add a Fetish edge (p.293).

COLOURS AND PATTERNS:
black, tan, cognac (dark brown), tattersall check, Newmarket stripe, red, hunter green, white

FABRICS: leather, suede, tweed, twill, wool, velvet, silk

GARMENTS AND ACCESSORIES:
tailcoat, breeches, jodhpurs, shirting, jacket with back vent, riding hat, bowler hat, knee-high riding boots, Chelsea boots, stock, tie, cravat, gloves

DETAILS: leather straps, horse bits, crop, spurs, frilled cuffs, stirrups

Rural

● COUNTRY, ARISTO
◐ BIKER, MILITARY, ACADEMIA, BOURGEOISIE, SLOANE
◑ HERITAGE, PREPPY, CLASSIC

Pastoral life requires its own specialized wardrobe, the luxe version in which you are stalking across your country estate with a pair of hounds, as opposed to milking cows at dawn. The popularity of the upstairs-downstairs television drama *Downton Abbey* (2010–15), and fashion's enduring fascination with the British aristocracy and its royal family, have elevated such traditionally functional items as waxed cotton jackets (see also Biker, p.67) and wellington boots (see Cowboy, p.79, and Military, p.91). A quilted jacket in a conservative colour, such as hunter green or navy blue, is a must-have and, as an unintentional style icon, Queen Elizabeth II was known for pairing hers with a silk headscarf, a look that was channelled by the British designer Richard Quinn on the London Fashion Week catwalk in 2018, before he received the inaugural QEII Award for British Design.

Heritage fabrics (p.23) are appropriate, such as tweed in a variety of traditional checks, among them the large squares of the windowpane check, the classic, finely detailed herringbone, and the earthy weave of the gamekeeper's tweed (also beloved of earnest professors; see Academia, p.188). The Glen plaid check features a criss-cross of fine black-and-white houndstooth stripes and was popularized by King Edward VII, who took a liking to the uniforms of the Countess of Seafield's estate keepers at her property in the valley of Glen Urquhart in the Highlands of Scotland. It became known as the Prince of Wales check after Edward VII's grandson Edward VIII, who abdicated a year after acceding the throne, to marry twice-divorced Wallis Simpson. Stepping down from the top job of 'The Firm' gave Edward licence to indulge in his favourite pastime, socializing, and he adapted the classic fabric with overchecks in bold colours, setting trends in the beau monde.

With its roots in the class-based style, the polished aristo look filters down to upper-middle-class aesthetics, such as Bourgeoisie

Queen Elizabeth II at the Royal Windsor Horse Show, 13 May 1989.

(p.202), specifically the much-maligned 1980s Sloane look (p.205). It also influences such Anglophile designers as Ralph Lauren and diffuses into the Ivy League look of Preppy style (p.191).

In general, streetwear on a (country) estate is a no-no. Heaven forbid you should turn up wearing urban regalia and impractical high-heeled shoes.

COLOURS AND PATTERNS: dark green, dark brown, mid-brown, navy, tweed, argyle knit, herringbone tweed, gamekeeper's tweed, Prince of Wales check, tattersall check

FABRICS: tweed, wool, waxed cotton, rubber, corduroy

GARMENTS AND ACCESSORIES: quilted jacket, tweed suit, shooting jacket, breeches, wellingtons, gilet, boots, flat cap, silk scarf, wool scarf, knitted jumper, brogues, deerstalker, overcoat

DETAILS: padding, shoulder guard for gun

Polo

● TENNIS
● GAUCHO, MILITARY
● ATHLEISURE, HIP HOP, PREPPY, NORMCORE

Polo, the world's oldest team sport, dates from the Eurasian nomads around 600 BCE and became a pastime of Persian nobility during the Sasanian Empire (224–651 CE) as a form of cavalry training. Women played, too, and there are early references to the Armenian princess Shirin meeting her future husband, the Persian king Khosrow II (590–628 CE), while playing the sport. The game had spread to India by the thirteenth century, and was later adopted by British Military personnel (p.91), who formed the first polo club in Silchar, Assam, in 1859. Polo players on the Indian subcontinent wore short-sleeved shirts to beat the heat, some with button-down collars to prevent them from flapping in the wind as they galloped after the ball.

A key component of smart-casual dress, today's polo shirt has two iterations. The original was designed by John E. Brooks, grandson of the founder of the American heritage brand Brooks Brothers, who attended a polo game in England in 1896 and noted that the players wore their collars buttoned down. Brooks incorporated this feature into a shirt made from oxford cloth, which gives us the modern-day oxford shirt.

The transition to what we now recognize as a polo shirt came via the game of tennis, which in the early 1920s was played in long-sleeved, starched white shirts. The seven-times Grand Slam-winning French player René Lacoste found the design too restrictive, and when he played a game with his friend the Marquis of Cholmondeley, who stepped on to the court wearing his polo shirt, Lacoste was struck by the practicality of the design. The semi-formal cut retains the smart feel of the collar, useful when turned up for protection against the sun, with a sportier piqué cotton fabric and short sleeves. He asked his tailor to run some up in cotton and wool, making them longer at the back so that they stayed tucked in even when reaching for the ball, and in honour

Lacoste Spring/Summer 2018 Womenswear, Paris Fashion Week, 27 September 2017.

Polo cont.

of his nickname, 'Le Crocodile', he included a playful emblem on his chest. Incidentally, in the same decade polo spread to Argentina, where the skilled horse-riding Gauchos (p.82) took naturally to the sport.

In 1933 Lacoste went into business with the knitwear manufacturer André Gillier, and the shirts, marketed as suitable for tennis, polo, golf and the beach, were an instant success. Lacoste was hailed as the first 'celebrity'-owned fashion company, as well as arguably the first brand of clothing to display the logo on the outside. In 1951 the manufacturer Izod was granted the licence to produce and distribute Lacoste shirts in the United States, and early examples of influencer seeding on such names as John F. Kennedy, Dwight D. Eisenhower and Bing Crosby ensured that these garments became a symbol of wealth for college students and sports enthusiasts.

In 1972 an enterprising young immigrant from the Bronx, previously called Ralph Lifshitz and now making a name for himself as Ralph Lauren, emulated the design in a wide selection of colours, each with the aspirational polo pony emblem. The polo shirt remains a key component of Preppy style (p.191), and made a resurgence in the 1990s as part of Hip Hop style (p.142). Note that the unequivocal rule is never to pop the collar.

COLOURS AND PATTERNS: royal blue, navy blue, red, emerald green, primary yellow, white, harlequin, broad stripes

FABRICS: piqué cotton, oxford cloth

GARMENTS AND ACCESSORIES: polo shirt, chinos

Cowboy

● WESTERN, AMERICANA
● GAUCHO, MILITARY
● BIKER, ROCKABILLY, METAL

The history of the cowboy is rooted in the haciendas of the Iberian
Peninsula. On Christopher Columbus's second trip to the West
Indies, in 1493, he took cattle and fine Andalusian horses; more
cows were imported by Gregorio de Villalobos, and after the
Spanish conquest of the Aztec Empire by Hernán Cortés in 1521
there were enough of both species to start a breeding programme
in Mexico. Those that escaped bred prolifically in the wild.

Cattle-ranching culture spread from the plains of Mexico north
to the prairies of North America, and south to the pampas of
Argentina, Uruguay, Brazil and Chilean Patagonia. By the time of
the archetypal Old West in the years between the end of the Civil
War in 1865 and 1912, when the remaining western territories were
admitted into states (apart from Alaska and Hawaii, which were
ratified in 1959), the herders were known variously as cowboys,
vaqueros and Gauchos (p.82). They were of mixed Spanish, Native
American and/or African descent, and farmhands involved in the
care and preparation of the horses alone were called 'wranglers'.
What came to be known as a 'western' shirt was based on a
Mexican *guayabera*, known for its brightly embroidered details
and reinforced yokes; durable press studs replaced the buttons
of the traditional shirt.

Leather or suede 'chaps' that encased the legs provided
protection from the thorny scrub vegetation, known as *chaparral*,
and prevented saddle sores on the inside of the thighs. Fringing is
common and, although later employed by stars of Metal (p.120) for
theatrical effect, is in fact a design feature invented by Indigenous
Americans to help rainwater drain away. For dry days, a long,
loose-fitting 'duster' coat could be worn to keep clothes free from
the dirt of the trail, a silhouette that is still popular in outerwear.

In 1853 the Bavarian merchant Levi Strauss followed the gold
rush from New York to San Francisco, where he opened a dry-

Cowboy cont.

goods store that sold, among other items, the hardwearing French twill cloth from Nîmes, known as *serge de Nîmes*, referred to colloquially as 'denim'. In 1873 he and a local tailor, Jacob Davis, patented their reinforced workwear overalls, complete with riveted pockets all the better to carry the weight of gold nuggets found by lucky prospectors. Before long, these blue trousers had replaced the gauchos' style of *bombachas* riding trousers. Coincidentally, it was the Nîmes textile manufacturers' attempts to re-create a popular fabric from the Italian city of Genoa (Gênes to the French) that gave us the name 'jeans'. Blue jeans remain a key motif of Americana and reappear as part of the Biker subculture (p.67).

Dsquared2 Autumn/Winter 2018 Menswear, Milan Fashion Week, 14 January 2018.

The distinctive shape of the cowboy boot emerged over time from several sources. It is primarily credited to the style of riding boot worn by Arthur Wellesley, 1st Duke of Wellington, when he defeated Napoleon Bonaparte at the Battle of Waterloo in 1815. Even before Waterloo, Wellington had had his bootmaker adapt highly polished, tasselled, knee-high military-issue Hessian boot of the Regency period (1795–1820) to make it tighter to the leg, simpler in design, cut from soft calf leather, and lower around the calf to make it suitable for riding as well as evening events. The boots were widely adopted by such fashion-forward dandies as George 'Beau' Brummell (see Dandy, p.247). The slightly pointed toe helped riders to guide their feet into the stirrups, and the stacked heel prevented the foot from getting caught in the stirrup and the rider being dragged in the case of a fall (the heel on all modern shoes dates from the Mongolian riders of the twelfth century, who invented it for the same purpose). The wellington boot style was imported to the United States and was one of the first items to be mass-produced to outfit the US cavalry (see also Military, p.91).

Cowboys and vaqueros adapted it to have an exaggerated point on the toe, scalloped front and back, and tabs that made the boot easier to pull on in a hurry; fancy stitching across the leather upper helped the boot to keep its shape when drying.

Although highly functional at the beginning, the cowboy look was given a Hollywood makeover for on-screen costumes, with stars of country music and rodeo riders progressively adding more embellishments and fringing, crystallizing the look, literally and figuratively, with the liberal application of rhinestones.

COLOURS AND PATTERNS:
blue, tan, silver, tan, cow print

FABRICS: leather, denim, suede, cotton, calico, linen

GARMENTS AND ACCESSORIES:
western shirt, straight-cut jeans, cowboy boots, Stetson, sombrero, poncho, bandana, chaps, duster coat, bolo tie, cowboy belt with large silver buckle

DETAILS: fringing, embroidery, leather tooling, collar tips, rhinestones

Gaucho

- SOUTH AMERICAN RANCHER
- COWBOY
- CRUISE, TAILORING, BOHEMIAN

The gaucho style is a distinctively South American take on cattle-ranching culture. The gauchos were skilled horse riders, semi-nomadic in their way of life, traversing the pampas – over a million square kilometres of low grassland that sweeps across Argentina, Uruguay, Brazil's Rio Grande do Sul and part of Chilean Patagonia. In folklore, such as the epic poem *El Gaucho Martín Fierro* by the Argentine writer José Hernández (published originally in two parts in 1872 and 1879), they were eulogized as the last exponents of a disappearing way of life, restricted in their liberty by neither fences nor the law.

The gauchos retained more traditional folk dress than many of the Californian cowboys, including the loose-fitting, comfortable *bombachas* trousers, cuffed at the hem and tucked into traditional riding boots, rather than the shorter, pointed cowboy boots.

The Iberian style wide-brimmed, flat-topped hat is often called a *bolero*. This is not to be confused with the cropped, open-fronted jacket the gauchos wore, also referred to as a bolero jacket, although both were named after the energetic Spanish dance. The other preferred hat was a *boina*, which looks like a cross between a knitted beret and a flat cap. A rectangular cloth called a *chiripá* was wrapped around the groin area in the manner of a nappy (diaper), belted to provide extra padding and comfort in the saddle on long rides (unsurprisingly, this garment has yet to be appropriated by fashion designers). The *chiripá* was fastened with a patterned fabric sash called a *faja* (where the gaucho's infamous knife was usually stashed), with a leather coin belt buckled over it.

Items had to be multipurpose if the rider was to travel light, and the simple, hands-free poncho was made from heavy-duty wool and could be worn for warmth or slept on as a blanket. Ponchos are found across the south of the South American continent, often woven with traditional geometric designs of the Indigenous people. One of the best-represented symmetrical

Jean Paul Gaultier for Hermès Spring/Summer 2011 Women's Ready-to-Wear, Paris Fashion Week, 6 October 2010.

Gaucho cont.

patterns is 'Guarda Pampa' (People of the Earth), which represents the Andes mountains reflected in the lakes of the area, as created by the Mapuche people of Argentina and Chilean Patagonia.

On modern catwalks, the gaucho look is epitomized by Gabriela Hearst, who grew up on her family's 6,900 ha (17,000 acre) ranch in Uruguay before completing her fashion training in New York. She elevates the look with leather midi skirts and lace blouses, tooled-leather trench coats, knee-high riding boots, robust metal hardware and bold, patterned knits in vibrant earth tones. Hearst is an advocate for sustainability, and has pledged to stop the use of virgin materials in her collections, using deadstock fabrics and showing via carbon-neutral shows. During her tenure as creative director there, Chloé became the first luxury brand to attain B Corp status. This independent certification poses 300 questions to ascertain a brand's commitment to people, the planet and purpose, alongside profit. In 2021 the pass rate for businesses was just 4 per cent.

A similarly purpose-driven brand with B Corp status is TOMS, a mid-range producer of traditional-style *alpargatas*, the rope-soled, jute-upper slip-on shoe, also known as an espadrille, with which Argentine gauchos would alternate their riding boots.

COLOURS AND PATTERNS: black, tan, red, white, Guarda Pampa

FABRICS: suede, cotton, leather, knitted wool

GARMENTS AND ACCESSORIES: poncho, *bombachas*, *bolero* hat, bolero jacket, *boina* hat, chaps, riding boots, *alpargatas*, leather belt, *faja* belt

DETAILS: fringing, embroidery, leather tooling, silver belt buckle

Prairie

- COWGIRL
- NEO-VICTORIANA, STEAMPUNK, HIPSTER, ROMANTIC
- RETRO, COWBOY, COTTAGECORE, BOHEMIAN, MODEST

Prairie style, although similar to the inherently West Coast American Cowboy style (p.79), channels settled life on the frontier, a mixture of old-fashioned manual labour, growing crops, tending livestock and raising a family at a remote outpost. The heyday of the Wild West was during the Victorian era (see also Neo-Victoriana, p.26, and Steampunk, p.42), and there are similarities in the prairie style of dress, such as the voluminous ruffled skirts worn over petticoats, the lace trim and the modest necklines. Perhaps not the most practical of barnyard utility wear, it appeals to nostalgia for a simpler time.

On the homestead, dress patterns were simplified and cut from less expensive cloth, such as calico, a coarse, unbleached cotton. Favoured patterns were desaturated, faded floral prints that disguised the dirt, and the homespun charm of a gingham check. For the most part, these clothes were home-made – a far cry from the polished construction of Paris's world-famous ateliers. This is sometimes demonstrated in catwalk versions of prairie style in patchwork designs and handkerchief-hem skirts, which feeds into the movement towards upcycling fabric deadstock as part of a sustainable approach.

There are elements of prairie style in the emergence of Cottagecore (p.161), which is primarily concerned with self-sufficiency and the genteel bucolic ideals of the English country garden. The hero piece for both styles is the 'prairie dress', typified by its floor-skimming maxi-length skirt, full sleeves and feminine frills. Smocking – originally a way to allow clothes to move with the wearer, before the invention of elastic – is a key design feature. This 'big dress energy' is a signature of the London designer Molly Goddard, with her dramatic tulle gowns, and the Royal College of Art alumnus Erdem Moralıoğlu, who is known for his intricate naturalistic prints; it is encapsulated in the American heritage of the New York label started by Batsheva Hay (an ex-lawyer purposefully

reacting against New York City's saturation point of black Minimalism, p.252) and in the Romantic (p. 263) silhouettes of the Vampire's Wife, founded by Susie Cave, wife of the singer-songwriter Nick Cave.

The free-spirited, loose layers of the prairie style also bear some similarities to the Bohemian aesthetic (p.217) that was popular in the 1970s, and layering long-chained necklaces and swapping out a Stetson for a wide-brimmed, floppy hat will push the look towards the Retro (p.20) end of the style spectrum. Cottagecore and prairie are versatile styles that can be adapted between seasons with the addition of boots for winter: Chelsea boots, wellington boots or knee-high boots for the former and cowboy boots for the latter.

The male-gendered version of the look channels the belt-and-braces gumption of the early settlers, with rough-hewn denim trousers or corduroys, work boots, waistcoats, unbleached cotton shirts sporting a 'grandad' or mandarin collar, with sleeves rolled up, accessorized with a pocket watch, a bandana, and a beard for extra ruggedness points. Transplanted to the city limits, this definitive Hipster look (p.226) was popular around the turn of the millennium.

COLOURS AND PATTERNS: white, floral print, buttercream, sky blue

FABRICS: linen, cotton, calico, broderie anglaise, lace, gingham, suede

GARMENTS AND ACCESSORIES: dress, poet shirt, cowboy boots, duster coat

DETAILS: ruffles, smocking, high neck, balloon sleeves, maxi length, ribbons, pie-crust collar

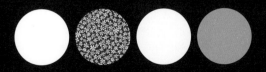

Gorecore

● GORPCORE, HIKING & CLIMBING
● ATHLEISURE, NORMCORE
● RETRO, RURAL

Gorecore style tells the world that you could survive in the wild, even if you're pounding the city streets to forage a takeaway meal. It follows the same etymology as its mid-2010s precursor Normcore (p.199), and in many ways it is similar in its basic, anti-fashion approach to style. It is named colloquially after the waterproof, breathable fabric Gore-Tex, although some fashion writers refer to the trend as Gorpcore after the hiker's term for trail mix, 'good old raisins and peanuts' or 'granola, oats, raisins, peanuts', depending on who you ask. Camping and hiking notably appeared on the catwalk in 2016 at Prada, and, influenced by the ubiquitous Athleisure movement (p.60), this style is further evidence of the ongoing casualization of modern dress.

Three major climbing films, *The Dawn Wall* (2017), *Free Solo* and *Silence* (both 2018), brought the sport and its fearless spirit into popular culture. This, combined with the introduction of climbing at the 2020 Olympics, has meant a dramatic increase in participants and interest in such traditionally outdoor brands as Rab, Arc'teryx, Columbia, Stone Island, Helly Hansen, Tevas, Birkenstock, Moncler and Mammut. Of note is Patagonia, the American brand founded by the climber and environmentalist Yvon Chouinard, which was an early pioneer of corporate social responsibility, pledging a self-imposed 1 per cent tax for the planet. The company's Black Friday 2011 advertising campaign 'Don't Buy this Jacket' in the *New York Times* struck an anti-consumerist chord with the eco-conscious values of Gen-Z and millennial consumers.

The global pandemic reinvigorated the love of the outdoors and hiking (indeed, for many it was the only available pastime during endless lockdowns). The look reached its zenith in 2021 with a collaboration between the technical outfitter North Face and the Italian luxury house Gucci, which infused the look with a dash of 1970s Retro (p.20).

Versace Spring/Summer 2017 Womenswear, Milan Fashion Week, 23 September 2016.

Gorecore cont.

Key items in the gorecore kit bag are the anorak and the parka, both originally developed by the Inuit, the Indigenous people of the frozen Arctic. The anorak is technically a hooded, waterproof, pull-over design, and many contemporary versions have a large front pocket for storing essentials, and a drawstring to waist and hood. The parka is padded for cold weather, and hip length. In the 1950s the US Air Force introduced the heavy-duty N-3B 'snorkel' parka with a fur hood that can be pulled tight, for flight crews stationed in cold environments (see also Aviator, p.63), while the US Army developed the M-51 'fishtail' parka, with its distinctive split back (see Combat, p.95). The latter became a favoured item of 1960s Mod subculture (p.228) and influenced 1990s Britpop. Combining the waterproof qualities of the anorak and the length of the parka, a knee-length, unlined, hooded, usually zip-front waterproof raincoat that can be folded for travelling is called a 'cagoule' in British English, or a 'windbreaker' in the United States and Canada.

COLOURS AND PATTERNS: black, sand, grey, orange, sky blue, olive green, argyle, tartan, plaid, gingham, check

FABRICS: fleece, Gore-Tex, nylon, Econyl, cable knit, softshell, gabardine, rubber, spandex

GARMENTS AND ACCESSORIES: T-shirt, anorak, cargo trousers, puffer jacket, waterproof jacket, cardigan, jumper, leggings, gilet, parka, cagoule

DETAILS: drawstring, buckles, beanie hat, backpack, bucket hat, lace-up, cord laces, hiking shoes and socks, hood, snap-closure buckle, sandals, bumbag (fanny pack)

Military

◉ ARMY, REGIMENTAL, SOLDIER
➡ HERITAGE, CYBERPUNK, EQUESTRIAN, NAUTICAL
⊕ ROCK & ROLL, DANDY

The amalgamation of decoration and functionality in military dress has had a lasting impact on fashion and popular culture. Brightly coloured army jackets were made famous by the Beatles for their concept album *Sgt Pepper's Lonely Hearts Club Band* (1967). Jimi Hendrix bought and performed in a vintage pelisse jacket (see below), and the self-proclaimed 'King of Pop' Michael Jackson wore both authentic and sequinned costume versions on stage. On the catwalk, the French designer Olivier Rousteing's figurative Balmain 'Army' came to life in his career-defining collection for Spring/Summer 2010, which featured all the hallmarks of regimental military jackets decorated with fancy gilt buttons, statement shoulders and grandiose embroidery.

Dutch cuirassier (left) and trumpeter of the 3rd Regiment, 1823. Etching by Dirk Sluyter after a drawing by Bartholomeus Johannes van Hove.

The distinctive military-style jacket of Western origin has changed little since those of the hussars, daring Hungarian military horsemen who were noted for their bravery. By the seventeenth century they had shed heavy armour in favour of a vivid jacket called a *dolman*, resplendent with rows of buttons, intricate cord braiding known as *passementerie* (which encompasses embroidery, fringing and tassels) and frogging – fastenings of a style that originated in China, where they are known as *pankou* or *haniou*, meaning 'flower button' (see also Heritage, p.23). Over their left shoulder, the hussars threw a short, braided, fur-trimmed

Military cont.

over-jacket called a *pelisse* to protect them from sword cuts, or as an extra layer in freezing temperatures.

By the eighteenth century European military forces were all wearing similar uniforms inspired by the hussars, consisting of tailcoats and breeches (see Equestrian, p.70), waistcoats and knee-high riding boots or buttoned gaiters. The differences lay in the colour of the coats and their facings: collars, cuff turn-backs, coat-tail trims and passementerie. Rank insignia was unheard of at the time, and officers – usually aristocrats – were reluctant to wear a livery as such because they saw it as a demeaning sign of employment, as worn by their servants. Some officers wore a metal throat covering called a gorget symbolically, as a throwback to medieval armour. And when it comes to armour, metal plates make an appearance in more Avant-Garde (p.244) collections and are a house signature at Paco Rabanne, intersecting historical elements with the space age from 1967 to current collections; and flowing chainmail-type metallic mesh fabric was reinvented by Gianni Versace as Oroton in 1982.

From 1768 British army officers were ordered by warrant to display their rank via epaulettes (from the French *épaule*, 'shoulder'). The tasselled epaulette secured weapons via shoulder belts and was based on earlier decorative ribbons, such as those worn by Louis XIV. The shoulder strap, which is stitched across the seam from the collar to the top of the sleeve, is technically called a *passenten*, but fashion writers often refer colloquially to these as epaulettes, and the same goes for any flat shoulder mark denoting rank on present-day uniforms. Navies (see Nautical, p.98) also adopted shoulder insignia, and buttons denoted an officer's rank and company.

A simplified version of the hussar jacket with shorter tails, called a coatee, was favoured in the nineteenth century. The Grande Armée of Napoleon Bonaparte added non-functional buttons to the cuffs, allegedly ordered by the emperor so that soldiers could not wipe their noses (or tears from their eyes, many of them being merely boys) and spoil their smart appearance. The tin buttons, which were also used to close the jacket, may even have contributed to Bonaparte's defeat in Russia in 1815; in freezing temperatures the metal became brittle and powdery, leaving his army to freeze.

Lily Stewart in John Galliano Autumn/Winter 2016–17, Paris Fashion Week, 6 March 2016.

Military cont.

    Greatcoats (also known as watchcoats) of the time were remarkably like those fabricated by modern fashion houses: made of thick wool, calf-length, double-breasted with metal buttons for extra pomp, and roomy enough to fit over a jacket. Some greatcoats have an attached cape, and flamboyant Regency Dandies (p.247) would flounce about with up to ten capes per coat. These overcoats were warm but not waterproof, and a solution to the problem of rain was found in the trench coat. Although named in the trenches, it was invented before World War I by two British heritage brands: Aquascutum, which was established in 1851; and Thomas Burberry, who founded his label in 1856 and invented lightweight, waterproof gabardine fabric in 1879. The trench coat was a success for both military and civilian use, and became the hallmark of 1940s film noir detectives and later neo-noir protagonists (see Cyberpunk, p.38).

COLOURS AND PATTERNS:
scarlet, grey, midnight blue, forest green, gold, brass, silver, chevrons

FABRICS: wool, velvet, fur, leather, chainmail

GARMENTS AND ACCESSORIES:
jacket, greatcoat, breeches, trousers, kepi hat, shako hat

DETAILS: double-breasted, buttons, frogging, embroidery, fringing, tassels, stars, eagles

Combat

◓ ARMY, MILITARY
◒ GORECORE, NAUTICAL, SAFARI, PREPPY, HIPPY, MOD
◕ PUNK, HIP HOP, GOTH

In the era of hand-to-hand combat, brightly hued uniforms helped to distinguish friend from foe on the battlefield, but the advent of long-range weapons during World War I meant that concealment became the name of the game. Ornate military jackets were relegated to ceremonial dress as cheaper, more casual and less eye-catching designs were favoured.

The British armed forces were the first to introduce khaki uniforms (see Safari, p.105), in 1848, and the trend for drab battle fatigues spread across the world, with most countries adopting a mixture of khaki, grey and/or dull green. On the catwalk, this earthy palette with the addition of utilitarian pockets, often styled with chunky, lace-up combat boots (see also Goth, p.220, and Punk, p.125), signifies to the fashion aficionado that the designer is looking to the army for influence. Of course, combat style is now so pervasive that it has taken on a non-violent meaning.

We owe this primarily to the counterculture Hippies (p.223) of the 1960s, many of whom were disillusioned US Army veterans returning from the Vietnam War (1954–75), who subverted their military-issue garb, often the M-65 field jacket, with symbols of peace. John Lennon, who was famously a vigorous proponent of the anti-war message, wore casually around town, performed in and was often photographed in a US Army OG-107 fatigue utility shirt given to him by a fan in the early 1970s. In England, brooding Mods (p.228) procured US Army M-51 'fishtail' parkas (see also Gorecore, p.88) from surplus and supply stores to keep their dapper Tailoring (p.195) immaculate while riding their scooters.

Chinos, the easy-to-wear yet smart trousers with a flat front and tapered leg that are a mainstay of Preppy style (p.191), had a rugged beginning born out of conflict, when the US Army was stationed in the Philippines during the Spanish-American war of 1898. Troops wore trousers made from imported Chinese twill, and

the garment was known as *pantalones chinos*, 'Chinese trousers'. During the same struggle, the humble pull-on T-shirt was first marketed as a 'bachelor undershirt', targeted at single men without wives to fix their buttons. It became part of the uniform of the US Navy in 1913 (see Nautical, p.98).

Cargo trousers, also known as 'combat trousers' – more utilitarian than the chino in appearance, with a loose fit and practical thigh pockets – were introduced in 1938 by the British and adopted by the Americans two years later. Their combination of toughness and insouciance made them a hit with Hip Hop (p.142) and later Gorecore for pure utility; along with cargo shorts, they are an anti-fashion Normcore staple (p.199).

The defining print of combat style is camouflage, a disruptive pattern first designed during World War I by the French fine-art painter Lucien-Victor Guirand de Scévola and some Cubist artists, such as André Mare, Jacques Villon and Georges Braque. The print appeared in the post-apocalyptic couture of John Galliano for Christian Dior Spring/Summer 2001, and neon-hued at Versace Spring/Summer 2016, and it reappears from season to season as a house signature in the luxe streetwear looks of Off-White. Liberated from its past in hiding, camouflage print is now a sure-fire way to stand out.

COLOURS AND PATTERNS:
olive, grey, green, grey-green, camouflage, black

FABRICS: wool, cotton, nylon

GARMENTS AND ACCESSORIES:
T-shirt, field jacket, field shirt, cargo trousers, combat boots, wristwatch

DETAILS: pockets, straps, buckles

Nautical

◈ NAVAL, SAILOR, SHIPSTER
● FLAPPER, GORECORE, MILITARY, COMBAT, HIPSTER
⊕ CRUISE, PREPPY, PIN-UP

More so than that of the other armed forces, naval style has a touch of the rogue: travel and tradition with a tinge of rum, tattoos and debauchery. Scarcely a resort season goes by (see Cruise, p.164) without a fleet of pea coats, crisp blue-and-white stripes, wide-legged trousers, hardy rope belts and dazzling gold buttons sailing down the runway. Jean Paul Gaultier has built a perfume empire on his erotically charged Le Mâle fragrance, which comes complete with a striped torso and suggestive bulge. Gaultier was originally inspired by the seaman protagonist of Rainer Werner Fassbinder's art-house movie *Querelle* (1982), which features murder, drug dealing and sodomy – not necessarily in that order.

The archetypal striped *marinière*, or Breton top as it is known in English, has 21 stripes, allegedly to represent each of Napoleon's victories over the British. In 1858 it was incorporated into the uniform of the French Navy, and the stripes were functional, too: a form of early high-vis to help sailors locate their comrades who were swept overboard. Coco Chanel is credited with popularizing the look after the war. Her nautical collection in 1917 was inspired by the sailors' collars she saw from her coastal residence in the South of France, La Pausa in Roquebrune-Cap-Martin, and her love of the sea was also reflected in the opening of her first boutique at Deauville on the Normandy coast. Incidentally, the distinctive sailor collar, with its deep V front, wide lapels and square back, is said to have been a nod to the eighteenth-century custom of sailors smearing their ponytails or pigtails in tar, to keep their hair out the way of rigging; the broad collar was a way to keep the rest of the uniform clean.

Graphic stripes were universally fashionable in the 1920s (see also Flapper, p.30), and versions of the *marinière* have since been worn by such iconic actors and artists as Brigitte Bardot,

Leon Dame in Maison Margiela Spring/Summer 2020 Womenswear, Paris Fashion Week, 25 September 2019.

Nautical cont.

Audrey Hepburn, Marilyn Monroe, James Dean, John Wayne, Pablo Picasso and Andy Warhol.

The classic pea coat, ostensibly named by the seafaring Dutch after *pije*, a coat made from thick wool, is double-breasted for warmth and cut to the hips for ease of movement (differentiating it from the long coat worn by the captain on the bridge), and sports a wide collar that can be turned up against the elements. It was incorporated into the British Royal Navy uniform in 1890 for use by petty officers (which in turn led to its nickname, the 'P-coat'). For Yves Saint Laurent's first show after leaving Dior in January 1962, he presented as his first look a ladies' version of the pea coat, styled with white wide-legged trousers. Authentic pea coats have buttons bearing the 'fouled anchor' emblem, which is an anchor caught in the rope, representing the trials and tribulations of daily life at sea.

Sailors wore capacious bell-bottomed trousers so that they could roll them up easily when wading in shallow water, with a button-up apron front so that if the sailor fell overboard they could be hauled off quickly (imagine removing tight fabric underwater). The baggy legs would also fill with air, and might serve as an emergency flotation device. The distinctive flare was changed to a straight-cut Combat style (p.95) only in the late 1990s, much to the outrage of some traditionalists.

In recent times, in much the same way that Gorecore (p.88) has taken hold, fishermen have been providing fashion inspiration for urban professionals in temperate climates. The spate of craggy beards, micro beanie hats, roll necks, cable-knit jumpers, extreme turn-ups and rubberized macs among craft beer-quaffing creatives led some fashion writers to dub this trend the 'Shipster' (see Hipster, p.226). The duffle coat, named after the heavy-duty cloth of the Belgian town Duffel, has a rope-and-toggle fastening that is easy to use even when wearing gloves in frozen conditions. Similarly, the vulcanized-rubber mackintosh (now an eponym for any raincoat), which was invented by Thomas Hancock and Charles Macintosh in drizzly Scotland more than 200 years ago, has seen a resurgence, especially in classic yellow. It's an ideal garment for deckhands working in misty climes, and perfect for lifting the spirits.

The commonplace navy blue-and-white uniform of many navies was introduced by the British Royal Navy in 1748, designed primarily to look different from the red coats of the land army (see Military, p.91). Indigo dye was readily sourced from Britain's territories in India, and true navy blue is almost black. Summer and tropical versions of naval uniforms tend to be pure white, attributed variously to their ability to reflect the sun's rays and the colour's status as a universal symbol of peace for seafarers encountering new lands and peoples.

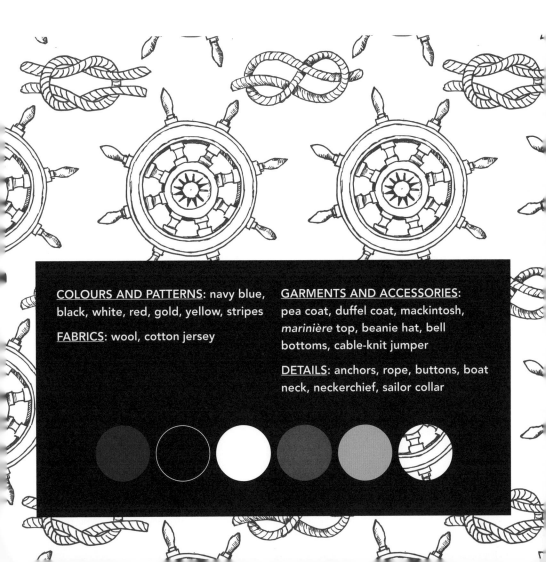

COLOURS AND PATTERNS: navy blue, black, white, red, gold, yellow, stripes

FABRICS: wool, cotton jersey

GARMENTS AND ACCESSORIES: pea coat, duffel coat, mackintosh, *marinière* top, beanie hat, bell bottoms, cable-knit jumper

DETAILS: anchors, rope, buttons, boat neck, neckerchief, sailor collar

Pirate

● BUCCANEER
➖ MILITARY, PUNK, COTTAGECORE
➕ BOHEMIAN, ROCOCO, ROMANTIC

While 'pirate' as a form of modern utility dress might be a bit far-fetched (swashbuckling your way to the supermarket, anyone?), it can be filed under Nautical (p.98) and has a history of being plundered by fashion and music for its anarchic aesthetic.

When the grande dame of punk, Vivienne Westwood, needed a new direction, it was to pirates that she turned for her iconic collection of the same name in 1981. The hard-edged Punk aesthetic (p.125) had run its course, and New Wave, the umbrella term for everything post-punk, needed a more Romantic (p.263) interpretation. Westwood's partner Malcolm McLaren, manager of the Sex Pistols, helped to restyle the musician Adam Ant in the pirate style during the months before the fashion show, complete with an ornate hussar jacket (see Military, p.91). Models swaggered down the catwalk in buckled boots and bicorne hats, with lace epaulettes and oversized blouses for both men and women.

Westwood was the first to show pirate style on the catwalk, but by no means the last. John Galliano presented highly sexed bodices, thigh-high gaiters and crotch-skimming sash skirts in his Spring/Summer 1993 ready-to-wear collection. Sash belts were originally for holding weapons, and as lumbar support. In a case of life imitating art, the blockbuster film *Pirates of the Caribbean* (2003) coincided with Alexander McQueen's 'high fashion for the high seas' spring ready-to-wear collection the same year, featuring shipwrecked, windswept sirens clad in leather and tulle. The bodice-ripping sentiment of pirate style has a historical source; it is said that female pirates exposed their breasts as their foes lay dying, to show they had been slain by a woman. In 2007 the New York designer Anna Sui presented a more playful take on the style with girlish off-the-shoulder printed dresses, some pieced together by patchwork in a similar way to the handcrafted nature of Cottagecore (p.161), styled with ripped tights.

Pirate cont.

Skull motifs, as seen at Libertine Spring/Summer 2018, were indeed used by pirates to strike fear into the hearts of those who encountered them. The Jolly Roger flag was originally blood crimson, named after the French term *joli rouge*, 'pretty red'. Earrings were trinkets celebrating successful voyages, stacked in multiples down the earlobe with pride. While we envisage fictional pirates in blousy shirting, in reality they did not wear what they called 'long clothes', since anything loose-fitting would be in danger of catching in the rigging.

COLOURS AND PATTERNS:
black, red, navy blue, skull prints

FABRICS: silk, leather, cotton

GARMENTS AND ACCESSORIES:
knee-high cavalier boots, breeches, thigh-high boots, poet shirt, military jacket, bicorne hat, earrings, scarves and bandanas

DETAILS: distressed, ripped, off-the-shoulder

Safari

◉ EXPEDITION, SAVANNAH
➡ <u>COWBOY</u>, <u>MILITARY</u>
➕ <u>CRUISE</u>, <u>CLASSIC</u>

As sure as 'florals for spring' is 'safari for summer', and fashion has a long history of appropriating this warm-climate aesthetic. The style has its origins in the khaki drill uniform worn by the British Indian Army Corps of Guides, which was introduced in 1848 (*khaki* is Urdu for 'dust-coloured') and rolled out to the rest of the British Armed Forces (see <u>Military</u>, p.91) before the Second Boer War (1899–1902). The safari or bush jacket was made from lightweight yet hard-wearing unlined cotton, sporting a wide <u>camp collar</u>, and was tied with a cotton belt rather than leather, for comfort. Four large 'bellows' pockets with box pleats could expand to hold all the accoutrements of adventure, such as map and compass, binoculars and gun cartridges. When paired with matching trousers or shorts, the safari jacket becomes a safari suit. Khaki drill remained combat dress until 1949 for desert and tropical service, and is still used by the British Armed Forces stationed in non-combatant hot climates.

Dolce & Gabbana Spring/Summer 2020, Milan Fashion Week, 22 September 2019.

The enigmatic writer Ernest Hemingway (also an avid hunter of big game, who packed notebooks along with gun cartridges in his oversized pockets) penned several works set in Africa, including *Green Hills of Africa* (1935), a non-fiction travel book inspired by a ten-week trip he made with his wife, Pauline, and *The Snows of Kilimanjaro*, a short story first published in Esquire magazine

Safari cont.

in 1936. Perhaps surprisingly, Hemingway was outfitted by
Abercrombie & Fitch, which was then – somewhat differently
from its later middle-of-the-road image – a brand for adventurers
and explorers. Advertisements from the time describe the
safari jacket as a 'coat-shirt', what fashion writers today refer
to as a hybrid 'shirt-jacket', or 'shacket', a useful trans-seasonal
wardrobe staple.

By the 1940s and 50s, safari themes had become a well-
trodden path in Hollywood, and a spate of films adopted the
aesthetic. The aptly titled *Safari* (1940) sizzled with Douglas
Fairbanks Jr and Madeleine Carroll, then in 1952 Gregory Peck,
Susan Hayward and Ava Gardner starred in the movie adaptation
of *The Snows of Kilimanjaro*, again showcasing the merits of the
safari jacket. *Mogambo* (1953), starring Clark Gable and Grace
Kelly, underlined the timeless appeal of the style. The book *Born
Free* (1960) by Joy Adamson, and the movie of it in 1966, starring
Virginia McKenna and Bill Travers as the couple raising wild lion
cubs, kept the African dream in the public eye.

The Algerian-born French designer Yves Saint Laurent had a
special affinity for the African continent. He first showed a safari
jacket in 1967 for his couture collection, and over the next two
years he developed two designs: a risqué lace-front version that
infused the look with 1960s sex appeal, and the military-style
'Saharienne' four-pocket, belted one that remains a signature piece
for the house (under its Saint Laurent rebrand) and is reinvented
from season to season. Yves Saint Laurent's original design for a
large circle-link belt also crops up in homage on catwalks today.

In the 1970s and 80s Roger Moore, as spy lothario James
Bond, brought to the fore myriad safari jackets and shirts, including
a cream silk and linen jacket and a sage-green camp shirt in
The Man with the Golden Gun (1974), a beige cotton shacket in
Moonraker (1979), which had the addition of a western shirt-style
yoke (see <u>Cowboy</u>, p.79), and a beige cotton military shirt and tan
wool shacket in *Octopussy* (1983). In 1984 Prince Charles became
an unlikely style icon in a version of the safari jacket by his Savile
Row tailor, Anderson & Sheppard, for a trip to Papua New Guinea
(Princess Diana sported a collarless, two-pocket skirt suit), and in
1985 Meryl Streep and Robert Redford continued the style in the
sweeping romantic drama *Out of Africa*.

On the runway, the military look is softened with diaphanous silk and satin fabrics that ooze loose-fitting comfort. Linen is another of the safari style's defining fabrics, being more hard-wearing than cotton and a better conductor of heat. Made from the flax plant, it is the world's oldest known textile (it has been found in ancient Egyptian tombs and was mentioned in the Bible, and a few scraps from prehistoric caves are more than 36,000 years old). Perhaps ironically, though, for a fabric otherwise suited to travel, it tends to crease disturbingly as soon as you step out of the door.

Given safari style's past as military and big-game hunting dress, and its problematic colonial connections, it serves stylists well not to interpret the look too literally. Pith helmets, guns or big cats on set, tempting though they are to underline the aesthetic, are not appropriate. You have been warned.

COLOURS AND PATTERNS: khaki, sand, beige, tan, drab, olive, rust, snake print, zebra print, leopard print, giraffe print

FABRICS: cotton, gabardine, drill, linen, Aertex, poplin, suede, worsted wool, moleskin

GARMENTS AND ACCESSORIES: shacket, shorts, short-sleeved shirt, Borsalino hat, Tilley hat

DETAILS: pockets, shoulder straps, bellows pockets, cartridge loops, circle belt, rope, raffia and straw

Music

The visual language of music is fashion. Almost without exception, for every genre of music, there is an associated style of dress.

Styles can be pinpointed to the decade in which they emerged. The 1950s were rock and roll, and rockabilly, with their blue jeans, gingham, swing skirts and post-war optimism. The 1960s brought a new groove with the exhibitionism of funk, a precursor to the sequins, hedonism and nightlife of disco. In upstate New York in 1969, the Woodstock festival changed history as a mass event of peace and free love. From there the classic sound of rock continued to flourish, liberally dusted with sex and drugs, tight leather trousers and big hair. It spoke to the devil on everyone's shoulder.

Rock's state shifted from hard rock into metal in the 1970s, alloyed with <u>Fetish</u> (p.293) and <u>Combat</u> (p.95) symbolism along the way.

3.

& Dance

In the four short years of its reign, 1970–74, glam rock punched above its weight, blessed with the likes of David Bowie as Ziggy Stardust, Marc Bolan of T. Rex, and the theatrics of Queen. It was a peculiarly British phenomenon that shone back over the Atlantic to inspire glam metal. Counter to this shiny, glittery aesthetic came the DIY anarchist ideology of punk, which raged long enough to become mainstream before imploding. Punk died, but the indie spirit lived on.

The 1980s brought the voice of hip hop and its fusion of breakbeats and MCing, the democratization of trends and the birth of streetwear. The role of the DJ continued to grow, and later in the decade electronic music became a genre at the dawn of the rave. By the 1990s rock had unpeeled the layers of artifice it had accrued, returning to a low-fi grunge aesthetic.

In the twenty-first century few people listen to only one musical genre, the same way few people stick to only one clothing style. Whether we listen across digital streaming platforms, congregate in muddy festival fields or dance alongside carnival parades, we will always be hardwired to enjoy the ritualistic experience of sound and rhythm, and find our music-based tribes.

Rock & Roll

⊖ 1950S AMERICANA, ROCK
● <u>RETRO</u>, <u>COMBAT</u>, <u>PREPPY</u>
⊕ <u>BIKER</u>, <u>VARSITY</u>

There are as many nuances of the rock clothing style as there are divergences in the musical genre itself. Rock and roll emerged from antecedent forms of African-American rhythm and blues, and gospel, as well as the folk sounds of country and western. Early contenders for the first rock song include 'Good Rockin' Tonight' (1948) by Wynonie Harris (re-recorded by Elvis Presley in 1954), and Jimmy Preston's boogie-woogie track 'Rock the Joint' (1949), although the latter was missing the crucial electric guitar element that characterizes rock and roll. The distinctive foot-tapping swing sound, energetic electric guitar and lead performer showmanship elements of the genre were developed by Chuck Berry, who recorded 'Maybellene' in 1955, the year Bill Haley's 'Rock around the Clock' topped the US Billboard chart.

Although the terms 'Rock & Roll' and '<u>Rockabilly</u>' (p.113) are sometimes used interchangeably by fashion writers and members of the contemporary rockabilly community to describe their retro form of dress (see <u>Retro</u>, p.20), the original rock and roll aesthetic is pure 1950s Americana with bowling shirts, denim jeans, penny loafers and Hawaiian shirts. Some adopters emulate the more conservative <u>Preppy</u> (p.191) look of the day in chinos (see also <u>Combat</u>, p.95) and sports jackets. The sports jacket, also known as a sports coat, was originally an invention of the hunting and shooting fraternity (see also <u>Rural</u>, p.74). It is a stand-alone jacket available in a variety of <u>tweeds</u> and plaids, differentiating it from the solid block colours of the <u>blazer</u> (see <u>Varsity</u>, p.193). Both are worn with trousers that complement, rather than match, the colour of the jacket, as opposed to the two- or three-piece suit, in which all pieces are cut from the same cloth.

Professionals who were out of their teens (such as many of the music artists themselves) favoured boxy, unstructured Brooks Brothers sack suits, the first mass-produced suits, which featured

Models wearing 1950s-style fashion. Undated photograph.

Rock & Roll cont.

a simple two-panel construction, no darts to the chest, and straight, unpleated trousers, and were designed to fit a variety of male body types off the peg (see also Tailoring, p.195). For younger fans, the 1950s Varsity (p.193) look was often seen in collegiate letterman jackets, while women of all ages wore tight sweaters, wide-legged and boyish 'Marlene' trousers, inspired by the actor Marlene Dietrich. Full circle skirts with nipped-in waists were favoured for dancing, paying homage to the silhouette of Christian Dior's New Look of 1947.

Worn by movie stars, featured in magazines, widely credited as being the first teenage girls' fashion trend, and an early example of trickle-down trend diffusion, these skirts – initially home-made – were the brainchild of an enterprising young actor from New York City, Juli Lynne Charlot, who needed a party outfit on a budget but lacked sewing skills. Made from a circle of felt, which was easy to cut and didn't require hemming, Charlot's conversation-starter designs featuring appliquéd poodles, hot rods, flamingoes and oversized blooms went into production for major department stores in the United States. They remain an iconic garment of the decade for vintage collectors.

COLOURS AND PATTERNS:
daffodil, pink, turquoise, teal, crimson, jungle green, atomic prints

FABRICS: wool, cotton, felt, denim

GARMENTS AND ACCESSORIES:
two-piece suit, blue jeans, bowling shirt, penny loafers, suede shoes, chinos, Hawaiian shirt, circle skirt, poodle skirt, cardigan, jumper, sports

Elvis Presley, c. 1958.

Rockabilly

- ◕ NEO-GREASER
- ◑ RETRO, BIKER
- ⊕ COWBOY, NAUTICAL, PIN-UP

Rockabilly, which had strong country music (hillbilly) inflection from the American Deep South, pioneered by Elvis Presley, built on the original Rock & Roll (p.110) aesthetic by adding such homespun fabrics as gingham, sweetheart necklines and cardigans for the girls, with western shirts and bootlace-style bolo ties for the boys (see Cowboy, p.79). The Greaser look (see Biker, p.67) was adopted by the rebellious teenage advocates of rock and roll with turned-up denim jeans, muscular T-shirts and tough biker jackets popularized by the iconic movie stars Marlon Brando and James Dean. As with rock and roll, broad-striped bowling shirts are a rockabilly favourite, as are whimsical poodle skirts.

The 1950s heralded a new era in women's sexuality, and liberated girls started to show more skin, encouraged by the appeal of such screen sirens as Marilyn Monroe, Bettie Page and Sandra Dee, who were known for their Pin-Up style (p.290) and penchant for a saucy take on a sailor's outfit (see Nautical, p.98). Tight pencil skirts, seamed stockings, cleavage-enhancing bustiers and peep-toe high heels add a frisson of sex kitten.

A key component of the look is down to hair, make-up and grooming. For the gents this means choosing from one of the cuts of the day, such as the pompadour (where all the hair is brushed skywards into a precision bouffant), quiff (where just the forelock is slicked back), or 'jelly roll' or 'elephant's trunk' (where the forelock is flopped forward and curled). These styles can be combined with the 'ducktail', where the hair on both sides is scraped into a V-shape at the nape. An alternative to the ducktail is the Boston, where the hair is cut straight across the neckline.

Contemporary rockabellas are known for their glamorous take on the 1950s aesthetic, with pin curls and flower hairpieces, and scarlet lipstick as an essential. 'Victory rolls', where the hair is swept up into barrels on the crown, are named after the manoeuvre

Rockabilly cont.

World War II pilots would pull after shooting down an enemy aircraft. For a simple daytime look, a low side ponytail, bandana or headscarf suffices.

In her lifetime, the British soul singer Amy Winehouse was known for matching her retro sound with a fusion of 1950s and early 60s rockabilly fashions. After her passing in 2011 (another star to join the tragic '27 club'), the fashion designer Jean Paul Gaultier paid tribute to her on his Spring 2021 couture catwalk with rockabilly pencil skirts and models sporting her signature beehive and winged eyeliner.

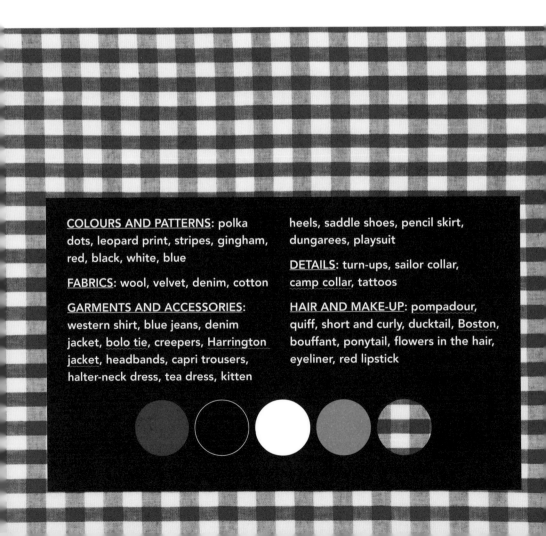

<u>COLOURS AND PATTERNS</u>: polka dots, leopard print, stripes, gingham, red, black, white, blue

<u>FABRICS</u>: wool, velvet, denim, cotton

<u>GARMENTS AND ACCESSORIES</u>: western shirt, blue jeans, denim jacket, bolo tie, creepers, Harrington jacket, headbands, capri trousers, halter-neck dress, tea dress, kitten heels, saddle shoes, pencil skirt, dungarees, playsuit

<u>DETAILS</u>: turn-ups, sailor collar, camp collar, tattoos

<u>HAIR AND MAKE-UP</u>: pompadour, quiff, short and curly, ducktail, Boston, bouffant, ponytail, flowers in the hair, eyeliner, red lipstick

Teddy Boys
& Teddy Girls

● NEO-EDWARDIAN, TEDS, JUDIES
➔ NEO-VICTORIANA, ROCK & ROLL, ROCKABILLY, PUNK, DANDY
⊕ TAILORING

While Rock & Roll (p.110) and Rockabilly (p.113) were born in the USA, a parallel youth subculture was emerging in the UK. On Savile Row, London, in 1954 tailors reacted to the end of rationing with a new drape suit with structured, sloping shoulders based on a style of evening jacket worn by Edwardian Dandies (p.247). It was single-breasted, often with a velvet shawl collar and contrasting French cuffs, box cut at the back with no vent, loose and unshaped at the waist in a style reminiscent of American 1930s zoot suits, and paired with slim, tapered trousers (see also Tailoring, p.195). It was aimed at upper-middle-class and aristocratic youth; however, for the most part, they rejected the trend. Instead, the suits were appropriated by dapper working-class lads, who grafted to afford the tailor's fittings, sometimes paying in weekly instalments.

The suit evoked the grit of American gangster movies, or the frock coats of Victorian-era gunslingers in the Wild West (see Neo-Victoriana, p.26), and these youths dressed as neo-Edwardians were dubbed 'Teddy Boys' in the press. They paired the suits with white shirts sporting a 'Mr B' collar (a high roll style patented by the singer Billy Eckstine), lavish brocade waistcoats, and narrow 'Slim Jim' ties or western-inspired bolo ties, and exhibited haircuts in the heavily pomaded American rockabilly style. They wore 'creepers', suede shoes similar to those used by World War II soldiers in North Africa; the name was attributed to the combination of its thick crepe sole and the craze for a slow-shuffle dance called 'The Creep' after the Ken Mackintosh song of the same name in 1954.

Teddy Girls, known as 'Judies', were almost exclusively working class, and although they socialized with the Boys they were still bound by contemporary gender expectations to help

Teddy Boys' Picnic, Tyneside, northern England. Back row: Rockin Jim Newark (29), Boppin Brian Dixon (19), Jumpin John Hunter (20), Rockin Ron Lewis (19), Alan 'The Jet' Duel (22). Front row: Laurie the Lar Bell (22), Mick Rankin Pink Panther (26), Chris Crazy Legs Magee (23). Undated photograph.

in the home. Most had left school as teenagers to work as reception staff or in factories, and while they were the first post-war teenage demographic to have some disposable income for discretionary goods, such as records, the Equal Pay Act of 1970 was still a long way off. Their affected upper-class dress was a testament to their imagination of a refined lifestyle: tailored jackets, masculine shirts and ties or Edwardian cravats, with slim-fitting pencil or hobble skirts, cropped, turned-up denim jeans, and circle skirts later in the decade. They carried umbrellas whatever the weather, often incongruously bare-toed in espadrilles, with straw boater hats or conical Asian 'rice paddy' hats, cradling elegant clutch bags.

Originally the Teds danced to jazz and skiffle, but when rock and roll landed in Britain, they knew they had found their sound. The films *Blackboard Jungle* (1955) and *Rock Around the Clock* (1956), with their rock and roll soundtracks, inspired exuberant dancing in the aisles and damage to cinema property. Teddy Boys started to be vilified in the press as delinquents, and when a contingent was present at the Notting Hill race riots in 1958, it tarred them all collectively.

Teddy Boy style gave way to the sleeker Mod aesthetic (p.228) of the 1960s, before being revived in the 1970s, this time characterized by drape jackets in brighter colours, paired with drainpipe jeans and loud shirts. Young Punks (p.125) clashed with older Teds on the streets of London in defence of their music choices, a conflict that was hyped by the press, but by the late 1970s and 80s their fashion and music styles had merged as part of the post-punk New Wave aesthetic.

COLOURS AND PATTERNS: black, navy, houndstooth, classic tweed checks

FABRICS: Wool, velvet, denim, brocade, cotton

GARMENTS AND ACCESSORIES: Boys: drape jacket, drainpipe jeans, bolo tie, winklepickers; Girls: circle skirt, pencil skirt, tailored jacket, cropped jeans, straw boater, clutch bag, espadrilles; Both: cravat, white shirt, umbrella

DETAILS: half-moon pockets, pocket watch and chain

HAIR: quiff, pompadour, Boston, ducktail, Tony Curtis quiff, sideburns

Classic Rock

Steven Tyler and Joe Perry of Aerosmith, London, 28 June 2014.

◐ ROCK
➡ HIPPY, SURF, POLITICAL
⊕ INDIE, FESTIVAL, ANDROGYNOUS

By the late 1950s rock had lost its roll. Elvis had joined the army, and on a fateful day in February 1959 (immortalized in 1971 as 'The Day the Music Died' in the song 'American Pie' by Don McClean), rock and roll stars Buddy Holly, Ritchie Valens and Jiles Perry Richardson Jr, known as 'The Big Bopper', were killed in a plane crash. At the start of the 1960s pop, Motown and Surf rock (p.234) were ruling the airwaves. That was until the 'British Invasion' of 1964.

There was a contrast between the Beatles wanting 'to hold your hand', and the Rolling Stones, who couldn't 'get no satisfaction'. The Stones were hell-bent on cultivating a gritty image to go with their hard electric blues sound, and as a point of difference from the relatively clean-cut Fab Four, they didn't wear suits on stage. Tousled, backcombed hair was a prerequisite. Mick Jagger snarled and peacocked across the stage, snake-hipped in leather; lovable rogue Keith Richards was never photographed without a cigarette hanging precipitously from his lips; Bill Wyman slapped his bass; and Charlie Watts brought drumming into the spotlight. Before his untimely death at the age of 27 (another pop-cultural icon to join the infamous '27 club'), the virtuoso multi-instrumentalist Brian Jones had fathered at least five children by different women, and accumulated several addictions. This trifecta of philandering, narcotics and music artistry set the bar for the heyday of rock, which spanned the next two decades.

In San Francisco, perhaps unexpectedly, it was anti-consumerist Hippy bands (p.223) pioneering psychedelic rock, such as Jefferson Airplane and the Grateful Dead (more specifically their producer, Bill Graham), who first hit upon the genius idea of selling merchandise to supplement the artists' incomes. The age of the band T-shirt had begun. Throughout the 1960s, as people renounced the Vietnam War, the humble T-shirt also became

the medium for <u>Political</u> messages (p.260), a format that has
continued into recent designer collections.

   As the theatrics of rock inflated to preternatural proportions in
the 1970s, it swelled into <u>Glam Rock</u> (p.122), a shiny bubble burst
by the angry counterculture of <u>Punk</u> (p.125), which fed into <u>Grunge</u>
(p.134) in the 1990s. Classic rock split into various subgenres, such
as progressive rock, alternative rock, power pop and soft rock.

   The symbiosis of rock music and designer fashion was
underlined when the French designer Hedi Slimane, as the creative
director of Yves Saint Laurent from 2012 until 2016, controversially
dropped 'Yves' from the brand name and moved the traditionally
Parisian house's design atelier and fashion shows to Los Angeles.
Around this time, several designers investigated the band tee
trope, including Versace for Spring/Summer 2014 and Vetements
for Autumn/Winter 2016. Rock remains a pervasive influence on
style, and cycled back as part of the lo-fi <u>Indie</u> aesthetic (p.131)
in the 2000s. While rock waxes and wanes as a musical genre, the
rock-star image is timeless.

<u>COLOURS AND PATTERNS:</u>
black, red, grey, white, gunmetal,
silver, stripes, polka dots, leopard
print, paisley

<u>FABRICS</u>: velvet, leather, cotton

<u>GARMENTS AND ACCESSORIES:</u>
denim jeans, T-shirt, band T-shirt,
ripped jeans, leather jacket, skinny
scarf, hat, biker jacket, sunglasses,
round glasses, leather trousers,
waistcoat, <u>Chelsea boots</u>, cowboy
boots, silver jewellery

<u>DETAILS:</u> Cuban heel, ripped,
flared, skinny, tattoos, plectrums,
guitars, fringing

<u>HAIR AND MAKE-UP:</u> shaggy hair,
curly hair, long hair, eyeliner

Metal

≈ HARD ROCK, HEAVY METAL, HEADBANGER

● COMBAT, ROCK & ROLL, GLAM ROCK, PUNK, BOHEMIAN, CAMP, FETISH

✛ BIKER, GOTH

The rock sound was forged through hellfire into heavy metal in the late 1960s and 70s, influenced by the guitar-shredding solos of blues-infused psychedelic rock artists Eric Clapton and Jimi Hendrix. The British bands Led Zeppelin, Deep Purple and Black Sabbath led the way into the abyss via a style initially touted as 'hard rock'. Defined by their sped-up drums, operatic vocals and diabolical themes, metal albums also contained moments of quiet, folky introspection. In the United States, Alice Cooper and MC5 turned hard rock into proto-Punk (p.125), while Gene Simmons et al. of Kiss viewed it through the lens of Glam Rock (p.122). In 1973 the Australian hard rock/metal icons AC/DC formed, although the band always insisted that their sound was still simply Rock & Roll (p.110).

In the 1980s the New Wave of British Heavy Metal (NWOBHM) spawned the juggernauts Iron Maiden, Motörhead and Saxon, all with a predilection for gothic lettering and Viking warrior motifs. The band Judas Priest, fronted by Rob Halford, is credited with developing the scene's affiliation with leather, incorporating elements of Fetish (p.293), Biker (p.67) and gang culture with leather jackets, belts, studded gauntlets and cut-off kutte jackets, also known as 'battle vests', in denim or leather embellished with patches, chains and studs. In Los Angeles and California, Guns N' Roses developed an American sound, Van Halen introduced virtuosity, while Mötley Crüe and Aerosmith leaned towards glam, earning the nickname 'hair metal'. The 'Big Four' Metallica, Megadeth, Anthrax and Slayer made the case for thrash metal.

Fans would emulate the style of the artists themselves, with jeans ripped from sliding across the stage; spray-on leather trousers or a biker jacket and layers of jewellery; skinny silk scarves and fringing to emphasize movement on stage; a billowing shirt reminiscent of Bohemian style (p.217), or in a loud pattern, thrown

Guns N' Roses in London, 1986.

over a muscle vest; and extravagant hats and eyeliner verging on
Camp (p.275), with a lift from a Cuban-heeled cowboy boot. The
band T-shirt is ubiquitous in its purpose of proclaiming allegiance
to a specific tribe. At the heaviest end of metal, fans tend to be
fiercely anti-fashion, wearing cargo shorts in camouflage sourced
from army-surplus stores (see Combat, p.95).

　　More so than classic rock, metal bands seem impervious to
musical fads. Many of the original bands continue to perform with
frontmen in their seventies.

COLOURS AND PATTERNS: black,
white, red, camouflage, gunmetal

FABRICS: leather, black denim,
spandex

GARMENTS AND ACCESSORIES:
black jeans, blue jeans, band T-shirt,
bullet belt, biker jacket, combat
boots, platform biker boots,
cargo shorts, cargo trousers, shirt,

kutte jacket, skater shoes, Converse,
gauntlets, gunmetal jewellery, choker

DETAILS: studs, straps, buckles,
gothic fonts, stretched earlobes,
piercings, rips

HAIR AND MAKE-UP: long hair,
blue- or red-dyed hair, beard, eyeliner,
body paint

Glam Rock

● GLITTER ROCK
● METAL, PUNK, HIPPY
⊕ FUTURISM, AVANT-GARDE, ANDROGYNOUS, CAMP

The year 1971 was a tough one for the British. Unemployment reached a post-war high of nearly 815,000, the pound went decimal, inflation was at a 30-year high, Rolls-Royce went into receivership, the United Kingdom opted out of the Space Race, and the Troubles in Northern Ireland reached boiling point with bloodshed on both sides.

On the other hand, rock music was going strong. The first Hard Rock Cafe opened in London, the Reading Festival made its inaugural appearance, the Who released its iconic album *Who's Next*, and on *Top of the Pops*, Marc Bolan of T. Rex performed 'Get It On' wearing a silver lamé jacket with sculptural shoulders, pink trousers, a gold brocade waistcoat and a liberal dusting of glitter across his cheekbones. It was both musically and aesthetically a departure from their earlier folky, Hippy style (p.223). Glam rock had entered the building.

David Bowie's alter ego Ziggy Stardust defined the genre: a fictional character based on the narrative of an Androgynous (p.270), bisexual alien who falls to Earth to save humanity, is worshipped as a messiah, then destroyed by his followers. Dressed in metallic jumpsuits, with heavily made-up eyes, glossy red lips, a sun-like gold disc on his forehead and a shocking crimson mullet, he set trends for men and women alike. The symbolism ran deeper than its glittering facade; Ziggy was a comment on the archetype of the self-indulgent rock star, with elements of Dada absurdism and Futurism (p.33), as well as the exaggerated movements of mime and Japanese kabuki theatre. Bowie had a strong affinity for Japanese culture, and some of Ziggy's most memorable, Avant-Garde (p.244) costumes were designed by Kansai Yamamoto.

The look was pervasive, and influenced such acts as Queen and Def Leppard while spawning Roxy Music, Sweet, Alvin Stardust and Mott the Hoople (for whom Bowie wrote a song), as well as Slade before it became known solely as the purveyor of a famous Christmas song. Although this was a mainly British phenomenon,

Jean Paul Gaultier Spring/Summer 2013, Paris Fashion Week, 30 September 2012.

Glam Rock cont.

there were some American artists at the fringes, such as Suzi Q, who made the silver leather jumpsuit her own, and those who dived right in, such as Alice Cooper, and Kiss, who took it to shock-rock, glam-metal extremes (see Metal, p.120).

Glam rock had a complicated relationship with Punk (p.125), which similarly wanted to move away from 1970s rock's indulgent and increasingly mainstream nature while denouncing its more glam sound. A few bands, such as the New York Dolls, managed to bridge the gap with glam punk.

Bowie killed off Ziggy in 1973, re-emerging as Aladdin Sane, now with the iconic lightning-bolt motif across his face, with a more blues-driven sound inspired by the Rolling Stones and by his time in the United States. The artist's glam-rock incarnations, including his *Diamond Dogs* album-era persona of 1974, have been referenced directly on catwalks from Jean Paul Gaultier Spring/Summer 2013 to Philipp Plein Resort 2019, indirectly at Balmain Autumn/Winter 2011, and consistently in the collections of the London designer Pam Hogg.

A post-pandemic glam-rock revival was instigated by the Italian band Måneskin, which thundered its way to victory in the Eurovision Song Contest in 2021 to become a worldwide sensation wearing Bowie-esque red leather one-pieces.

COLOURS AND PATTERNS: red, silver, gold, white, geometric, stripes, stars

FABRICS: spandex, lamé, lace, brocade, lurex, vinyl

GARMENTS AND ACCESSORIES: jumpsuit, platforms, knee-high boots

DETAILS: lightning bolts, sci-fi and space themes, power shoulders, asymmetric, one-shoulder

HAIR AND MAKE-UP: mullet, glitter

Punk

⊜ PUNK ROCK
⊖ <u>FUTURISM</u>, <u>TEDDY BOYS & TEDDY GIRLS</u>, <u>METAL</u>, <u>GLAM ROCK</u>, <u>INDIE</u>, <u>HIPPY</u>
⊕ <u>HERITAGE</u>, <u>CYBERPUNK</u>, <u>STEAMPUNK</u>, <u>DIESELPUNK</u>, <u>COMBAT</u>, <u>POLITICAL</u>, <u>FETISH</u>

Of all the styles in this book, punk is among the most commonly referenced in global fashion collections. As much as it is a subgenre of rock music (see <u>Rock & Roll</u>, p.110), it is also a subculture (see section 6, <u>Subcultures & Countercultures</u>, p.212, where this entry could have easily sat).

Ironically, fashion's love for punk is unrequited, given that punk as a movement is nonconformist, anti-consumerist and anti-capitalist. While it rejects and is anti-fashion in terms of seasonal trends, it has a strong sense of style based on contravening social norms, is proactive in its DIY ideology, and uses found objects, such as safety pins, with craft-based zips, studs and hand-painted slogans. It takes traditionally conservative <u>Heritage</u> fabrics (p.23), such as tartan, and imbues them with anti-authoritarian meaning, juxtaposing them with slick leather and PVC.

Punk was conceived in opposition to mainstream, self-indulgent hard rock and the easy-going flower power of the <u>Hippy</u> (p.223) movement, starting in 1971 with the proto-punk band the New York Dolls, who were managed by Malcolm McLaren and fused elements of David Bowie and T. Rex's <u>Glam Rock</u> (p.122) with the primal energy of the Stooges. The Ramones – widely credited as the first post-rock band – formed in New York City in 1974, and the sound spread with such bands as the Clash in London (1976), the Saints in Brisbane (1973) and Buzzcocks in Manchester (1976). (Buzzcocks were also the first real <u>Indie</u> band, p.131, taking the DIY ideology to its logical conclusion by pressing their own records.)

McLaren had a shop on the King's Road, Chelsea, which had been selling <u>Teddy Boy & Teddy Girl</u> (p.115) fashions since 1971, as well as designs by his girlfriend Vivienne Westwood (who had been working as a primary-school teacher). The shop was

Punk cont.

rebranded 'SEX' in 1974, and a year later a 19-year-old John Lydon auditioned for the Sex Pistols by singing along to Alice Cooper's 'I'm Eighteen' on the store's jukebox, alongside records and rails of Fetish wear (p.293), while Chrissie Hynde, later of the Pretenders, worked behind the counter.

Lydon's transformation into his alter ego Johnny Rotten, with bleached orange-red spiky hair, was complete by the time he opened the controversial track 'Anarchy in the UK' (1976) with the declaration, 'I am an anti-Christ, I am an anarchist.' That wasn't the half of it, though, and the bass player John Simon Ritchie (also known as Sid Vicious) exemplified the out-of-control extremes of punk. He died of a heroin overdose at 21 years old while on bail for assault and for the murder of his girlfriend, 20-year-old Nancy Spungen, a groupie and seasoned heroin addict, who was found dead on their hotel bathroom floor with a single knife wound to the abdomen. He confessed, then retracted the statement, saying he had passed out on the bed. The identity of the murderer remains a mystery.

Unlike mainstream rock, punk encouraged female artists, since they were by nature anti-establishment – such as the New Yorker Patti Smith, who released the seminal punk poetry album *Horses* in 1975. In the UK, 1976 was a pivotal year for female-fronted punk bands, spearheaded by Siouxsie and the Banshees and X-Ray Spex. Siouxsie Sioux, born Susan Janet Ballion, befriended the Sex Pistols, attended gigs and contributed to the aesthetic development of punk as well as Goth (p.220) with her jagged, raven-black hair, heavily kohled cat-eye make-up, scarlet lipstick and layers of black, bondage-inspired clubwear often sourced from SEX. She was a poster girl for the DIY philosophy: an audience member who decided she could be on the stage, too, and who – despite having no formal training – displayed a powerful four-octave vocal range. Later that year SEX was renamed and refitted once again, this time to 'Seditionaries: Clothes for Heroes', as Vivienne Westwood's designs evolved to include deconstructed mohair sweaters, chains, Combat gear (p.95), artfully ripped pornography-printed T-shirts and detachable 'bum flaps' (a kind of reverse loincloth, seemingly without purpose), alongside her popular bondage trousers complete with zipped crotch and hobble straps.

At the same time emerged Marianne Joan Elliott-Said – soon to be known by her stage name, Poly Styrene – who had previously

A punk boy in Trafalgar Square, London, early 1980s.

released a reggae record and who became X-Ray Spex's songwriter and lead vocalist. One of the few punk artists of mixed heritage, with British-Somalian parents, Poly Styrene wore her hair naturally curly and interpreted punk through a lens of Futurism (p.33), using upcycled synthetic materials and wearing vivid colours, making her clothes herself or sourcing them second-hand before 'vintage' was a term. Her costumes covered more than they showed, and she refused to be reduced to a sex symbol. The famous line, 'some people think little girls should be seen and not heard,' before a screamed, 'but I think "Oh bondage, up yours!"', from the band's debut track, 'Oh Bondage Up Yours!' (1977), is often cited as pre-empting the Riot Grrrl movement of the 1990s, which generated such bands as Bikini Kill and the Slits. Female punks pioneered third-wave feminism and its focus on intersectionality and reproductive rights.

Punk rears its head on the catwalk with unfailing certainty from year to year, reinvented as a metaphor (a hackneyed one, some fashion writers would say) for youth culture and rebellion, from

Punk cont.

Versace's titillating gold safety-pin dresses for Spring/Summer 1994 to Junya Watanabe's patchwork of British heritage textiles for Autumn/Winter 2017, via Jean Paul Gaultier's Spring/Summer 2011 couture collection, and an enduring fixation with buckles, chains, spikes and pins at Alexander McQueen. Punk's distinctive aesthetic has also been incorporated into myriad retrofuturistic styles, including the technological, neo-noir sensibilities of Cyberpunk (p.38), the gothic Victoriana of Steampunk (p.42), and the roaring engines and post-apocalyptic chug of Dieselpunk (p.45).

Of course, Vivienne Westwood – who became part of the establishment, with a damehood bestowed by Queen Elizabeth II – will always be thought of as the undisputed godmother of punk. Towards the end of her life the designer reiterated the anti-consumerist message for a new generation with the aphorism 'Buy less, choose well, make it last.' In the 1970s, punk was the bitter pill the mainstream needed, and the more commercialized today's youth culture becomes, the harder punk will surely hit when it inevitably returns.

COLOURS AND PATTERNS: black, red, emerald green, tartan, pinstripe, leopard, horizontal wide stripes

FABRICS: leather, PVC, fishnet, tweed, mohair

GARMENTS AND ACCESSORIES: corset, leather trousers, biker jacket, biker boots, Doc Martens, combat boots, creepers, kilt, choker, blazer, studded belt

DETAILS: safety pins, chains, spikes, studs, distressed, rips, hand-painted slogans, zips, turn-ups, piercings and body modifications

HAIR: mohawk, dyed

Emo

- EMOTIONAL HARDCORE, ALT-ROCK, POP-PUNK
- PUNK
- E-BOY & E-GIRL, SKATE

Emo is punk's musically gifted, introverted adolescent sibling, who shies away from violence (towards others). It evolved out of the mid-1980s hardcore punk sound of Washington State, dubbed 'emotional hardcore' and later abbreviated to 'emo', with such bands as Rites of Spring (founded 1983) and Jimmy Eat World (1993) taking hardcore introspective.

By the millennium, emo and pop-punk bands were almost indistinguishable. As a case in point, see My Chemical Romance (founded 2001) and the Red Jumpsuit Apparatus (2003), who helped to define the harmonic, confessional interludes that are interspersed with sections of hardcore punk. However, many of these bands rejected the label 'emo'.

The emo style owes a lot to such punk tropes as studded belts and spikes, but paired with younger elements, including denim jeans, band hoodies, band badges and Skate shoes (p.231). The fingerless gloves or arm warmers are used by some emos to cover scars from self-harming, continuing punk's legacy of self-mutilation left by Iggy Pop of the Stooges. Others just like the look. Emo has evolved over time, with such artists as the sexually fluid Yorkshire-born Dominic Harrison (also known as Yungblud) cycling back emo for the TikTok generation with a nod to E-Boy & E-Girl style (p.51).

Even emo has a subgenre in Scene, which focuses on the clothing rather than the musical style. Scenesters are to all intents and purposes happy emos, and the style was popular with teenagers in the United States from the mid-2000s to the early 2010s. There

Demna Gvasalia for Vetements Spring/Summer 2017 Haute Couture, Paris Fashion Week, 24 January 2017.

Emo cont.

is no musical subgenre referred to as 'scene' itself; rather, its followers enjoy a variety of styles connected to emo, including crunkcore, happy hardcore, screamo, emo pop and pop punk. At first glance a scenester may look emo, but there are some subtle differences to the stereotype: striped neon hair extensions, a cartoon skull-print T-shirt or hoodie, tulle tutu skirt, bright leggings or mismatched socks, white denim jeans, plastic bead jewellery and shutter shades are all popular. They are often highly Androgynous (p.270), channelling the spirit of David Bowie and Glam Rock (p.122), and have more piercings than emos, especially stretched lobes, septum piercings, or snakebite and labret piercings that frame the lips.

For all emos and scenesters, eyeliner, asymmetric haircuts and tattoos are key elements of the look. As points of difference, emos may reference the introspective intellectualism of Academia (p.188), with thick horn-rimmed spectacles that are rarely seen on the scene. They will also display original band merchandise and are genuine music fans.

COLOURS AND PATTERNS: black, grey, black-and-white stripes, pink, purple, green, tartan

FABRICS: denim, PVC, leather

GARMENTS AND ACCESSORIES: skinny jeans, tight T-shirt, band T-shirt, hoody, Vans, Converse, Doc Martens, fingerless gloves, fishnet tights, choker, chain belt, PVC trousers, black spectacles, arm warmers

DETAILS: studs, spikes, skulls, layered jewellery, rings, piercings, tattoos

HAIR AND MAKE-UP: long fringe, backcombed hair, red or blue streaks, chipped nail polish, thick eyeliner

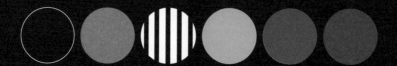

Indie

- INDIE-ROCK, INDIE-POP, INDEPENDENT
- E-BOY & E-GIRL, PUNK, EMO
- POLO, CLASSIC ROCK, GRUNGE, RAVE, HIPSTER, MOD

Indie-rock (and its radio-friendly version indie-pop) is essentially a subgenre of rock, and as such carries a few of the same Classic Rock (p.118) totems, among them spray-on jeans, band T-shirt, Biker jacket (p.67), chunky boots, skinny scarf, and jaunty trilby or fedora.

Punk (p.125) granted artists permission to go in any direction. Some went the alt-rock and art-rock route, like Sonic Youth. Some decided to go independent of a major record label, such as Buzzcocks, who are credited as being one of the United Kingdom's first 'indie' bands to release their own material, pressing 1,000 copies of their debut EP, *Spiral Scratch*, in 1977 and selling it directly to record stores. It went on to sell 16,000 copies and made the UK Top 40, launching the band's career. The album cover was shot on Polaroid by their manager, Richard Boon, and this low-fi, unpretentious nature was part of the burgeoning genre's charm.

Early indie was influenced musically by the bittersweet lyrics and jangle-pop strumming of the Smiths in the United Kingdom, and by R.E.M.'s alt college-rock sound in the United States. Stylistically understated, the look combined black blazers with blue jeans and oversized shirts, either plain or vertically striped, and an unbuttoned waistcoat.

In the 1990s Grunge (p.134) stamped indie with the souls of tortured artists (and ubiquitous plaid shirts), and at its fringes, Emo (p.129) added a flicker of dark introspection. In the United Kingdom, Britpop divided fans between the swagger of Oasis in their signature parkas and floral shirts inspired by Mod subculture (p.228) and the 'Madchester' indie dance scene (see Rave, p.146); and the art-school sensibility of Blur with their array of knitwear, shirts, Harrington jackets and striped polos (see Polo, p.76).

As the indie mindset expanded, it shifted consumer behaviour away from high-street brands and designer labels towards

Indie cont.

Hedi Slimane for Yves Saint Laurent Autumn/Winter 2013–14 Menswear, Paris Fashion Week, 20 January 2013.

independent designers and vintage-store hauls. Young, creative millennials started questioning where their clothes came from, and this lit the touchpaper of the sustainable fashion movement. It was also the birth of the Hipster (p.226), whose uniform consisted of thrifted sheepskin coats, denim trucker jackets, well-worn sweaters and suede or flannel shirts thrown over faded tees and jeans and paired with Doc Martens or Converse high-tops.

The golden age of indie, around the millennium, saw the emergence of such transatlantic bands as the Arctic Monkeys, Bloc Party, Dirty Pretty Things, the Killers, the National, the Strokes, the Libertines, the Horrors, the Rapture, the Stills and the Fratellis, among many others that took the definite article. This was notably a white boys' club, and there were few Black, queer or female bands or artists; Kate Nash, Warpaint, Anna Calvi and Beth Ditto were some of the exceptions. The homogeneity reached saturation point, referred to by some in the music press as 'indie landfill', and although the music scene died down, fashion will always have a penchant for the 'I'm with the band' look.

On the catwalk, it was Hedi Slimane who looked to the music scene of his home town, Los Angeles, for Saint Laurent's Autumn/Winter 2013 menswear collection, which offered leather, plaid, red leopard and ripped blue denim for a low-key rock royalty look. In 2022 fashion writers hailed the return of 'indie sleaze', a hybrid of grunge and decadent 1980s rock with an affected nod to Retro (p.20), which had originally spread like wildfire across the 2010s social-media platform Tumblr as an early internet aesthetic (see also E-Boy & E-Girl, p.51).

COLOURS AND PATTERNS: black, grey, red, white

FABRICS: denim, knit, leather

GARMENTS AND ACCESSORIES: hoodie, ripped jeans, skinny jeans, oversized knitwear, fedora, beanie hat, blue denim hotpants, biker jacket, band T-shirt, parka, plaid shirt, skinny scarf, knitted wool scarf, suede jacket, denim jacket, military jacket, Doc Martens, biker boots

DETAILS: crumpled fabric, fringing

HAIR AND MAKE-UP: tousled hair, smudged eyeliner, tattoos

Grunge

◉ SEATTLE SOUND
◓ <u>NAUTICAL</u>, <u>METAL</u>, <u>GLAM ROCK</u>, <u>PUNK</u>, <u>NORMCORE</u>, <u>ANDROGYNOUS</u>
⊕ <u>E-BOY & E-GIRL</u>, <u>BIKER</u>, <u>INDIE</u>, <u>BOHEMIAN</u>

It's Christmas Eve 1988 in the Pacific Northwest seaport of Seattle, and it's barely above freezing as Nirvana head into the studio to record their debut album, *Bleach*, for the sum of $606.17. The record goes on to sell more than 2 million copies worldwide. Their signature stop-start sound, which veers between angry nihilist and down-tempo, wistful disappointment, is typical of the grunge genre. The 'Seattle Sound', as it is known in the music press, is influenced by American <u>Punk</u> (p.125) bands, including Black Flag, and such 1970s <u>Metal</u> (p.120) bands as Black Sabbath – the anthesis of the exhibitionist <u>Glam Rock</u>-inspired (p.122) hair metal that is saturating the charts. Out of this cultural Petri dish oozes grunge, characterized by its rawness and low-tech production, with melancholic electric guitars distorted through a simple wah-wah pedal. Tellingly, grunge also has moments of melodic pop and fragile optimism.

Grunge style wasn't specifically anti-fashion, as punk was; it was more akin to a 1990s version of <u>Normcore</u> (p.199) in that it didn't want to make a statement (although paradoxically, as with most anti-statement modes of dress, it later became one). Kurt Cobain was the poster boy of the genre, and with his shaggy, dirty-blonde hair and kohl-lined eyes, he wasn't without style. The dishevelled, thrifty aesthetic of the genre is seen in ripped jeans, faded band T-shirts, chunky boots, thermal underwear and plaid lumberjack shirts or oversized woolly knits. He also famously wore a woman's dress for his iconic cover for *The Face* magazine in 1993 (see <u>Androgynous</u>, p.270), yet often opted for such classics as a striped *marinière* top (see <u>Nautical</u>, p.98).

The grunge scene was an epicentre of heroin addiction, which coincided with the mid-1990s 'heroin chic' look for catwalk models – characterized by the waiflike Kate Moss – who lacked the athletic vigour of such early 1990s 'supers' as Linda Evangelista, Naomi

Kurt Cobain of Nirvana, Chicago, 1993.

Grunge cont.

Campbell and Cindy Crawford. Courtney Love, lead singer of the rock band Hole (and Cobain's wife), popularized the Kinderwhore look, a feminist reinterpretation of demure baby-doll dresses, good-girl <u>Peter Pan collars</u> and <u>Mary Jane shoes</u>, given a gritty, fallen-from-grace edge.

Marc Jacobs's Spring/Summer 1993 collection for Perry Ellis was one of the first examples in which a trend had bubbled up from the street to the catwalk, to be reinterpreted in luxe fabrics at high price points, for elevated versions of everyday staples. It received negative reviews, which led to Jacobs being fired, although in time the collection was considered prescient. Other designers, such as Anna Sui, flirted with grunge, to a lukewarm reception. When Hedi Slimane did grunge for Saint Laurent's Autumn/Winter 2013, he divided the fashion press, some reviews praising in glowing terms his attunement to cultural capital, others horrified that he was taking the French house's heritage downmarket. It did, however, get the approval of Love herself. The inevitable resurgence of 1990s trends 20–30 years after their origin ushered in a new era of grunge that resonated with another generation of disaffected youth in the 2020s. Grunge, in the words of Nirvana's anti-materialist, inclusive lyrics, gives permission to 'come as you are'.

<u>COLOURS AND PATTERNS</u>: red, black, plaid, floral prints (micro), thin horizontal stripes

<u>FABRICS</u>: denim, cotton, corduroy

<u>GARMENTS AND ACCESSORIES</u>: jeans, flannel shirt, band T-shirt, minidress, skater skirt, Doc Martens, combat boots, cardigan

<u>DETAILS</u>: rips, black opaque tights, silver jewellery, choker, mirrored lenses, denim shorts over tights, layering, long necklaces

Funk

- ⬭ GROOVE, BOOGIE, GO-GO
- ➡ <u>MILITARY</u>, <u>CLASSIC ROCK</u>, <u>TAILORING</u>, <u>HIPPY</u>
- ⊕ <u>FUTURISM</u>, <u>AFROFUTURISM</u>, <u>COWBOY</u>, <u>DISCO</u>

The earliest use of 'funky' as an adjective came through jazz slang around the turn of the nineteenth century, meaning a strong, earthy smell to evoke the primal, pungent odour that lingers after physical exertion and sex. The word's use was considered improper for the delicate sensibilities of white America, but for African-American jazz audiences, the sweat of the performer was something to be celebrated. For the same reason, artists would encourage one another to 'get down' and put some 'stank' ('stink' and funk) on it. 'Funk' as a style of music was coined in 1959, and by the 1960s the word 'funky' had come to mean unconventionally stylish and modern. Musically, funk came from soul and R&B, and was a reaction to the pretentions and complexities of modern jazz. Funk emphasized groove, and was characteristically down-tempo, suggestive and pleasurable to dance to.

James Brown, the undisputed Godfather of Soul, epitomized funk's divergence from the polished aura of Motown: Black performers, styled to be palatable for the more conservative white audiences of the time in elegant gowns and dinner jackets (see <u>Tailoring</u>, p.195). Brown brought to the aesthetic a raw carnal energy with sequined jumpsuits slashed to the navel (often emblazoned with the word 'SEX'), shimmering metallic jackets and platform shoes. George Clinton and his Parliament-Funkadelic collective,

Halpern, London Fashion Week, 15 February 2020.

Funk cont.

including the wildly extrovert bass player Bootsy Collins, added psychedelic influences (see Hippy, p.223) with touches of science fiction-inspired Afrofuturism (p.48) and cosmic motifs. Jimi Hendrix was a pioneer of funk rock (see Classic Rock, p.118), and his proclivity for a vintage Military hussar jacket (p.91) gave the genre another expression.

   In the 1970s these threads were woven into the Disco aesthetic (p.139). However, as a point of difference, funk had live performances, while disco DJs span discs ('disco' is an abbreviation of *discothèque*, a word coined by the French during the Nazi occupation, when live music was banned).

   Funk samples and breakbeats have been instrumental in both Hip Hop (p.142) and dance music, with its influence through Rave culture (p.146).

COLOURS AND PATTERNS: fuchsia, turquoise blue, mustard, bright orange, lime green, plaid

FABRICS: satin, polyester, nylon, lamé, velvet

GARMENTS AND ACCESSORIES: platform shoes, jumpsuit, dungarees, bell-bottom trousers, three-piece suit, headband, skinny scarves, round sunglasses, roll neck, fedora, rings, fur coat

DETAILS: sequins, low cut, wide lapels, fringing, camp collar

Disco

◉ CLUB
⊖ <u>FLAPPER</u>, <u>FUNK</u>, <u>RAVE</u>
⊕ <u>RETRO</u>, <u>BODY-CONSCIOUS</u>

Modern club culture, with superstar DJs, extravagantly themed venues and aspirational dress codes, started with the dawn of disco in the 1970s. Musically a fusion of <u>Funk</u> (p.137) and soul, jazz (see <u>Flapper</u>, p.30), gospel and R&B, disco was originally a safe space where American minority groups – those of Black, Hispanic and Italian origin – as well as LGBTQI+ communities could express themselves.

The nightclub Studio 54, which opened its doors in 1977 on 54th Street in Midtown Manhattan, has reached an almost mythological status in pop culture. Many of its legendary stories are true: Bianca Jagger really did ride in on a white horse led by a man who was naked save for body paint, on her birthday; cocaine and Quaaludes (dubbed 'disco biscuits') were rife; sex was conducted openly on the balconies and in the VIP rooms; and for a New Year's Eve party, the dance floor was buried under 4 tons of glitter. Its clientele was a who's who of A-list celebrities, and everyone from David Bowie to Cher, Eartha Kitt, Jacqueline Kennedy Onassis, Grace Jones, Mick Jagger, Liza Minnelli, Margaux Hemingway, Andy Warhol, Elton John and former first lady Betty Ford (who later helped fellow substance abuse addicts to get clean at her clinic) partied there.

Notable fashion designers who frequented this den of iniquity include Diane von Fürstenberg, whose signature wrap dress was easy to wear while dancing (and, to paraphrase her own words, easy to put back on without disturbing a sleeping man in the morning); the ever-glamorously attired Valentino Garavani; American wunderkind Tom Ford (who later made high-octane eveningwear his hallmark); and perhaps most notably Halston, who redefined languid glamour and partied harder than most. Less well known as hedonists were Calvin Klein, Norma Kamali and Carolina Herrera.

As with today's clubwear, the name of the game was to get noticed while being comfortable, so fashions were <u>Body-Conscious</u>

Diana Ross, *c.* 1970.

(p.287), revealing, or loose and louche. Sequins found their spiritual home under the glittering disco ball, and jewel-toned fabrics added to the sense of luxury.

On today's catwalks, disco is a key reference point for eveningwear, and the twenty-first century has, for example, brought a resurgence of the trend for Spring/Summer 2018 at Paco Rabanne, Saint Laurent, Christian Dior and Balmain. For Autumn/ Winter 2019 Michael Kors themed his collection directly around

Studio 54; Versace for Spring/Summer 2020 used the diva
Dua Lipa to open and close the show; while the British designer
Michael Halpern polished it up for Autumn/Winter 2020. For
the first fully post-pandemic summer of freedom, 2022, many
designers captured the party-going mood with disco-themed
collections, among them Fendi, Dolce & Gabbana and Philosophy
di Lorenzo Serafini. The bumpy relaunch of the house of Halston
in 1997, and again in 2006, has since found its stride with
contemporary interpretations of disco style from season to season.

Disco as a musical genre, however, came to an abrupt halt
at the close of the 1970s, officially killed off on Disco Demolition
Night, 12 July 1979. What started as a marketing ploy by the
Chicago baseball team the White Sox to boost their dwindling
attendance ended up with crates of disco records being blown up,
nearly 50,000 disco sceptics storming the pitch and another 20,000
outside the gates rioting to get in. Out of the ashes of disco came
house music and the rise of electronic dance music, which gave
way to the Rave (p.146) culture of the late 1980s and 90s.

COLOURS AND PATTERNS:
pink, purple, white, gold, silver,
leopard print, snake print,
zebra print, tiger print

FABRICS: satin, polyester, nylon, fur,
lamé, velvet

GARMENTS AND ACCESSORIES:
hot pants, platform shoes, jumpsuit,
bell-bottom trousers, disco pants,
halter-neck top, miniskirt, shirt,
crop top

DETAILS: sequins, glitter, low cut,
hood, wide lapels, bias cut, flared,
asymmetric

HAIR: Afro, long curls

Hip Hop

● OLD-SCHOOL
● <u>DISCO</u>, <u>MAXIMALIST</u>
⊕ <u>AFROFUTURISM</u>, <u>ATHLEISURE</u>, <u>BOURGEOISIE</u>

Hip hop is more than just music. While it is primarily associated with rapping and MCing, it also encompasses DJ skills in sampling, mixing and scratching; breakdancing; and graffiti art. It emerged from the block parties of the Bronx, New York, a multicultural melting pot of African Americans, Caribbean Americans and Latino Americans, and musically has its roots in the performance energy of funk, the party beat of <u>Disco</u> (p.139) and the new sound of electronic music, with Caribbean elements of vocal toasting, reggae and dub, jazz scatting, and the meaningful lyrics of spoken word and talking blues.

Breakbeats came first – and the idea of isolating and mixing the breaks of two hard funk tracks to create an extended segment for dancing or MCing is credited to DJ Kool Herc, who was born in Kingston, Jamaica, and grew up in the Bronx. One of the first records to define the sound was 'Rapper's Delight' (1979) by Sugarhill Gang, which laid on to vinyl for the first time the 'hip-hop' refrain that named the genre, although Keef Cowboy of the Furious Five coined the term. The legendary Grandmaster Flash and the Furious Five set the tone for later socially conscious rap themes in 'The Message' (1982).

In its early forms, the old-school hip-hop aesthetic channelled some of the excesses of the 1980s, as well as the paintbox-bright palette of the 1990s, as it moved into the golden age of hip hop, incorporating Afrocentric patterns, <u>dashiki</u> shirts and West African kufi hats made out of <u>kente cloth</u> (see <u>Heritage</u>, p.23), styled with light-wash denim (think Will Smith and Jazzy Jeff). The central hip-hop aesthetic took its cues from the everyday comfort of sportswear, what is now called <u>Athleisure</u> (p.60), and this was underlined by Run-DMC's track 'My Adidas' (1986). At the same time, themes of <u>Afrofuturism</u> (p.48) were explored by such artists as Afrika Bambaataa in his album *Planet Rock* (1992) with the electro-funk collective Soulsonic Force.

Wu-Tang Clan at a red-carpet event in Hollywood. Undated photograph.

In the 1990s the American clothing manufacturer Starter had
a monopoly on merchandise for North America's three biggest
sports: the National Basketball Association, National Football
Association and National Hockey League. Letterman or varsity
jackets (see Academia, p.188) were based on the original bomber
style (see Aviator, p.63), and although they were not luxury items,
they commanded a premium price of around $150 and as such
were the status symbol of the everyman.

American prep brands (see Preppy, p.191) worn by the
privileged attendees of Ivy League universities were major fashion
players in the 1990s, and with them came aspirations of country
clubs, weekends in the Hamptons, sailing trips and skiing holidays.
Rappers were living the American dream and subverted the
traditional white Anglo-Saxon Protestant connotations of these
brands, something that was wholeheartedly embraced by the

Hip Hop cont.

designers themselves, such as Ralph Lauren, whose polo shirts (see Polo, p.76) were a badge of honour, and Tommy Hilfiger, who also cultivated the connection with the urban music fraternity. The look permeated contemporary R&B, and Aaliyah in particular remains an enduring style icon. Tragically killed in a plane crash at just 22 in 2001, she had railed against the girlish catwalk fashions of the time by adopting baggy jeans, tracksuits and crop tops, styled with hoop earrings and Androgynous (p.270) tomboy elements.

By the turn of the millennium, many hip-hop stars were at their commercial zenith and the riches of their success were flaunted via diamond-encrusted chains, jewellery and watches in a Maximalist (p.254) display of conspicuous consumption, as proof that the artist had 'made it'. The 'bling' look typified by such artists as T-Pain, 50 Cent and Lil Wayne was a defining aesthetic of the mid-2000s and remains a key look in rap styles that evolved out of hip hop, such as gangsta rap and trap music.

The influx of rappers into the fashion industry paved the way for the modern streetwear-luxe aesthetic, with Sean 'Puff Daddy' Combs creating the label Sean John in 1998, Jay-Z founding Rocawear in 1999, Pharrell Williams following their lead with Billionaire Boys Club in 2003, and Kanye West rewriting the history books with his multi-billion-dollar brand Yeezy, which launched in 2006 and was known until 2022 for its collaboration with Adidas.

Today's logomania trend has its roots in hip hop, in part credited to the work of the Harlem fashion designer Daniel Day, also known as 'Dapper Dan', who in the mid-1980s cut up and reworked leather bags from such labels as Gucci, Fendi and Louis Vuitton into oversized bombers and tracksuits for clients Mike Tyson, Floyd Mayweather, the gold medal-winning Olympic athlete Diane Dixon, and Salt-N-Pepa. Unsurprisingly, it sparked a flurry of cease-and-desist lawsuits, forcing him to close shop in 1992. He was ahead of his time, though, in attaching luxury-brand monograms and logos to streetwear, and in an interesting plot twist, Alessandro Michele for Gucci's 2018 cruise collection knocked off Dapper Dan's self-proclaimed 'knock-ups'. All this had a happy ending in an official collaboration, and the Italian house underwrote the relaunch of the notorious Harlem design studio.

COLOURS AND PATTERNS: red, white, blue, black, yellow, paisley

FABRICS: nylon, polyester

GARMENTS AND ACCESSORIES: tracksuit, oversized T-shirt, bucket hat, baseball cap, bomber jacket, Timberland boots, shirt, baggy jeans, red leather jacket, dungarees, basketball shirt, paisley bandana, beret, newsboy cap

DETAILS: chains, jewellery, grills/fronts

Rave

● ACID HOUSE, EDM, GARAGE, JUNGLE, TECHNO
● FESTIVAL
⊕ KIDCORE

Raves, in the context of wild parties, were referred to first in the 1950s by London's Soho Beatnik set (p.214), and by the Mods (p.228) in the 1960s, before the term fell out of parlance until the 1980s. At that point they became a stylistic mash-up of European techno and American house music seen through the ecstasy-fuelled lens of the late 80s 'Madchester' dance scene, before being re-exported to the States in the 1990s. The first raves were secret, illegal 'free parties', proto-festivals held in fields or warehouses, and the style was more akin to that of tree-hugging Bohemian hippies (p.217).

Acid house grew out of Chicago house, evolved to incorporate the squelchy, bass-heavy sounds of the Roland TB-303 synthesizer. The name 'acid' was originally a way to describe how the music disseminated into expansive patterns, like fractals, but before long it coincided with the use of the psychedelic drug itself. Recreational drugs were (and still are) a big part of the rave scene, referenced directly in the designs of Raf Simons, and indirectly in the use as a motif of the dummy (pacifier), which alleviated teeth-grinding and gurning while high. This and other Kidcore motifs (p.175), such as rainbows, butterflies and hair clips (see also Kawaii, p.170), are often to be seen at raves as a nod to escapism from the mundane responsibilities of adult life, and regression into childhood.

The second Summer of Love occurred in 1987 in the UK as spaced-out adolescents found community and empathy in such clubs as Shoom and Astoria in London, and the Haçienda in Manchester, which brought together warring factions of football hooligans (an ethical quandary for the local police force). As in the original Summer of Love in 1967, devotees of rave favoured tie-dye and peace signs as countercultural symbols (see Hippy, p.223).

Anouk Schonewille on the catwalk for Prada Autumn/Winter 2018–19 Womenswear, Milan Fashion Week, 22 February 2018.

Shoom, founded by the DJ Danny Rampling, used the smiley-face symbol on its promotional artwork. Below deck, drug dealers stamped it on their pills and wore armfuls of childish bead bracelets as a code to advertise their wares. These home-made bracelets became an important element of rave culture, as partygoers dubbed 'kandi kids' exchanged them with new-found friends on the dance floor as a sign of peace, love, unity and respect. This practice is still common on the American electronic dance music scene.

In the 1990s electronic music evolved to include jungle and garage, and in urban clubs punters upped the style stakes. The

Rave cont.

influence of Hip Hop (p.142) was felt in the wave of designer logos from the catwalks of Milan, such as Versace and Moschino.

Detroit techno and the industrial German sound lent raves a futuristic edge. Promotional posters by such artists as the east London icon Pez, who was employed in 2019 by the American mid-range brand Coach to design fly-poster artwork, featured trippy op-art patterns and extra-planetary visuals to evoke the mind-expanding, escapist nature of the rave. Space themes were a common source of reference, and there are similarities with the Cyberpunk style (p.38). Neon fabrics are perfect for attracting attention on the dance floor, and glow enjoyably under UV lights.

Sure enough, fashion's penchant for reinventing styles 20–30 years after their time means that rave style has come back hard, particularly in the context of 1990s and Y2K fashion, and the early 2020s brought a resurgence in bucket hats, spaghetti-strap camisoles, crop tops, platform trainers and baggy jeans. Rave is often seen in the context of free-spirited Festival wear (p.149), and, when given an erotically charged interpretation, is a version of Body-Conscious (p.287). Ultimately, the rave aesthetic is a reminder that we should drop beats, not bombs.

COLOURS AND PATTERNS: neon yellow, neon pink, neon blue, yellow, iridescence, op art

FABRICS: satin, polyester, nylon, faux fur, denim

GARMENTS AND ACCESSORIES: logo T-shirt, platform trainers, crop top, micro sunglasses, bucket hat

DETAILS: smiley faces, space and planetary themes, pacifiers, glow sticks, cut-aways

HAIR AND MAKE-UP: space buns, face stickers

Festival

◉ FIELD DAY
◑ <u>MILITARY</u>, <u>COMBAT</u>, <u>ROCK & ROLL</u>, <u>ROCKABILLY</u>, <u>INDIE</u>,
   <u>BODY-CONSCIOUS</u>
● <u>CYBERPUNK</u>, <u>DIESELPUNK</u>, <u>GORECORE</u>, <u>RAVE</u>, <u>BOHEMIAN</u>, <u>HIPPY</u>

There was a time in 2005 when the height of British cultural capital
included Kate Moss wading through the mire at the Glastonbury
Festival of Performing Arts with her boyfriend of the time, Pete
Doherty of the band Babyshambles, which he had formed while
banned from the Libertines for escalating drug abuse. Drink in one
hand, cigarettes in the other, looking as though they hadn't slept
in two days, Moss wore a gold lurex jumper with endless legs and
wellington boots, and Doherty a black leather biker jacket, band
T-shirt with the slogan 'I am a shambles', skinny black jeans and
his signature <u>trilby</u>. It was the heyday of <u>Indie</u> (p.131) and the
dishevelled rock-star look (see <u>Rock & Roll</u>, p.110, and <u>Rockabilly</u>,
p.113), which threatened to make a full comeback in 2022 with
<u>Gen-Z</u> mining the aesthetics of such early social-media platforms
as Tumblr for what is now called 'Indie Sleaze'.

  Music and arts festivals have been popular since the times of
ancient Greece, but gained momentum in popular culture in the
mid-twentieth century, starting with the Newport Jazz festival in
Rhode Island, which was founded in 1954. Glastonbury (originally
called Pilton Pop, Folk and Blues Festival) was founded in 1970,
and that year its 1,500 visitors paid a mere £1 entry and received
free milk provided by Worthy Farm's permanent four-legged
residents. By 2022 it had swelled to over 200,000 visitors each
paying £280 for the ticket alone. That pales in size and scale to such
near-mythological events as Woodstock, during which up to half
a million people descended on Bethel in upstate New York for four
days in 1969 to spread the message of peace and love at the height
of the Vietnam War. Woodstock's legacy of <u>Hippy</u> culture (p.223)
continues to be felt at today's music festivals with the prevalence of
CND symbols, <u>Military</u>-issue shirts and jackets (p.91), chunky boots
(see <u>Combat</u>, p.95), flower crowns and trippy psychedelic prints.

Dsquared2 Spring/Summer 2012, Milan Fashion Week, 26 September 2011.

Traditionally, festivals called for <u>Bohemian</u> style (p.217), typified by eclectic layering, floaty <u>poet shirts</u>, 1970s-inspired maxi dresses in floral prints, flares and crochet vests, but the subsequent return of the 1990s as a major trend and the increasing popularity of electronic music mean that <u>Rave</u> style (p.146) often takes centre stage. A safe bet is to dress according to the music of the event.

British festivals are known for their inclement weather and can be a sea of rain-soaked ponchos (see <u>Gaucho</u>, p.82) with <u>Gorecore</u> (p.88) anoraks and rubber boots one minute, stripped down to bikini tops, cut-off denim shorts and fringed vests the next. On the other hand, the Coachella Valley Music and Arts Festival, held on the sun-drenched fields of the Empire Polo Club in Indio, California, and arguably the most commercialized of all festivals, becoming the first to gross $100 million in 2017, is a veritable catwalk show of pristine coordinated tops and bottoms, sheer Body-Conscious dresses (p.287) and unexpectedly high heels. Coachella attendees have also in the past been called out for the cultural appropriation of Native American headdresses and Hindu bindis (see Heritage, p.23), although they are by no means the only guilty parties. The commercialization of festivals rumbles on, with many fast-fashion brands churning out poorly made, disposable items every summer and marketing them at young revellers.

At the apex of festival style is the heavily memed Burning Man, a self-proclaimed act of 'radical self-expression' and an exercise in self-reliance held on a dried salt lake *playa* in the remote Black Rock Desert in northwestern Nevada. 'Burners' congregate to incinerate their artistic effigies, and while clothing is optional, many choose post-apocalyptic tribal Dieselpunk (p.45) and the futuristic neon of Cyberpunk (p.38).

COLOURS AND PATTERNS: tropical prints, psychedelic prints

FABRICS: denim, crochet, nylon, fishnet, vinyl

GARMENTS AND ACCESSORIES: poet shirt, biker jacket, PVC trousers, disc belts, slip dress, denim hot pants, wellington boots, rain poncho, bucket hat, bumbag (fanny pack), Doc Martens, flat shoes, combat boots, Converse, Hawaiian shirt

DETAILS: feathers, sequins, wristbands, fringing, flower crowns, layered necklaces, studs

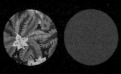

Carnival

◉ MARDI GRAS
➡ HERITAGE, GORECORE, FESTIVAL, ROCOCO
⊕ ATHLEISURE, RAVE, BODY-CONSCIOUS

Carnival is a truly global party, with more than 50 major events across the world from Rio de Janeiro to London, Goa to New Orleans, and Venice to Trinidad. Although many different nations take part, they are connected by a common thread.

In ancient Egypt 4,000 years ago, there began a pagan agricultural feast at the end of the winter to use up stored food before it spoiled, and to welcome spring. The festivity spread across ancient Greece and the Roman Empire, where it became associated with the feast of *Navigium Isidis* (meaning the 'vessel of Isis'), which honoured the goddess Isis and heralded the start of the sailing season. Revellers were carried on boats through the streets, and that is thought to be the basis of the tradition of carnival floats. It also drew on the hedonistic wine banquets of Dionysus and Bacchus, before being appropriated by Christianity as the last feast before the fast of Lent. The word 'carnival' comes from the Italian *carne levare*, 'to remove meat', which through folk usage became *carne vale*.

The Venice Carnival, which began in the eleventh century, instigated the tradition of costume and masquerade to protect the wearer's anonymity while indulging in sins of gluttony and lust. From the sixteenth century onwards, the Portuguese took the festival (along with millions of enslaved Africans) to Brazil, where over time a fusion of music and dance styles gave birth to samba. The first Rio Carnival was held in 1723. French colonists took the celebration of Mardi Gras (literally translated as 'Fat Tuesday', and also known as Shrove Tuesday) to the island of Trinidad in 1783, but excluded slaves from the celebrations; so these enslaved people started having their own parties. They mimicked and mocked their oppressors in elaborate gowns, adding elements of their lost African culture to the sounds of calypso and, later, soca. Trinidad ended up in the hands of the British during the

Marc Jacobs Spring/Summer 2019, New York Fashion Week, Park Avenue Armory, 12 September 2018.

Carnival cont.

Napoleonic Wars in 1814, and once slavery was abolished in the 1830s, Carnival became a meaningful festivity of emancipation. The Notting Hill Carnival in London was founded in 1966 as an offshoot of the Trinidad and Tobago Carnival to celebrate Caribbean culture after a period of racial tension and violence in the capital, and as such it has become a secular event held during the last weekend of August.

Carnival style is divided into two camps: those taking part in the processions and on the floats, and those in the spectating crowds. For those taking part, the costume can cost several hundreds of pounds, depending on where they are placed in the band: back line, front line, as a section leader, or as an individual. Apart from Venice, which is typified by Rococo-style dress (p.257) and elaborate masks, the key takeaway for spectators is to keep it bright and tight. It should go without saying, for those on the sidelines, not to plunder another person's culture for fashion inspiration (see Heritage, p.23).

Trimmings that emphasize a dancer's movement, such as feathers and fringing, are a good option. Trainers are a must, as are bumbags (fanny packs) to enable you to dance hands-free (a key item also for a Festival, p.149). Sequins glisten in the sunshine, and for those attending the Notting Hill Carnival, it is always worth checking the weather forecast to see if you will need a raincoat (see Gorecore, p.88).

In the early hours of a Caribbean Carnival on the opening day (known colloquially as *J'ouvert*, from the French *jour ouvert*, daybreak) is the tradition of 'ole mas', the first opportunity for revellers to play at 'masquerade' and escape the usual restraints of society. Topical events are addressed through witty political commentary, and a host of characters appear from the depths of hell to re-enact the story of slavery and the evil inflicted by white colonists. Whirling imps, bats and blue-painted devils haunt the streets to scare the uninitiated and demand money from passers-by. The *jab molassie* (molasses devil; the word 'jab' from the French *diable*, meaning 'devil') is the character of a ghost inspired by the grim story of a slave who fell into a vat of boiling molasses at a sugar factory. Players of this mas (masquerade) are covered in tar, oil or grease, and may have chains around their necks.

Over time the ole mas transitioned into 'dirty' (or 'dutty', in Creole) mas, involving the throwing of paint, water, chocolate, mud or oil, with some carnivals using more indelible substances than others. This connects back to the ancient Portuguese tradition of *entrudo* (Shrovetide), from the pagan spring fertility festival, whereby people would dress up as devils and demons and throw water, mud and sometimes even urine at each other. This was a key feature of the earliest carnivals held in Brazil.

For most people, the most widely recognized incarnation of Carnival is the 'pretty mas' with its spectacle of embellished bikinis, beads, feathers and rhinestones, but watch out for the combative 'jab jab' or double devil, who seeks other jab jabs to fight. Dressed in the manner of a medieval jester, in striped satin with a shield on their chest, with down trimmings to disguise the arm movements, and mirrors to blind and distract opponents, they wield a fearsome whip.

COLOURS AND PATTERNS:
red, yellow, pink, orange, green, blue, tropical prints, gold, leopard print

FABRICS: denim, crochet, nylon, fishnet

GARMENTS AND ACCESSORIES:
hot pants, trainers, bikini, shorts, mask, bumbag (fanny pack)

DETAILS: feathers, sequins, embellishment, crystals, beads, ribbons, shells, glitter

Play

There are more nuances than ever before to working and non-working clothes. The Covid-19 pandemic catapulted many people into an uneasy existence between home and office, and, as any hybrid worker knows, there is a world of difference between dressing for the office, on-camera days working from home, and off-camera days when comfort is key.

Off-duty style encompasses all points on a wide scale of lounging, from standing on the deck of a cruise ship wearing a silky kaftan that wafts in the breeze, to staying at home on a winter's evening wrapped in cosy knitwear and chunky socks. How we choose to dress when off the clock is telling about our personality. This is perhaps nowhere more creatively shown than in Tokyo's Harajuku district, which is world-famous for its lasting impact on street style and fashion design. Below the cityscape of towering glass and concrete, streets crowded with neon signs, a distinctly cute style emerged in kawaii, which offers a spectrum of pastels and saturated hues.

Keep piling on more accessories, with heart- and moon-shaped stickers stuck down with the zest of a child enjoying craft play, and the look becomes decora. The frilly confections of Lolita style are inspired by doll-like perfection, while cosplay caters to the audience who enjoys role-playing and never grew out of the dressing-up box. In the West, kidcore style evolved, with a deep-seated nostalgia for

4.

cartoons, plastic accessories and bright, crayon-inspired hues.

Playful dressing can be sophisticated, too. The Dolce Vita style, which was distilled from the 1960 Italian movie of that name, gave us a timeless reference moodboard for summer city breaks with little black dresses and perfectly cut suits.

From city to countryside, the dream of rolling fields and the smell of cut hay and freshly baked bread inspired the cottagecore look, which trended hard at the beginning of the pandemic and circles back with perennially rustic charm and diaphanous floral dresses, most commonly as a summer look. For the winter, the Danish aesthetic hygge is an altogether cosier aesthetic, embracing the art of comfortable living. Toying with fashion is a hard-earned pleasure.

Cosplay

● FANCY DRESS, COSTUMING, DRESSING UP
● DIGITAL FASHION, CARNIVAL, AVANT-GARDE, DRAG
⊕ FUTURISM, CYBERPUNK, STEAMPUNK, DIESELPUNK, NAUTICAL, KAWAII

Costuming as a cultural phenomenon owes much to the Venetian masked balls held from the seventeenth century onwards during Carnival (p.152). By the eighteenth century such entertainments had become fashionable at royal courts across Europe. Although cosplay is not an aesthetic in the same way as other entries in this book, the selecting and embodying of characters arguably acts as an expression of self-identity more obviously than the adopting of seasonal fashions. It also mirrors humans' use of avatars to inhabit the metaverse (see Digital Fashion, p.54), as well as clearly indicating a subculture to other members of its community.

Cosplayers can impersonate any character from science fiction or fantasy literature, television, video games, anime or manga, and the cosplay scene is centred on major conventions or 'cons'. At the very first World Science Fiction Convention, or Worldcon, held in New York in 1939, the literary agent, magazine editor and coiner of the term 'sci-fi', Forrest J. Ackerman, wore a Futuristic costume (p.33) designed and created by his girlfriend Myrtle R. Douglas, also an avid fan of the genre and publisher of her own fanzine. Their costumes channelled the work of the illustrator Frank R. Paul, as well as the film *Things to Come* (1936), based on H.G. Wells's novel *The Shape of Things to Come* (1933). Ackerman said later that he thought everyone would be dressed up. Although he and Douglas were the only ones to do it that year, the trend (referred to at first simply as 'costuming') caught on quickly.

The word 'cosplay' is attributed to the Japanese reporter and manga publisher Nobuyuki Takahashi in an article for *My Anime* magazine in 1983, covering the scene at Tokyo's Comiket convention. He considered the Western notion of 'masquerade' to be too old-fashioned in sentiment, and brainstormed several terms along the lines of 'costume show' and 'hero play' before settling on

Cosplay girl at Comic Fiesta, Kuala Lumpur, Malaysia, 2019.

Cosplay cont.

'cosplay', *kosupure* in Japanese. When the hit anime *Sailor Moon* aired in 1992–7, based on superheroine princesses reincarnated as schoolgirls, it instigated a wave of teenagers dressing up in Kawaii (p.170) cosplay get-up, especially school uniforms and sailor outfits.

Crossplay is a version of cosplay in which the wearer inhabits a character of another gender. In Japan this is more commonly female-to-male, owing to societal pressure, and in the West there are proportionally more male-to-female cosplayers. However, crossplay varies from Drag (p.278), which focuses on the expression of gender traits and original characters rather than recognizable ones from pop culture.

At the 'fancy dress' parties of the nineteenth century, guests would base their dress on such abstract themes as insects, flowers and darkness, and these ideas occasionally crop up on catwalks today in Avant-Garde collections (p.244). Some of these hyper-conceptual designs are more art than fashion, impractical for daily life, but others are more wearable, such as the statement orchid and butterfly dresses of Moschino's Spring/Summer 2018 collection. For a more practical take on cosplay, there have been several anime and streetwear collaborations, among them Akira x Supreme, MSGM x Attacker You!, and BAPE's threefold collaboration with One Piece, Dragon Ball and Pokemon (see Athleisure, p.60).

Cottagecore

● NEO-AESTHETICISM
● E-BOY & E-GIRL, HYGGE
⊕ NEO-VICTORIANA, PRAIRIE, LOLITA, BOHEMIAN

Cottagecore is one of the newer aesthetics to emerge from the maelstrom of the internet, first appearing around 2010 on the social-media platform Tumblr and exploding in popularity on Instagram and TikTok during the Covid-19 pandemic from 2020. It is an example of neo-Aestheticism, mirroring the Aesthetic movement of the Victorian era (see Neo-Victoriana, p.26), which, spearheaded by the writer Oscar Wilde, prized beauty above all else and had a deep nostalgia for a simpler time. There are many parallels between Aestheticism and cottagecore, which is more than just a styling direction. It signifies an interest in humble pleasures, such as baking, crafting, sewing, knitting and sustainable consumption, and idealizes the bucolic English countryside. In common with the Arts and Crafts movement, Aestheticism sought to find meaning in handmade objects as a reaction to the Industrial Revolution – although, of course, the imagined rustic charms of the Middle Ages were far from its plague-riddled reality.

The pandemic pressed 'reset' for many people, and ignited a new-found love of country walks and the idea of self-sufficiency. FOMO became FOGO, fear of going out, and if people did venture to the shops, they were likely to encounter rows of empty shelves. After the pandemic, as supply chains continue to be a problem in a world of war, climate change and explosive population growth, the appeal of home-made products is easy to understand.

The associated style of apparel encompasses smocked floral milkmaid dresses in natural fabrics (such as cotton or linen), breezy peasant blouses, workmanlike dungarees, waistcoats and the romanticized lace-up corsets of yesteryear, always with a basket of freshly cut roses and a straw hat. It is homely and escapist, like the more wintry Hygge (p.183). When given an American twist, often just by swapping Mary Janes, oxford shoes or brogues for cowboy boots, cottagecore becomes Prairie style (p.85).

Jacquemus Spring/Summer 2020, Valensole, France, 24 June 2019.

In common with those of some of the other internet-based 'core' aesthetics – among them 'fairycore', which is based on motifs of fairies and woodlands; 'farmcore', which idealizes farm living; and 'goblincore', which focuses on the ugly end of nature's beauty, typified by mushrooms, frogs, toads and insects – cottagecore creators often use image-editing software, such as Photoshop or the tools available on social-media apps, to curate an online persona using filters and post-production techniques alongside props. The images presented are, by and large, those of a single-person protagonist, such as those posted by the E-Boy & E-Girl community (p.51), and cottagecore provides a safe space for the queer community of women-loving women and non-binary-loving women.

Cottagecore as a philosophy champions progressive liberal values and sustainability through circularity. The circular economy in fashion emphasizes a move from a linear model of production and consumption, whereby goods are made, used and disposed of, towards one that extends the life cycle of a garment through durable fabrics, repair, upcycling, resale and rental. The last two, resale and rental, are set to reshape the fashion industry over the coming decades.

COLOURS AND PATTERNS: floral, gingham, sage green, dusky pink, cornflower blue

FABRICS: cotton, linen, macramé, crochet, raffia, broderie anglaise

GARMENTS AND ACCESSORIES: milkmaid dress, cardigan, peasant blouse, dungarees, waistcoat, straw hat, Mary Jane shoes, oxford shoes, corset

DETAILS: ruffles, knitted, home-made, embroidery, off-the-shoulder, sweetheart neckline, mushrooms, strawberries, flower garlands, lace-up

Cruise

● RESORT, HOLIDAY
● NAUTICAL
⊕ DOLCE VITA, BOURGEOISIE, CLASSIC, SURF, LADYLIKE

Cruise fits into the fashion lexicon as a bonus collection, or retail drop, on top of the traditional biannual fashion collections. The womenswear Spring/Summer shows, during what insiders call 'fashion month' (the fashion weeks of New York, London, Milan and Paris combined), are presented on the catwalk in September for delivery in store the following January, and the Autumn/Winter (Fall) shows, which are on the runway in February, are delivered in store in August. This leads to the bizarre sight of heavy wool coats when it's still as hot as summer and skimpy shorts on rails when there's snow on the ground. Menswear collections traditionally show in June and December, again to be in-store six months later, but mixed-gender shows are increasingly the norm.

Historically, the six months' lead time allowed editors to photograph garments for editorials, and the magazines to be printed and distributed, while buyers would order looks relevant to their target customers and give the designer time to fulfil and manufacture the order. The see-now-buy-now model trialled by Burberry in 2017, whereby customers could purchase items directly from the catwalk to capitalize on the hype created by social media and live-streamed shows, failed to become the norm as brands increasingly move towards a more sustainable made-to-order model that minimizes overproduction.

Resort or cruise collections began as a holidaywear capsule for customers who travel frequently, either on vacation or to homes in hotter climates. However, luxury consumers are today found across the world, and markets in the southern hemisphere, such as Brazil, Australia and South Africa, experience the seasons in reverse, while some near the equator, such as Malaysia, have monsoon seasons. African markets, such as Nigeria and Kenya, are increasingly important and have their own unique climates. Consumers there require working wardrobes outside the seasonal drops at northern latitudes.

Chanel cruise collection, Paris, 3 May 2018.

Cruise cont.

Coco Chanel is credited with starting the resort trend with her 'Cruise' collection in 1919, shown in the coastal town of Deauville rather than in Paris. That collection also set the standard for the Nautical (p.98) influences seen in holidaywear, with rope details and the prevalence of a chic navy-and-white palette (see Classic, p.209).

These days, cruise collections are likely to contain a variety of trans-seasonal garments, such as coats, workwear separates, denim, evening gowns and tuxes, alongside the more expected bikinis, beach shorts, swimsuits and sliders. Brands use mid-season collections to sell more commercial pieces that would sit less well in their conceptual mainline shows, and – since these garments are not tied to a particular season – there is less pressure to offer markdowns, allowing them to be sold at full price for longer. Some brands make up to 60 per cent of their revenue from cruise collections.

Shown outside the fashion weeks, around May or June, and in store between late October and December, collections labelled resort or cruise are not bound to the major fashion capitals and have become an extravagant marketing tool. Notable venues for these mid-season collections have included Louis Vuitton's expedition to Rio de Janeiro for Resort 2017, Chanel's installation of a full-size ocean liner at the Grand Palais in Paris for Resort 2019, Gucci's takeover of a Roman necropolis in Provence for Cruise 2019, and Dior's Andalusian extravaganza of 110 looks in Seville for Resort 2023, involving flamenco icons and 40 backing dancers.

The sped-up nature of the fashion cycle promotes consumption and has its critics among designers in the industry. Many high-profile designers, such as Riccardo Tisci, who exited Givenchy in 2017 after a 12-year tenure, cite exhaustion from the toxic pressure of deadlines. The mental health of fashion designers was thrown into the spotlight after the suicide of Alexander McQueen in 2010, and the nervous breakdowns the next year of both Christophe Decarnin and John Galliano, at the time the creative directors of Balmain and Dior respectively. Taking heed of this, the late Tunisian couturier Azzedine Alaïa was the first to offer seasonless collections, refusing to be caught on the never-ending carousel of newness. The house of Alaïa now offers Winter/Spring and Summer/Autumn pieces, as well as permanent collections, such as its 'Black Dress' staples.

COLOURS AND PATTERNS: white, navy blue, tropical prints, pink, yellow, sky blue

FABRICS: cotton, silk, linen, lace

GARMENTS AND ACCESSORIES: bikini, swimsuit, espadrilles, sliders, sunglasses, sunhat, luggage

DETAILS: rope, raffia

Dolce Vita

● MOVIE STAR, ITALIAN GLAMOUR
◐ TAILORING, MOD
● CRUISE, CLASSIC, ROMANTIC, LADYLIKE, PIN-UP

It is a testament to the work of the costume and art director Piero Gherardi, who won the Academy Award for Best Costume Design for his work on Federico Fellini's *La Dolce Vita* (1960), that more people are able to talk about the movie's style than about its plot. The film follows the protagonist, gossip columnist Marcello Rubini (Marcello Mastroianni), around Rome at a time when people were turning away from the Catholic Church towards hedonism and celebrity idols. Over the course of a week, his philandering takes in the A-list Swedish actor Sylvia (Anita Ekberg, virtually playing herself), the socialite Maddalena (Anouk Aimée) and Marcello's long-suffering, self-pitying fiancée, Emma (Yvonne Furneaux).

From a fashion perspective, the film is an ode to the hardest-working items in the wardrobe: the little black dress and the perfectly cut black suit (see Classic, p.209). Mastroianni's character must be able to flit seamlessly between day and night and various levels of formality, so a single-breasted black suit is selected for him (see Tailoring, p.195), worn with a crisp white shirt, elegant French cuffs and oversized cufflinks. A pair of classic tortoiseshell Persol sunglasses completes the look, worn day and night (a celebrity trope to this day, and one we owe to this movie). For Sylvia, the costume of a gravity-defying sleeveless black gown for the evening, or a sheer black lace blouse for day. The heiress Maddalena wears two versions of an elegant black shift dress with a rounded neckline and long sleeves, and for Emma, Gherardi keeps it simple with either a long black camisole dress or a black scoop dress with cap sleeves.

Fellini was channelling the transformative qualities of the Spanish couturier Cristóbal Balenciaga's black sack dress of 1957, which allowed the wearer freedom of movement and was resoundingly modern in its simplicity. Its minimal silhouette later influenced the clean geometry, A-line shape and mini hemlines of 1960s Mod fashions (p.228). Other highlights from the film are the sundresses

Anita Ekberg in the film *La Dolce Vita*, 1960.

with polka dots or broad black-and-white stripes. When combined with the film's black-and-white cinematography, the high-contrast monochrome palette of the costumes adds to the iconic aesthetic.

'Dolce Vita' has become synonymous with timeless Italian style, and evokes the romance of summer days spent flitting around picturesque Roman landmarks. It remains one of the most enduring references for people looking for timeless holidaywear inspiration (see Cruise, p.164).

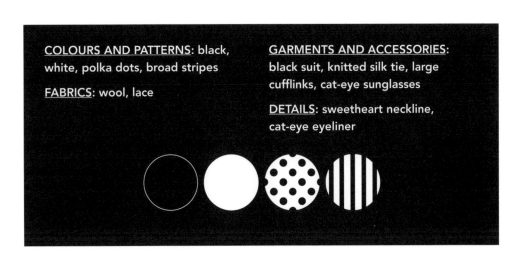

COLOURS AND PATTERNS: black, white, polka dots, broad stripes

FABRICS: wool, lace

GARMENTS AND ACCESSORIES: black suit, knitted silk tie, large cufflinks, cat-eye sunglasses

DETAILS: sweetheart neckline, cat-eye eyeliner

THE STYLE THESAURUS

Kawaii

● HARAJUKU
➜ E-BOY & E-GIRL, COSPLAY, DECORA, LOLITA
✦ ACADEMIA, MAXIMALIST

The Japanese term *kawaii* has permeated global consumer culture in a wash of sugary pastel hues and anthropomorphic animals, such as Hello Kitty, and Pikachu from Pokémon. Translatable as 'cute', the word also describes everything adorable, childlike and innocent.

The aesthetic started in the late 1960s as a protest by university students against prescribed learning and the rigorous expectations of a traditional Japanese education. They would miss classes to read manga comics, and there was also an emerging style for childlike handwriting that used looped characters and heart motifs, an analogue precursor to the emojis of today. The toy company Sanrio picked up on the trend and launched Hello Kitty in 1974, and since then this simple cat drawn from childish lines has appeared on everything from stationery to commercial airline livery; it even has its own theme park.

The emergence of the kawaii trend coincided with the emancipation and increasing power of women in the Japanese corporate environment in the 1970s and 80s. For those industrious office ladies, kawaii was a light-hearted way of rebelling against conservative traditions in society. They would affect cuteness, adopting ultra-feminine *burikko* mannerisms, such as girlish voices, covering the mouth when laughing, and childlike squeals of delight. This may be counterintuitive to Western notions of feminism, but it is worth noting that being called *kawaii* is generally considered a compliment, and the term can also be applied to men. These women's new financial independence allowed them to indulge in materialism and participate in the kawaii subculture on the street.

Kawaii crossed over to fashion on the streets of the world-famous Harajuku district of Tokyo, where girls would adopt baby-doll or pinafore dresses accessorized with bows and bunny ears, over-the-knee socks and dainty Mary Jane shoes.

170

LEAF XIA Autumn/Winter 2019, New York Fashion Week, 13 February 2019.

The aesthetic evolved into specific styles, such as Decora (p.173) and Lolita (p.177), as well as kogal, which involves wearing a high-school uniform (real or pretend) with a pleated miniskirt and rolled-down socks or legwarmers. Kogal girls refer to themselves as *gyaru*, 'gal', although this term is also applied to a Japanese version of the California Valley Girl look circa Y2K, summed up by conspicuous consumption, tanned skin, bleached blonde hair and long acrylic nails, with heavy make-up as a point of difference to the fresh-faced innocence of kawaii. Some kogal girls live at home with their parents into their twenties, thirties and beyond (and are referred to rather unkindly by social scientists as 'parasite singles'), and many have a generous shopping allowance.

Kawaii spread across social-media platforms among Gen-Z. Given its Japanese roots, it has heavily influenced E-Boy & E-Girl gamer style (p.51), especially its subgenre Erokawa (sexy-cute), an

Kawaii cont.

erotic version of kawaii with the flushed face of the orgasmic *ahegao* pose. Other variations include Yumekawaii (dreamy-cute), which incorporates fantasy and unicorn elements, and Fairy Kei, which has a nostalgic 1980s touch with references to the cult cartoon characters My Little Pony, Rainbow Brite and Care Bears, and to 1980s prints, such as polka dots. Edgier versions include Yamikawaii (cute with dark themes, such as mental illness) and Gurokawaii (horror and gore cute). Kawaii also influences the pastel tones and vulnerability of Soft Girl and Soft Boy aesthetics. Although kawaii looks are inherently Maximalist (p.254) and can appear costume-like, they fall short of full anime or manga character outfits, which would become Cosplay (p.158).

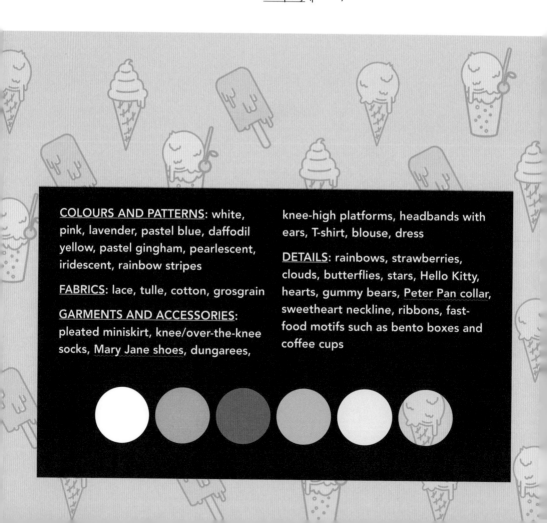

COLOURS AND PATTERNS: white, pink, lavender, pastel blue, daffodil yellow, pastel gingham, pearlescent, iridescent, rainbow stripes

FABRICS: lace, tulle, cotton, grosgrain

GARMENTS AND ACCESSORIES: pleated miniskirt, knee/over-the-knee socks, Mary Jane shoes, dungarees, knee-high platforms, headbands with ears, T-shirt, blouse, dress

DETAILS: rainbows, strawberries, clouds, butterflies, stars, Hello Kitty, hearts, gummy bears, Peter Pan collar, sweetheart neckline, ribbons, fast-food motifs such as bento boxes and coffee cups

Decora

◐ HARAJUKU
◑ RAVE, KIDCORE
⊕ E-BOY & E-GIRL, KAWAII, MAXIMALIST

In the mid-1990s the Kawaii style
(p.170) was pushed to the furthest end
of the Maximalist spectrum (p.254) in
the youthful Harajuku neighbourhood
of Tokyo, reaching its peak around the
turn of the millennium with the help of
the fashion photographer Shoichi Aoki.
Aoki, who founded *FRUiTS* magazine
in 1997, would take to the streets to
capture images of the most distinctive
and eclectic members of Tokyo's
various subcultures. Around this time
the teen pop idol Tomoe Shinohara
experimented with proto-decora style,
and her fans, known as 'Shinora', would
copy the look, many of them ending
up in *FRUiTS*. The look broke through
internationally in the mid-2000s via
such fashion bloggers as Kyary Pamyu
Pamyu, who was scouted by a music
producer and went on to become
a global J-pop star.

Girl dressed in decora street style, London, 17 September 2019.

     The 'more is more' mentality led street-style enthusiasts to
pile on ever more plastic toys, styling tulle tutus with cartoon-
emblazoned hoodies and mismatched socks. Accessories are
particularly important in decora style, with several hairclips,
heart- and star-shaped stickers dotted across the cheeks, glitter,
diamante, armfuls of plastic bangles, and sometimes a tiny plaster
positioned on the bridge of the nose. Home-made bead bracelets
and necklaces crop up in both decora and Rave style (p.146); in the
latter they are the signifier of the 'kandi kids'.

Decora cont.

The decora colour palette is often louder than the original kawaii, with neon hues and bright rainbow stripes that evoke the 1980s revivalist feel. For this reason it is often confused with Kidcore (p.175). However, decora is specifically about decoration, and technically it is possible to create monochrome decora looks.

Although it is not a common reference for fashion designers, decora made an appearance in the Spring/Summer 2018 Comme des Garçons show in sculptural accessories made from toy parts. In Autumn/Winter 2018 the beauty trend for stacking barrette hair clips spread across social media, and endured in product ranges as luxury brands sought to capitalize on these entry-point items.

COLOURS AND PATTERNS: neon pink, purple, bright green, bright yellow, pink-and-black stripes, purple-and-black stripes, rainbow stripes, cyan

FABRICS: jersey, tulle, plastic, faux fur

GARMENTS AND ACCESSORIES: cartoon patterned sweatshirt, tiered skirt, Mary Jane shoes, trainers, mismatched tights or socks, platform shoes

DETAILS: stickers, hair clips, headbands, plastic toys, soft toys, layering, plastic beads, plastic chains, pom-poms

Kidcore

⊘ NOSTALGIA
➜ <u>DECORA</u>, <u>MINIMALIST</u>, <u>LADYLIKE</u>
⊕ <u>RETRO</u>, <u>HIPPY</u>, <u>MAXIMALIST</u>, <u>CAMP</u>

While both <u>Decora</u> (p.173) and Kidcore incorporate themes of nostalgia, children's toys and television characters, with stickers applied to everything from trainers and backpacks to the apples of the cheeks, there are a few subtle signifiers that tell the looks apart. Decora was born on the streets of Tokyo in the 1990s, while Kidcore is a Western aesthetic from the 2010s, whereby <u>millennials</u>

Winnie Harlow in Moschino, New York Fashion Week, 9 September 2021.

Kidcore cont.

dress the way they did as kids in the 90s. Kidcore is still around, and now Gen-Z scours thrift shops for Disney merch and prints of puppies, kittens, unicorns and old cartoons. Decora is usually added to a base Kawaii outfit (p.170), with highly saturated hues of pink, purple and powder blue, and armfuls of bracelets. Kidcore, on the other hand, often incorporates such youthful denim pieces as dungarees, with primary colours and paintbox brights. While there may be a bangle or two, it's much more pared back than Decora.

Jeremy Scott at Moschino proved time and again that no theme is too kitsch to tackle on the runway. For his Spring/Summer 2022 show he looked to a menagerie of nursery-rhyme characters to design a collection that was one part Ladylike (p.281) elegance to one part dressing up. Kidcore divides taste, and although it's a miss for those in the industry who are devoted to a palette of all-black everything and Minimalist lines (p.252), its frivolous escapism serves as a reminder that there is still fun to be had with fashion.

COLOURS AND PATTERNS: primary red, yellow and blue, rainbow stripes, leopard print, tie-dye

FABRICS: denim, faux fur, sweatshirt jersey, crochet, sequins

GARMENTS AND ACCESSORIES: hoody, dungarees, cartoon T-shirt, jeans, ballet pumps, Converse, friendship bracelets, pyjamas, braces (suspenders), ankle socks, plastic chains

DETAILS: cartoon characters, plastic toys, micro bags, temporary tattoos, stickers, frills, Peter Pan collar, scalloped edges, animal ears

Lolita

◉ HARAJUKU, SWEET LOLITA
◉ <u>NEO-VICTORIANA</u>, <u>KAWAII</u>, <u>MODEST</u>
⊕ <u>STEAMPUNK</u>, <u>PRAIRIE</u>, <u>NAUTICAL</u>, <u>COTTAGECORE</u>,
   <u>GOTH</u>, <u>ROCOCO</u>

For many, the name 'Lolita' stirs up the image of the pre-teen
object of desire of the middle-aged protagonist in Vladimir
Nabokov's controversial novel from 1955. However, while it does
portray a childlike aesthetic, the Lolita style of Tokyo's Harajuku
district is based on <u>Ladylike</u> beauty and elegance (p.281) and
<u>Modesty</u> (p.284) in the manner of the Victorian age. It was distilled
from <u>Kawaii</u> style (p.170) in the 1990s, taking inspiration from
<u>Neo-Victoriana</u> (p.26) in its <u>pie-crust collars</u>, long sleeves and

Women dressed in Lolita fashion outside the Individual Fashion Expo.IV, Tokyo, 3 September 2008.

Lolita cont.

ruffled skirts, and pulling in such design details as sailor collars (see also Nautical, p.98).

Lolita incorporates Asian and European sensibilities, borrowing from the Rococo style (p.257) inextricably linked with Queen Marie Antoinette, whose extravagance in fashion and other areas contributed to the French Revolution of 1789. Voluminous skirts are tiered like wedding cakes and puffed up with frothy petticoats. Girls wear bows in their perfect, doll-like hair, and dainty bonnets tied with ribbons under the chin, their hands, encased in delicate lace gloves, carrying frilled parasols or fans. Macaroon-hued versions of the style are usually called Sweet Lolita, whereas an all-black look is a signifier of Gothic Lolita (see Goth, p.220).

Ultimately Lolita, in common with the other kawaii styles, is rooted in modern Japanese culture, which encourages young people to celebrate childhood rather than playing at being adults ahead of their time. Such nuanced preferences may in part explain why Mattel's Barbie dolls, with their highly developed physique, did not sell well in Japan.

COLOURS AND PATTERNS:
pink, cream, white, black

FABRICS: lace, tulle

GARMENTS AND ACCESSORIES:
A-line skirt, petticoats, Mary Jane
shoes, parasol, blouse, pearl
necklaces, fan

DETAILS: bows, ruffles, puffed
sleeves, ribbons, hearts, sailor collar

Lounge

- HOMEWEAR
- HERITAGE, NEO-VICTORIANA, FLAPPER, EQUESTRIAN, MILITARY, TAILORING, DANDY, ANDROGYNOUS
- ATHLEISURE, HYGGE, NORMCORE

It may seem that loungewear is a relatively modern invention, but in fact adapting one's dress from home life to public life was normal in the seventeenth, eighteenth and nineteenth centuries. Clothing for relaxing in the home was distinct from sleepwear, which one would never dream of wearing in company.

Some of the earliest loungewear was brought by the Dutch East India Company from the East in the seventeenth century in the form of the *banyan* (literally 'merchant'). This loose-fitting silk housecoat was based on Persian robes and the Japanese kimono and named after the trees under which such merchants used to sit to transact their business. In the eighteenth century the physician Benjamin Rush, one of the Founding Fathers of the United States, remarked that men with philosophical leanings were often painted in their libraries wearing these flowing gowns, worn so as not to impede the faculties of the mind.

The Regency-era Dandy Beau Brummell (p.247) pioneered the trend for the lounge jacket and trouser suit, the precursor of today's lounge suit (see Tailoring, p.195). The lounge jacket was cut shorter and straighter at the back than the morning coat (see Equestrian, p.70). Later in the evolution of the lounge suit, the American market invented the roomier 'sack suit', cut from two panels. The lounge suit migrated from entertaining within the home to casual events in public, and is now an appropriate form of smart business dress.

In the nineteenth century (see Neo-Victoriana, p.26) the Crimean War made Turkish tobacco fashionable, and the 'smoking jacket' evolved as a hybrid between the comfort of the *banyan* house robe and the tailoring of the lounge jacket. Gentlemen would change into these jackets so that their day clothes would not smell of smoke, and retire into a separate room to smoke

Dolce & Gabbana Spring/Summer 2009 Menswear, Milan Fashion Week, 21 June 2008.

their pipes. The silk-satin lapels of the jacket's shawl collar would prevent ash from sticking, and the men would change back before returning to the ladies.

The smoking jacket begets the tuxedo. In 1865 the future King Edward VII, then Albert Edward, Prince of Wales, asked his Savile Row tailor Henry Poole to make a new kind of dinner jacket that incorporated the silk lapels of the smoking jacket. It made an impression on the American coffee broker and financier James Brown Potter, who had one made for himself, debuting it at the Autumn Ball of the Tuxedo Park Country Club in New York. And so the tuxedo was born.

In some countries, a dinner jacket is called a smoking jacket, but this is a linguistic 'false friend'. A dinner jacket and a tuxedo are one and the same, usually of black or midnight-blue wool with satin lapels, and a smoking jacket has satin lapels but can be of quilted velvet and in jewel tones, such as teal, burgundy or emerald. To confuse things further, when Yves Saint Laurent designed his iconic tuxedo for women in 1966, he called it 'Le Smoking'.

The humble pyjamas entered the English language via the Hindi word *paijama* ('leg covering') during the Raj, the direct rule of India under the British Crown from 1858 to 1947. These clothes were worn by all classes and sexes, from peasants to the high-born, and became popular as loungewear (with the addition of a matching shirt) for men in Britain around 1870. After World War I it was the trendsetting designer Coco Chanel who popularized pyjamas for women, wearing a version of 'beach pyjamas' as early as 1918. They were scandalous in their Androgynous nature (p.270), although the look quickly caught on among aristocratic early adopters.

Pyjamas in red and black silk, inspired by Indo-Chinese designs and decorated with dragons, blossoms and butterflies, were quite literally in *Vogue* during the Roaring Twenties with the fashion for Orientalism, the taste for so-called exotic cultures (see Flapper, p.30). The colour-block satin pyjama set worn by Claudette Colbert in the comedy *It Happened One Night* (1934), before motion-picture censorship was instigated, moved the trend forwards.

The contemporary definition of 'lounging' rarely involves elaborate dinner parties, and after the Covid-19 pandemic we

Lounge cont.

are more adept than ever at dressing for the home. Contemporary loungewear often takes the form of <u>Athleisure</u> (p.60), such as tracksuits and hoodies, sometimes elevated with tactile fabrics, such as cashmere and velour. Sleepwear may also be lounged in, and there are some designers, such as Dolce & Gabbana, who recommend silk pyjamas for daywear, as seen on their Spring/ Summer 2009 runway.

<u>COLOURS AND PATTERNS</u>:
cream, purple, burgundy, midnight blue, black, gold

<u>FABRICS</u>: velour, satin, velvet, tracksuit jersey

<u>GARMENTS AND ACCESSORIES</u>:
pyjamas, tracksuit, hoody, cardigan, jumper, sliders, slippers, robe

<u>DETAILS</u>: elasticated waistband, drawstring waist, unstructured

Hygge

- COSY
- <u>BOHEMIAN</u>, <u>LAGENLOOK</u>
+ <u>LOUNGE</u>

As the nights draw in at northern latitudes and the temperature drops, the natural human instinct is to build a nest, pull up the covers and hibernate. 'Hygge' (pronounced 'hyoo·guh') is entrenched in the Danish and Norwegian way of life. As a generalization it means 'cosiness' and 'contentment', encompassing togetherness, comfort food and sweet treats, candle-lit ambience, roaring fires and tactile fabrics. During the Covid-19 pandemic, it accelerated into the global consciousness via social media as humans sought to find positives while under house arrest.

From a fashion perspective, hygge is observable in a palette of wintry, desaturated neutrals, thick woollen knits, sheepskin and fur (these days, faux, of course). The root of the word is the Old Norse *hugga*, meaning 'to comfort', from which comes the word 'hug'; envelop yourself in layers wrapped around the torso to create a top-heavy silhouette and you are halfway there.

In its approach to layering and comfort, Hygge bears similarities to <u>Lagenlook</u> (p.250), with its loose, unstructured garments assembled in a <u>Bohemian</u> manner (p.217). However, Lagenlook often involves several thin layers, longline down to mid- or maxi-length and crinkled or deconstructed, whereas hygge is usually about snug, homely fabrics (although, confusingly, a summer version of hygge might be almost indiscernible from Lagenlook).

With hygge as a lifestyle imperative, it's no wonder that the Danes repeatedly come in the top two of the United Nations World Happiness Report (with tough competition from Finland), despite having nights that last for 17 hours in the middle of winter, and shorter lifespans than their Scandinavian neighbours. On that last point, the CEO of the Happiness Research Institute in Copenhagen, and author of the global bestseller *The Little Book of Hygge: The Danish Way to Live Well* (2016), Meik Wiking, joked in an interview that perhaps all those delicious pastries and *gløgg* eventually take their toll.

Max Mara Autumn/Winter 2017, Milan Fashion Week, 23 February 2017.

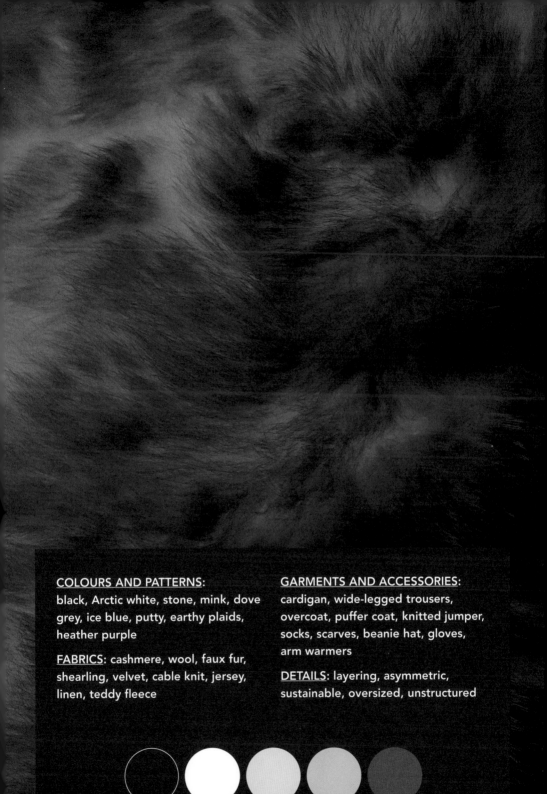

COLOURS AND PATTERNS:
black, Arctic white, stone, mink, dove grey, ice blue, putty, earthy plaids, heather purple

FABRICS: cashmere, wool, faux fur, shearling, velvet, cable knit, jersey, linen, teddy fleece

GARMENTS AND ACCESSORIES:
cardigan, wide-legged trousers, overcoat, puffer coat, knitted jumper, socks, scarves, beanie hat, gloves, arm warmers

DETAILS: layering, asymmetric, sustainable, oversized, unstructured

Conformists

As much as we hate to admit it, most of us are conformists most of the time. We hold down steady jobs, search for knowledge at institutions of learning, play on teams, trying to better the lives of ourselves and our families. For all that, we need clothes that have stood the test of time, clothes that are free of judgement.

From day to day, that might constitute a fail-safe combination of white T-shirt and blue jeans, innocuous baseball cap and comfortable trainers. For more formal occasions it could be a well-cut suit and polished oxfords. Tailoring is high-quality clothes-making, steeped in hundreds of years of using paper patterns to construct a three-dimensional garment from a two-dimensional length of fabric. When it's truly bespoke, the fabric is cut and sewn to the measurements of the client, but even off-the-peg suits carry a sense of inherent respectability. As a method of construction, tailoring finds its way into myriad other styles, accenting the look as acceptable anywhere.

There are some styles, such as bourgeoisie, that are preoccupied with social mobility and acceptance by other members of one's class. The phenomenon of the Sloane in 1980s London, with its haughty twinsets and pearls, was echoed across the Channel in Paris with the near-equivalent Bon Chic Bon Genre (BCBG) aesthetic that signified French old money.

Even the most diehard follower of trends will have some classic pieces

5.

in their wardrobe. Seasonless or decade-less pieces, such as a white cotton shirt, a beige trench coat, khaki chinos, a camel wool coat, simple white trainers and black biker boots, are worth investing in. This has more than just style implications, however. The second-hand and resale market is growing rapidly and is set to be worth $218 billion by 2026, up from $96 billion in 2021. The shift in the collective mindset from fast fashion to garments that hold their value and are worn, cared for and mended will benefit both the planet and our personal finances.

Academia

● LIBRARIAN, GEEK CHIC
◑ ATHLEISURE, COTTAGECORE, PREPPY
⊕ RETRO, KAWAII, TAILORING, CLASSIC, BEATNIK

The erudite style of the learned professor associated with Western universities is rooted in an education system that dates back almost a millennium (the oldest, the University of Bologna, was founded in 1088, followed closely by the University of Oxford, in 1096). As a contemporary cultural movement, Academia fetishizes knowledge and philosophy, fostering the idyllic image of books lining mahogany-shelved libraries, poetry, literature and analogue living.

The look is typified by a tweed blazer and waistcoat, neatly ironed white shirt and tie, deep V-neck sweater, tailored trousers or pleated tennis skirt, and polished brogues or oxford shoes, accessorized with a cross-body satchel full of well-thumbed books. The plain black or navy turtleneck beloved of the pseudo-intellectual Beatnik style (p.214) is also an Academia wardrobe essential, and wearers interpret the aesthetic through the lens of several Retro (p.20) decades, particularly the 1930s, 40s, 60s and 70s.

Academia is an example of an internet-based neo-Aestheticism that takes comfort in nostalgia, in much the same way as Cottagecore (p.161). In the digital sphere, this once elitist mode of dress, signifying the privilege and wealth of private education (similar to North American Ivy League Preppy, p.191) and criticized for being predominantly thin, white and cisgender, is increasingly subverted by a diverse audience. It is disseminated across social media and blogs as dark academia – which has a more gothic palette and channels secret clubs like that in *Dead Poets Society* (1989) and murder mysteries, such as Donna Tartt's *The Secret History* (1992) – and light academia, which is conceptually brighter in both palette and subject matter. The predominance of Tailoring (p.195) gives it an inclusive Androgynous edge (p.270), often with suits cut from British Heritage fabrics (p.23) such as muted tweeds, differentiating it from the charcoal-grey, black and pinstripe wool flannels that constitute a more executive look. Overall, Academia

Wales Bonner Autumn/Winter 2020–21 Menswear, London Fashion Week, 5 January 2020.

Academia cont.

is an inherently <u>Classic</u> style (p.209) that serves a variety of conservative functions, although it can be made younger by swapping formal shoes for trainers and adding a sweatshirt. This takes it into 'schoolcore' territory, essentially <u>Gen-Z</u>'s more woke (and less hypersexualized) take on *gyaru* school uniform, a form of <u>Kawaii</u> dress (p.170).

The academic look speaks in particular to a segment of consumers brought up on the British writer J.K. Rowling's tales of a young wizard. It is reassuring that the on-campus university experience and the comfort of old-fashioned libraries and paper pages have not lost their appeal now that those students are at ease in a hybrid learning environment.

<u>COLOURS AND PATTERNS</u>: black, grey, tan, brown, white

<u>FABRICS</u>: tweed, cotton, wool, cashmere, cable knit

<u>GARMENTS AND ACCESSORIES</u>: oxford shirt, blazer, turtleneck jumper, cardigan, check trousers, trench coat, duffle coat, brogues, loafers, <u>Chelsea boots</u>, Doc Martens, knee-high socks, ties, loafers, pleated miniskirt, satchel, waistcoat, knitted vest, cricket sweater, scarves, beret, kilt

<u>DETAILS</u>: spectacles, brooches, umbrella, watch, elbow patches, V-neck, <u>Peter Pan collar</u>, midi length

Preppy

◐ IVY LEAGUE, PREP
● RURAL, ACADEMIA, SLOANE, BCBG
⊕ EQUESTRIAN, POLO, NAUTICAL, HIP HOP

Are you yearning for an acceptance letter to Harvard, Princeton or Yale? Is your name Blair, Skip or Chase, perhaps followed by a Roman numeral? Does your family have a holiday home in the Hamptons or Martha's Vineyard? If the answer is yes to any or all of these questions, chances are you are already abreast of preppy style.

In the United States, a preparatory school is a private institution designed to equip pupils for a prestigious university education, and the 'preppy' look that has emerged from this demographic as they move from school to university and beyond pulls in, whether consciously or not, various signifiers of wealth that are styled in a youthful way and can be imitated. These include references to sports such as sailing (see Nautical, p.98), with a predilection for nautical stripes, pea coats with shiny gold buttons, and deck shoes; and Equestrian (p.70) details, such as trousers

Kendall Jenner in Versace Autumn/Winter 2020, Milan Fashion Week, 21 February 2020.

Preppy cont.

tucked into knee-high boots and tweed hacking jackets inspired by the British aristocracy (see also Rural, p.74).

Preppy style is brasher than the intellectual aesthetic of Academia (p.188), favouring bold hues of crimson, navy, lemon, duck-egg and sky blue, and polka dots. In the late 1980s and 90s it was taken over by the Hip Hop community (p.142), especially the classic Ralph Lauren polo shirt, and the uniform of beige chinos was paired with trainers for the first time.

Peak prep was achieved in 1980 with *The Official Preppy Handbook* (1980) by Lisa Birnbach, Jonathan Roberts, Carol McD. Wallace and Mason Wiley, as the United States embraced the financial optimism of the new decade. This satirical guide to navigating the upper echelons of the American class system covered everything from college interviews, through life as a young executive, to retirement at the local country club. It spawned a trend for similar publications, among them *The Official Sloane Ranger Handbook* by Ann Barr (1982), and indeed, as an old-money aesthetic associated with the upper classes, the preppy style bears similarities to the respective British and French styles Sloane (p.205) and BCBG (p.207).

COLOURS AND PATTERNS: Madras check, crimson, navy blue, duck-egg blue, sky blue, lemon yellow, polka dots, blue-and-white *marinière* stripes shirt, oxford shirt, deck shoes, loafers, tennis skirt, necktie, bowtie, cardigan, trench coat, pea coat, sunglasses, signet rings

Varsity

- COLLEGIATE
- AVIATOR, POLO
- ATHLEISURE, COWBOY

Although similar to Academia (p.188) and Preppy style (p.191) in its collegiate underpinnings, the Varsity look (an abbreviation of 'university') takes a sportier approach. American varsity champions the classic letterman team jacket of track and field cut in the style of the bomber jacket (see Aviator, p.63), while British varsity leans in to the peculiarities of particular sports, with the deep V-neck white cable-knit sweater of traditional cricketing clothing, the broad horizontal stripes of the rugby shirt, and the vertical stripes of rowing-team blazers. The classic tennis shirt (see Polo, p.76) is a staple, and the diamond pattern of argyle knits found in golf is universally popular.

The blazer, often confused with other types of jacket, is a stand-alone garment worn with contrasting trousers, and is usually brightly coloured or vertically striped. Blazers were originally designed in the 1850s for the rowing teams of Oxford and Cambridge universities (referred to collectively by the portmanteau 'Oxbridge'), to keep athletes warm on the chilly banks of the River Thames at the annual Henley Royal Regatta. The classic sporting garment often has contrasting buttons and a patch on the chest pocket denoting the club or college, and can be double- or single-breasted. These jackets were fashioned in distinctive colours and patterns so that spectators could easily distinguish one team from another, and it was the blazing crimson jacket of Cambridge's Lady Margaret Boat Club that first entered the vernacular as a 'blazer'.

Not to be outdone by its ancient rival, the University of Oxford lays claim to the genesis of the striped school tie. It is said that in 1880 members of the Exeter College rowing club took the ribbons from their straw boater hats and tied them around their necks to promote their allegiance to their college.

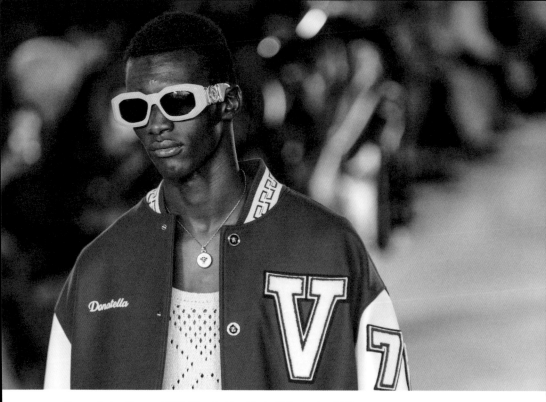

Versace Spring/Summer 2022, Milan Fashion Week, 24 September 2021.

It could be said that the Venn diagram of athletic prowess (displayed by those known in school-clique parlance as 'jocks') and booksmart academia (the nerds) meets in the varsity aesthetic. For other school cliques, see Goth (p.220), Hipster (p.226), Skate (p.231), Surf (p.234) and the artistic sensibility of Bohemian (p.217).

COLOURS AND PATTERNS: red, white, blue, navy blue, burgundy, collegiate stripes

FABRICS: cable knit, wool

GARMENTS AND ACCESSORIES: blazer, letterman jacket, polo shirt, rugby shirt, tennis skirt, ankle socks, baseball cap, trainers, loafers, miniskirt

Tailoring

⊖ SUITS, EXECUTIVE, BUSINESS

⊖ EQUESTRIAN, MILITARY, DISCO, DOLCE VITA, LOUNGE,
   BOHEMIAN, MOD, DANDY, ROCOCO

⊕ RETRO, HERITAGE, ROCKABILLY, TEDDY BOYS & TEDDY GIRLS,
   CLASSIC, ANDROGYNOUS

The ubiquitous business suit has taken several turns over the
course of history. Understandably, around the time of the French
Revolution in 1789, the trend for over-the-top extravagance in the
form of Rococo fashions (p.257) waned across Europe. In Britain,
a new style was attributed to the impeccable taste of one man,
George 'Beau' Brummell, whose colourful life had a lasting effect
on men's fashions.

Brummell was a pioneer of the Dandy aesthetic (p.247), which
– rather than being frivolous and foppish, as it is sometimes
perceived to be – was partly inspired by the functionality of Military
uniform (p.91). The jacket, an austere, dark tailcoat in the style
of a morning coat (see Equestrian, p.70), had a vent at the back
to hang over the saddle when sitting astride a horse. Constituting
the first occurrence of a matching set of jacket and trousers, it
was worn with full-length trousers (as opposed to breeches) in
white or black. At this time the suit was always a three-piece,
and the waistcoat provided valuable warmth before the advent
of central heating.

By the Victorian age, the combination of jacket and matching
trousers was known as a 'ditto'. A new, more casual style of Lounge
suit (p.179) did away with the impractical tails and was cut from
one piece of fabric with few darts for shape, different from a frock
coat, which had a seamed waist. By the Edwardian era, the lounge
suit was acceptable in more public situations, and the morning
coat became reserved for formal settings. In North America,
Brooks Brothers popularized the sack suit, the first mass-produced
suit, which had no darts at the waist and hung squarely over
the torso. Suits became synonymous with respectability and
accompanied the white-collar uniform of professionals.

Tailoring cont.

Of course, not all tailoring is worn solely by conformists, and cuts swing from one extreme to another. A good example is the contrast between the very wide-legged trousers known as 'Oxford bags', a fashion among university students between the 1920s and 1950s, and the svelte Italian cuts of 1960s Mods (p.228).

Zoot suits were popular by the late 1930s, especially among African Americans, as a form of expression, to show their love of jazz and to allow them to break free of the dull grind imposed by the lack of opportunities and meagre wages. Mexican-American men and women, who called themselves *pachucos* and *pachucas* respectively, also wore the flamboyant zoot suits with their long jackets and roomy trousers; the men styled theirs with rakish pork-pie hats and creeper shoes, and the girls with sheer blouses, high heels, make-up and bouffant pompadour hairstyles (see Teddy Boys & Teddy Girls, p.115).

However, after the United States entered World War II in December 1941, following the attack on Pearl Harbor, fabric rationing required a 26 per cent cutback on wool in men's suits. The voluminous zoot suit was now considered unpatriotic. Racial tension had escalated and, while *pachucos* and *pachucas* were labelled troublemakers by the media, it was in fact American soldiers, white civilians and the police who were the perpetrators of the Los Angeles Zoot Suit Riots of 1943. Over three days of violence, Mexican Americans were beaten and stripped, their much-loved suits symbolically burned. The riots were not just about the suits themselves, but this was a historic moment for the garment.

Women's suits, meanwhile, evolved from the English riding habit, the *redingote* (again, rooted in equestrian clothing). In the 1910s the 'Suffragette Suit' became a statement of emancipation; it was embraced in the 1920s by liberated Flapper girls (p.30), and Coco Chanel helped the cause by championing the wearing of suit jackets with skirts, and of trousers separately.

The 1930s and 40s were pivotal for the women's suit, as the screen icon Marlene Dietrich invented the Androgynous look (p.270) by wearing trouser suits and tuxedos in her films *Morocco* (1930), *Blonde Venus* (1932) and *Seven Sinners* (1940). Dietrich's look served as a precursor to Saint Laurent's famous 'Le Smoking'

Tailoring cont.

two decades later. *Vogue* featured the French designer Marcel Rochas's first ready-to-wear suits for women in 1939, and in the 1940s Katharine Hepburn's penchant for languid tailoring overlaid the look with feminine glamour.

In contemporary society, wearing tailoring is less and less about dress codes and prescribed formality. Suits are Classic garments (see p.209) that transcend occasions, and, as an expression of self-identity, tailoring always gives an impression of authority and refinement.

COLOURS AND PATTERNS: black, grey, navy blue, chalk stripe, pinstripe, windowpane check, herringbone, houndstooth, Prince of Wales check, bird's eye

FABRICS: wool, flannel, cotton

GARMENTS AND ACCESSORIES: two- or three-piece suit, tie, pocket square, waistcoat, shirt, cufflinks, cravat, brogues, oxford shoes, monkstrap shoes, loafers, watch, belt

DETAILS: single-breasted, double-breasted, peak lapels, notch lapels

Normcore

● DADCORE/MOMCORE
● <u>ATHLEISURE</u>, <u>HIPSTER</u>
⊕ <u>GORECORE</u>, <u>MINIMALIST</u>

Emerging in the mid-2000s in opposition to the omnipresent skinny jeans and skull-print scarves of <u>Indie</u> (p.131), where everyone wanted to be the band leader, Normcore came to define a look that embraced the basic, ordinary style of the American tourist. The term is attributed to the irreverent New York trend-forecasting agency/art project K-Hole (yes, really named after the ketamine-induced state of stupor) in its satirical report on consumer culture 'Youth Mode: A Report on Freedom' (October 2013) – the kind of report for which big brands pay real money in order to keep ahead of the zeitgeist. The short, downloadable PDF that was later displayed by galleries was full of such knowing witticisms as 'Once upon a time people were born into communities and had to find their individuality. Today people are born individuals and have to find their communities' and 'In Normcore, one does not pretend to be above the indignity of belonging.'

The wearers of this style aren't afraid to be one of the herd, and the actor and comedian Jerry Seinfeld serves as an unlikely style icon in the sports blousons, baggy overshirts, white trainers, plain T-shirts and stonewashed denim he wore for his eponymous hit TV show in the 1990s. Also pivotal to the development of the style was the founder of Apple, Steve Jobs, with his rotation of black rollnecks, straight-cut blue Levi 401 jeans and New Balance 992 sneakers.

Given that both champion cargo shorts, T-shirts layered under button-down <u>oxford shirts</u>, socks and sandals or ugly trainers, nylon backpacks and zip-up fleeces, what is the difference between the nondescript tourist look proper and normcore? The key is in stylistic intent. Normcore carries the same self-awareness as other <u>Hipster</u> (p.226) trends, but here the self-awareness recognizes that we are one of seven billion and not special, to paraphrase

Normcore cont.

Vetements Spring/Summer 2019, Paris Fashion Week, 1 July 2018.

Fiona Duncan's article on the aesthetic for the *New York Times* digital magazine site *The Cut* in 2014.

In the original report, normcore described a personality shift towards celebrating inclusivity (such as the enjoyment of being in the World Cup crowd, even if you're not a football fan), rather than clothes, which the writers categorized as 'Acting Basic'. Its true meaning became inconsequential once it had been misappropriated to mean a style of dress via Duncan's popular article, the fashion pack who latched on to it, and later an untold number of internet memes. What essentially started as a joke art project snowballed into one of the most culturally sticky trends of the twenty-first century.

It wasn't long before the trend bubbled up to the catwalk. Vetements pushed DHL T-shirts for Spring/Summer 2016, then revisited the idea with an anonymous uniform of denim jeans,

T-shirts and longline jackets for Spring/Summer 2019. The designer
Demna Gvasalia carried the idea over to Balenciaga and polished
it up for Spring/Summer 2019, accessorized with brown-paper
shopping bags. Prada Autumn/Winter 2022 made a case for the
return of the sleeveless white tank top, which then appeared on
the supermodel Kate Moss at Bottega Veneta for Spring/Summer
2023, paired with 'mom' jeans and a plaid overshirt (although
the shirt was actually made from intricately printed leather). The
London designer Martine Rose, of British-Jamaican heritage,
regularly leans into the city's style tribes for inspiration, and
normcore is her design signature, presented for Spring/Summer
2023 as chinos and track jackets, double denim and check shirts,
and jeans, T-shirts and beige raincoats, again with white trainers.

　　Dressing 'normally' is also the prerogative of the plain Girl/Boy Next
Door look, but here there is a lack of stylistic affectation. Similarly,
the Off-duty Model look elevates basic dressing to aspirational street
style, shot on long-limbed beauties outside fashion-week venues.

COLOURS AND PATTERNS: blue,
white, red, yellow, black-and-red
plaid, vertical stripes

FABRICS: blue denim, jersey, cotton,
nylon, polyester, Gore-Tex, fleece,
soft shell

GARMENTS AND ACCESSORIES:
chinos, trainers, T-shirt, hoody,
sweatshirt, Birkenstocks, white sports
socks, baseball cap, black rollneck,
blue denim trucker jacket, blouson
jacket, puffer jacket, overshirt, cargo
shorts, bumbag (fanny pack), oxford
shirt, circular glasses, football shirt,
Harrington jacket, polo shirt, bucket
hat, tank top

DETAILS: zips, stonewash denim,
bumbag worn across the body, cut-off
shorts

Bourgeoisie

- BOURGEOIS, BOURGIE, BOUGIE, BOUJI, BOUJEE
- NEO-VICTORIANA, DISCO, VARSITY
- HIP HOP, PREPPY, CLASSIC, DANDY

In contemporary slang, acting 'bougie' has a wealth of positive and negative meanings. From a fashion perspective, it implies that the person in question has great taste and looks well put together. It can also suggest that they are dressing above their station. Black popular culture has been applying the term since at least the 1980s, when Gladys Knight and the Pips recorded the Disco (p.139) track 'Bourgie, Bourgie' about a person from the wrong side of the tracks who is now a jet-set success story. Fast-forward to 2016 and the trap single 'Bad and Boujee' by the American trio Migos went quadruple platinum, its sentiment echoing the 'from nothing to something' story of many Hip Hop tracks (p.142). The music video shows the band dripping in diamonds, the ladies dressed immaculately in Moschino, lace, pearls and tailored blazers, as they eat fried chicken eaten out of faux Chanel fast-food boxes, washing it down with Cristal champagne.

'Bougie', however you choose to spell it, harks back to the Old French *burgeis* (town-dweller) and *burg*, the Old Frankish word for a fortified settlement (hence Johannesburg, Hamburg, Edinburgh, Pittsburg, Williamsburg and so on). The 'bourgeois' people of the town were primarily merchants and craftspeople who acted as intermediaries between the peasant farmers and the rich landowners for whom they toiled. This nouveau-riche segment was satirized by the French playwright Molière in his ballet-comedy *Le Bourgeois Gentilhomme* (*The Would-be Gentleman*; 1670) and became a vilified construct at the hands of Karl Marx in *The Communist Manifesto* (1848). Marx's argument ran that after the Industrial Revolution, the middle class, who owned the means of production and capital, exploited the proletariat (the rural and urban workers) for their own gain. The bourgeoisie of the Victorian age engaged in conspicuous consumption as they sought to enhance their social status

The rapper Saweetie arrives at a Dolce & Gabbana event, Venice, 29 August 2021.

Bourgeoisie cont.

through shop culture and decorative trinkets, mirroring the word's contemporary meaning.

On the street, the look is typified by logos and It bags, gold statement earrings and chain necklaces, worn with silk scarves, tailored blazers (see Varsity, p.193), or Ladylike (p.281) cardigans and pencil skirts. Bougie men lean in to Tailoring (p.195), with well-made dress shoes or loafers, or designer Athleisure (p.60), and often wear an impressive timepiece.

Donatella Versace quipped that in the 1980s and 90s people wanted to be chic, elegant and bourgeois. Whichever side you fall off this polysemous word, dressing bougie means dressing expensively, which is almost always a good look.

COLOURS AND PATTERNS: gold, silver, houndstooth check, camel, black, white

FABRICS: satin, velvet, velour, faux fur, silk, bouclé

GARMENTS AND ACCESSORIES: culottes, knee-high boots, gold jewellery, blouse, longline coat, sunglasses, designer handbag, designer shoes, faux-fur jacket, gloves, pearls, watch

DETAILS: pussy bow, pleats, frills, knee length, double-breasted, diamonds and fine jewellery, logos

Sloane

⊜ SLOANE RANGER, HOORAY HENRY
⊖ <u>RURAL</u>, <u>SAFARI</u>
⊕ <u>PREPPY</u>, <u>CLASSIC</u>

In London, the upper-middle- to upper-class social strata have their own tribe of maligned Alice-band-and-pearls-wearing ladies from the well-heeled Sloane Square intersection of the boroughs of Chelsea and Belgravia. Elevated from being merely <u>Bourgeois</u> (p.202), Sloanes are usually of considerable financial means, although few are genuine aristocracy as Lady Diana Spencer – the quintessential Sloane – was before she married Prince Charles in 1981.

Lady Diana Spencer at the Young England Kindergarten, London, 17 September 1980.

Resisting the nuances of seasonal (or even decadal) trends, the Sloane look is staunchly anti-fashion, and therefore inherently <u>Classic</u> (p.209). It is forever stuck circa 1982, when the humorous *Official Sloane Ranger Handbook* by the journalist Ann Barr was published, and is associated with its love of <u>pie-crust</u> and <u>Peter Pan collars</u>, gilets and waxed-cotton Barbour jackets borrowed off the peg from a weekend at the parents' <u>Rural</u> (p.74) abode, worn with Gucci horse-bit loafers and an Hermès scarf tied below the chin (which led to the Lone Ranger-inspired nickname). In warmer climes, the Sloane errs towards <u>Safari</u> style (p.105).

In much the same way as adherents of the American <u>Preppy</u> style (p.191), Sloanes would have been expected to attend a select list of private secondary schools. Kate Middleton (now the Princess of Wales), who is whispered about in some circles as 'The Sloane

Sloane cont.

on the Throne', in her pre-royal life indeed went to the right schools (Downe House and Marlborough College) and university (St Andrews), and was pictured on more than one occasion in classic Sloane cotton shirt and shooting vest, with skinny jeans tucked into wellies and a trilby sporting a jaunty feather. In the city, her go-to 2000s looks included pretty pastel cardigans, floral midi skirts, kitten heels and pashminas.

The male Sloane, also known as a 'Hooray Henry' (a slang term coined for the aggressively posh cheers the jazz trumpeter Humphrey Lyttelton received between numbers in the 1950s), usually works as a lawyer, banker or hedge-fund manager. Monday to Friday he wears a bold chalk-stripe or subtle pinstripe suit, roomy in the trouser leg and possibly a hand-me-down from his father, with polished oxfords and a natty silk tie. Come the weekend, he is to be found watching the rugby in the White Horse public house in Parson's Green (also known as 'The Sloaney Pony'), wearing salmon-red chinos, tan suede chukka boots, a collared shirt and a padded gilet, Labrador in one hand and pint in the other.

COLOURS AND PATTERNS: navy blue, gold, tartan, cream, mauve, Liberty floral prints, burgundy, gun check

FABRICS: wool, waxed cotton, cashmere, suede

GARMENTS AND ACCESSORIES: blouse, cardigan, cotton shirt, pearls, watch, silk scarves, skirt, shooting jacket, Alice band, tasselled knee-high boots, chukka boots, signet rings

DETAILS: pussy bow, pie-crust collar, pleats, frills, knee length, midi length

BCBG

⊜ BON CHIC, BON GENRE
◐ <u>PREPPY</u>, <u>SLOANE</u>
⊕ <u>CLASSIC</u>

In Paris there evolved a similarly highbrow aesthetic to the British
<u>Sloane</u> Ranger (p.205): BCBG (*bon chic, bon genre*, French for
'good style, good class'), which received its own handbook by
Thierry Mantoux, *BCBG: Le Guide du Bon Chic Bon Genre*, in
1985. In France, the word *bourgeoisie* describes the middle and
upper classes, historically organized into five social layers: the
petite bourgeoisie (true middle class), *moyenne bourgeoisie*
(upper middle class), *grande bourgeoisie* (upper-class gentry),
haute bourgeoisie (perceived nobility, with family dating back
as far as the Revolution) and *ancienne bourgeoisie* (provincial
landowning dynasties with a history preceding the Revolution).
BCBG stereotypes come from the *grande* or *haute bourgeoisie*,
own a familial property in the 7th, 16th or 17th arrondissements of
Paris, never talk about their origins (a point of difference to <u>Preppy</u>
Americans; p.191), have exceptional manners and are able to wear
clothes of the same size all their life.

The style is <u>Classic</u> (p.209) and similar to the Sloanes' landed-
gentry look, with <u>blazers</u>, knotted silk scarves (Hermès only) or
cravats, and British hunting <u>tweed</u>. Chic additions include cropped
cigarette trousers, pseudo-intellectual roll necks, cufflinked shirts
and always a signet ring bearing the family crest.

The style gives its name to the American brand BCBG Max
Azria, founded by and named after the Tunisia-born designer. Azria
was raised in Paris and set up the label in Los Angeles in 1989 as
an antidote to the excesses of the 1980s. The brand was a success
story in the 1990s, selling runway-quality commercial womenswear
for significantly less than its competitors: high-class designs for
middle-class prices. Whether true BCBG types would wear some
of the label's more skin-flashing creations is up for debate.

Karo Laczkowska in Celine Autumn/Winter 2019 Ready-to-Wear, Paris Fashion Week, 1 March 2019.

COLOURS AND PATTERNS:
black, white, navy, Loden green, herringbone tweed

FABRICS: cashmere, silk, cotton, linen, wool, tweed

GARMENTS AND ACCESSORIES:
blouse, cardigan, cotton shirt, pearls, watch, Hermès silk scarf, skirt, ballet pumps

DETAILS: pussy bow, frills, knee length, midi length

Classic

◉ CHIC, SOPHISTICATED, ELEGANT

⊖ ATHLEISURE, AVIATOR, BIKER, EQUESTRIAN, RURAL, COWBOY,
COMBAT, CLASSIC ROCK, PREPPY, VARSITY, BOURGEOISIE,
SLOANE, BCBG, BEATNIK, ANDROGYNOUS

⊕ HERITAGE, NAUTICAL, TAILORING, LADYLIKE, MINIMALIST

Trends come and go, but classic style is immortal. Elegant,
enduring garments made from good-quality fabrics are the
building blocks of the wardrobe and can be styled with accessories
to take them from day to evening. Classic can often be interpreted
as Minimalist (p.252) and even anti-fashion, with garments devoid
of season-specific details that would age them, but this is not
always the case; a pussy-bow blouse, for example, is classic but not
minimal. In general, classic veers towards conservative dressing,
but again there are exceptions. Biker jackets (p.67) and the black
leather trousers beloved of Classic Rock stars (p.118), for instance,
can be worked into a classic style. Classic can mean demure
and Ladylike (p.281), with knee-length skirts and cardigans;
Androgynous (p.270), with wide-legged, high-waisted trousers
à la Katharine Hepburn; or a polka-dot bathing suit evoking the
sex symbols of yesteryear (see Pin-Up, p.290).

Most styles have at least one associated classic product. Among
these are the beige trench coat and chinos of Combat (p.95), the
striped *marinière* top and double-breasted pea coat of Nautical
style (p.98), and the aviator and bomber jackets and sunglasses
of Aviator style (p.63). A pair of straight-cut blue denim jeans and
cowboy boots channel the western heritage of the Cowboy (p.79);
smart, plain blazers borrow from the Varsity look (p.193); and the
black roll neck of Beatnik style (p.214) is also a Normcore (p.199)
standard thanks to the influence of Steve Jobs. Footwear varies
from plain white trainers, the staple of Athleisure (p.60), to the
riding or Chelsea boots of Equestrian style (p.70). A white cotton
shirt is a must-have and can be paired with almost any style.

For many, the definitive image of a timeless style is the Little
Black Dress, LBD. This ubiquitous item dates back to 1926, when

Chanel Spring/Summer 1991 Ready-to-Wear, Paris Fashion Week, October 1990.

American *Vogue* published an illustration of a simple new design by Coco Chanel with a bateau neckline, long sleeves, a dropped waist and just-below-the-knee hemline, accessorized with a pearl necklace and matching stud earrings. *Vogue* labelled it 'Chanel's Ford', implying that – like the family car of the time – it was versatile and accessible to all. The LBD was immortalized on film in *Breakfast at Tiffany's* (1961) by the screen icon Audrey Hepburn wearing a Givenchy sheath dress, also accessorized with strings of marble-sized pearls. Pearls are often defined as 'classic' jewellery, and feature in the middle- and upper-class styles <u>Bourgeoisie</u>

(p.202), Preppy (p.191), Sloane (p.205) and BCBG (p.207), before remerging in 2020 in male jewellery as an androgynous trend. The aristocratic country looks of the Rural set (p.74) are often deemed to be classic, and resistant to the waxing and waning of urban fashions.

Equivalent to the LBD, the perfectly cut black suit is a perennial style classic. The combination of a black suit, white shirt and black necktie has been adopted across society from high-school proms to weddings and funerals (but note that black suits are generally not recommended in the corporate environment; navy or charcoal is preferred). Tailoring (p.195) in most of its forms and hues, especially two- and three-piece suits, blazers and outerwear in a palette of navy, camel, black, charcoal or Heritage check (p.23), also constitutes style classics that can be handed down from generation to generation.

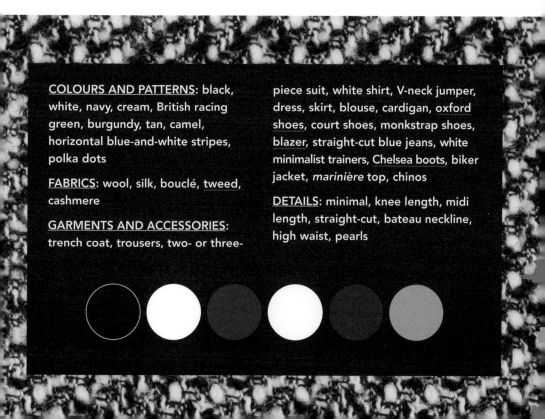

COLOURS AND PATTERNS: black, white, navy, cream, British racing green, burgundy, tan, camel, horizontal blue-and-white stripes, polka dots

FABRICS: wool, silk, bouclé, tweed, cashmere

GARMENTS AND ACCESSORIES: trench coat, trousers, two- or three-piece suit, white shirt, V-neck jumper, dress, skirt, blouse, cardigan, oxford shoes, court shoes, monkstrap shoes, blazer, straight-cut blue jeans, white minimalist trainers, Chelsea boots, biker jacket, *marinière* top, chinos

DETAILS: minimal, knee length, midi length, straight-cut, bateau neckline, high waist, pearls

Subcultures

The requirement for humans to comply with authority, whether legal or political, is by its very nature oppressive. The mainstream notion of acting as a cog in the machine was opposed by countercultures that believed in anti-materialism and anti-capitalism, such as the Beat Generation poets and the original hippies. Impoverished, wandering artistic types known as bohemians had been a visible section of Western society since the time of the French Revolution at the end of the eighteenth century. Not all bohemians are hippies, but almost all hippies are bohemians.

Contemporary revolutionaries defined by their style include the anarchic punk movement, which was as much defined by its musical style, and is explored in section 3, Music & Dance (p.108). Goth was spawned from a darker shade of punk and found a spiritual side.

There are also subcultures of communities united by a particular lifestyle or interest, such as surfers and skaters. These two groups in particular have a laid-back view of rules and of life in general.

The notion of cool is often attributed to subcultures and countercultures. Curiously hard to define, it is nevertheless chased by marketers, and successful companies emerge from, or home in on, subculture communities, or those who wish to emulate them. One subculture known for its ability to convey the next cool thing is the hipster, and the original hipsters were the beatniks, who channelled

6.

& Countercultures

the visual style of the Beat Generation. The culture split aesthetically, and by the end of the 1960s a psychedelia-loving faction was known as 'hippy'.

In Britain, another group shook off the austerity of their parents' generation and signalled the changing times with a modernist aesthetic. They became known as mods and found a natural enemy in the rockers, lovers of 1950s American Biker culture (p.67) and Rock & Roll (p.110). After them came the proudly working-class skinhead subculture, whose overall perception was later muddied by its appropriation by a faction of far-right supporters.

Despite the globalization of trends across social media, some subcultures are specific to a place. One of these is the African continent's Société des Ambianceurs et des Personnes Élégantes, known as La Sape. This community of Dandies (p.247) spans two cities separated by the River Congo, and elevates exquisite style to an ideology.

Beatnik

● BEAT GENERATION, BEAT
➔ NAUTICAL, ROCK & ROLL, HIPPY, HIPSTER, MOD
✛ ACADEMIA, BOHEMIAN, MINIMALIST

Out of post-World War II American consumer culture emerged the
Beat Generation, the earliest counterculture youth movement of
the twentieth century. Its creative output was defined by the unholy
trinity of Allen Ginsberg, William S. Burroughs and Jack Kerouac,
particularly their respective books *Howl* (1956), *The Naked Lunch*
(1959) and *On the Road* (1957).

Kerouac first used the phrase 'Beat Generation' in 1948 for
this underground movement that emerged in New York, first in
the halls of Columbia University and later on the liberal streets
of Greenwich Village. The equivocal word 'beat' was interpreted
as being tired and beaten down, with Catholic connotations of
beatitude (the state of bliss of the dead), as well as being musically
'on the beat'. These were rebellious intellectuals interested in
philosophy – particularly existentialism and the idea of living in the
moment, free to choose one's purpose in life – and recreational
drugs. They read widely of Jean-Paul Sartre, Friedrich Nietzsche,
Albert Camus, Simone de Beauvoir and Søren Kierkegaard, and
were interested in Eastern philosophy, mysticism and the occult.

The present-day understanding of 'cool' gained momentum at
this time, both in the Taoist sense of simplicity and going with the
flow, and according to African and Western notions of self-control,
detachment and sangfroid. The use of the word 'cool' originated
in the 1930s with African-American jazz musicians, and its use as
a positive affirmation is attributed to the tenor saxophonist Lester
Young, who also epitomized the laid-back sound of cool jazz.
(Incidentally, Young was a pioneer who subverted gender norms,
was Androgynous, p.270, in his dress, called his male friends 'lady',
and has been credited as the first person to use the words 'bread'
for 'money' and 'crib' for home.)

The Beat movement was anti-consumerist and its adherents
bought most of their clothes second-hand, adopting the French-

inspired details such as *marinière* tops (see Nautical, p.98) and
berets also beloved of artists and great thinkers. Women wore
above-the-knee painter's smocks with tights, which was shocking
to the general public (the miniskirt would not become fashionable
for another decade). They were known as 'hepcats' or 'hepsters',
and the Beats became the first Hipster tribe (p.226). They listened
to bebop and jazz, smoked marijuana, promoted sexual freedom
and engaged in spontaneous acts of performance art and poetry,
known as 'happenings'.

Dancewear, including tights and leotards, was popular with
the women, as were slim, cropped black trousers, worn with ballet
pumps. The look was immortalized by Audrey Hepburn in *Funny
Face* (1957), with a black roll neck, capri pants and white socks,
paired with black penny loafers. Men of the Beat Generation grew
moustaches and goatees and wore horn-rimmed spectacles to
emulate the virtuoso jazz trumpeter Dizzy Gillespie. Sandals were
worn by both sexes – when they wore shoes at all.

A brooding black palette was the norm, and beatniks favoured
unfussy, Minimalist designs (p.252). Simple modernist jewellery
(see Mod, p.228) – sculptural pendants or beads – was often the
only adornment, although they did popularize the wearing of
sunglasses indoors (an affectation that hipsters continue today).

'Beatnik' wasn't coined until the early 1960s to describe the
mass followers of the movement, who were ridiculed in much the
same way as the hipsters of the 2000s. The suffix 'nik' is said to be
both a Yiddishism introduced by the San Francisco journalist and
humorist Herb Caen and a homage to the launch of the Russian
satellite *Sputnik 1* in 1957. Ginsberg hated the term because it
described fashion rather than the movement's artistic ideals, but
it endures as the general description of the Beat aesthetic.

Culturally, the Beat movement was allied with desegregation
and heavily influenced later Rock & Roll musicians (p.110), such
as the Beatles and Bob Dylan, who elevated popular music to
an art form. Without the original Beat and the beatniks who
came after it, the Hippy movement (p.223), with its similarly
anti-establishment, anti-military and anti-capitalist ideals, would
not have emerged.

The model Vikki Dougan poses in Los Angeles, c. 1956.

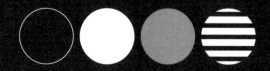

Bohemian

- BOHO, FOLK
- NEO-VICTORIANA, FLAPPER, INDIE, BOURGEOISIE, MAXIMALIST, ROMANTIC
- COWBOY, GAUCHO, PRAIRIE, FESTIVAL, HIPPY, SURF, LAGENLOOK

'Bohemian' has become the catch-all word for free-spirited wanderers, artists and anyone living an unconventional lifestyle, as well as for their eclectic style of dress. Etymologically it comes from the French *bohémien*, a term historically used for the colourfully dressed, nomadic Romani people who came to France from the medieval kingdom of Bohemia, now part of the Czech Republic. In fact, the Roma diaspora had originated in northern India and roamed across Europe, where they were generally unwelcome – except in Bohemia, where the king and Holy Roman Emperor Zikmund Lucemburský in 1423 granted a warrant asking for them to be protected and permitted rights. It was this endowment that is understood to have led to the mistaken belief that they came from Bohemia.

After the French Revolution of 1789–99, many artists lost their wealthy patrons and descended into poverty, sharing some perceived similarities with the Roma. In nineteenth-century Western painting and literature, bohemianism became synonymous with a subculture of artistic enlightenment, the opposite of the usually philistine and uncultured Bourgeoisie (p.202). *The Bohemian* (1868) by the Impressionist painter Pierre-Auguste Renoir depicts a girl dressed in a white, off-the-shoulder blouse and flowing skirt, with long curly hair – still a classic bohemian look today. The Victorian Pre-Raphaelites popularized flowing gowns and long strings of beads for their Arthurian muses (see also Romantic, p.263, and Neo-Victoriana, p.26), and subsequently the Flapper era (p.30) added to the bohemian palette with its love of exotic prints, intricate embroidery, harem trousers and unstructured dresses with fringing that expressed the wearer's movement when dancing.

Philosophically, bohemianism bears some similarities to the Beatniks (p.214) with their anti-materialistic focus on creativity and living in the moment, although the bohemian mode of dress

Chanel Métiers d'Art Pre-Fall 2023, Dakar, 7 December 2022.

is considerably more 'thrown together' and <u>Maximalist</u> (p.254). Bohemianism found its soulmate in the counterculture <u>Hippy</u> (p.223) movement of the 1960s and 70s, and there are parallels in the flowing garments of folk musicians. Men wore their shirts unbuttoned, while women wore so-called peasant blouses with voluminous <u>bishop sleeves</u> and smocking that revealed décolletage, alluding both to free love and to latent sexuality. Layered necklaces, crochet or suede waistcoats, hip belts, loose-fitting trousers and flower crowns were common between the sexes.

In the mid-2000s boho chic was an inescapable celebrity style trend as <u>Indie</u> (p.131) music ruled the airwaves, and it became the go-to look for <u>Festival</u> wear (p.149), with revellers dressed in floaty handkerchief tops, mirror-embroidered waistcoats, tiered ruffle maxi skirts or cut-off denim hot pants, with slouchy ankle boots, floppy wide-brimmed hats, and wide coin belts slung low on the hips. The look for summer often pulls from the airy dresses of <u>Prairie</u> style (p.85), while for winter the jeans-and-boots combination of <u>Cowboy</u> (p.79), wool ponchos of <u>Gaucho</u> (p.82) and shearling jackets of <u>Aviator</u> style (p.63) add warming layers.

The Y2K bohemian aesthetic cycled back in the 2020s, bringing with it the divisive dresses-over-jeans microtrend, as seen on the catwalk at Chanel Pre-Fall 2023. Bohemianism is part of the fabric of some design houses, such as Etro, Chloé, Ulla Johnson, Sea New York and Zimmermann. The aesthetic continues to speak to the evolving race of global nomads, at liberty to work wherever there is a Wi-Fi signal.

<u>COLOURS AND PATTERNS</u>:
terracotta, white, turquoise, naturalistic prints, ochre, paisley, ikat, tie-dye

<u>FABRICS</u>: jersey, hemp, cotton, chunky knits, lace, crochet, wood, leather, suede, sheepskin

<u>GARMENTS AND ACCESSORIES</u>:
blouse, maxi skirt, waistcoat, sandals, hoop earrings, camisole top, denim shorts, cowboy boots, ankle boots, wide-legged trousers, flared trousers, longline cardigan, long necklaces, body jewellery, espadrilles, moccasins, headbands, flower crowns, scarves, handkerchief skirt, flip-flops, poncho, wrap top, sheepskin coat

<u>DETAILS</u>: rope belt, off-the-shoulder, silver jewellery, unbuttoned, creased, flared, bishop sleeves, fringing, embroidery, maxi length, pom-poms, tassels, patchwork

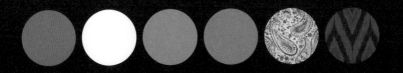

Goth

- GOTHIC, POSITIVE PUNK, DARKWAVE
- NEO-VICTORIANA, TAILORING, MINIMALIST
- CYBERPUNK, STEAMPUNK, ROCK & ROLL, PUNK, EMO, LOLITA, HIPPY, DANDY, ROMANTIC

The search for the origins of the Goth style has given rise to some misconceptions. One is that it is historical, perhaps related to the ornate style of architecture popular in medieval Europe, featuring gruesome and expressive stone gargoyles. Another is that it might stem from the time of the Gothic Revival, through the Romantic era (p.263) and into the Victorian, when horror fiction was popular. That would certainly explain why goths favour black and often wear lace, corsets, flowing skirts and capes (see Neo-Victoriana, p.26).

In truth, goth is far younger. As a subculture, it is inextricably linked to the style of music that evolved out of British post-punk in the late 1970s. There had been proto-goth artists, however: the album *The Marble Index* (1968) by the German singer-songwriter, actor and model Nico (real name Christa Päffgen), showcasing her haunting sound, ghostly face, jet-black hair and gloomy attire, helped to shape goth.

The label 'first gothic rock band' belongs to the experimental English band Bauhaus and their brooding single 'Bela Lugosi's Dead' (1979). The track 'Spellbound' (1981) by Siouxie Sioux and the Banshees (one of the last true Punk bands, p.125, to be signed to a record label), with its themes of witchcraft, helped to evolve the genre, and Sioux was styled in heavy black eye make-up, theatrical face powder and raven-coloured, backcombed hair. Post-punk New Romantic (p.266) bands added to the theatricality of the look with frilly fop shirts, and the Sisters of Mercy brought goth rock to a popular audience, with their palette of inky black.

In the United States, taking inspiration from mid-century visual and musical styles, Gothabilly emerged: a melting pot of goth, Rockabilly (p.113) and Pin-Up (p.290) styles with barrel curls, sleeve tattoos, a fascination with the paranormal and low-budget B-movies, halter-neck tops, circle skirts and seamed stockings.

In the late 1980s and 90s the Rave
scene (p.146) and the Y2K trend for
Cyberpunk (p.38) themes in popular
culture brought forth the Cybergoth
subgenre with its neon club-ready
dancewear, body modification,
platforms, faux-fur boots, fishnets and
synthetic locks, accessorized with
post-apocalyptic masks and goggles.

In the Harajuku district of Tokyo,
around 2007, goth fused with the Lolita
(p.177) trend. Street-style enthusiasts
were immaculately dressed in tiered
skirts, black lace and corsets, with Mary
Jane pumps or platforms, distilled into
an all-black palette with accents of
blood red and royal purple.

An aesthetically led subgenre of
goth called Nu-Goth started to gain
traction in the 1990s, with its own set
of interests, such as paganism and the
occult, and sleek, fashion-forward clothes. Pentagrams, crucifixes,
and moon and star signs are commonly worn with such 1990s
favourites as chokers, crop tops, round sunglasses, body harnesses
(see also Fetish, p.293), lace-up Doc Martens (preferably platforms)
and immaculate inky-black lipstick. There is some crossover with
Hippy Goths (p.223), who channel Fleetwood Mac's Stevie Nicks
in velvet platforms and chiffon.

The age of social media brought a younger generation of
nu-goths, known as Pastel Goths, who share some characteristics
with Sad Boys & Sad Girls (see E-Boy & E-Girl, p.51) and mix their
punk elements with soft pink and lilac tones. The distillation of
goth into consumer culture via shopping-mall brands, among
them Hot Topic in the United States, led to what trad goths call the
abomination of Mall Goths, who eventually collected around their
own nu-metal music scene, and as such are considered more part
of the Metal subculture (p.120).

Gothic fashion is alive and well as a reference on the catwalks,
elevated to what fashion writers labelled 'Haute Goth'. This was

Nova Malanova in Marc Jacobs Spring/Summer 2014, New York Fashion Week, 12 September 2013.

Goth cont.

seen with poignancy in the dark-themed collections and skull motifs of Alexander McQueen, and <u>Avant-Garde</u> (p.244) designers Rick Owens, Gareth Pugh and Yohji Yamamoto, as well as the more playful designers Anna Sui, Thierry Mugler, Jean Paul Gaultier and Christian Lacroix. Newer labels, such as the Vampire's Wife by Susie Cave, have made haute goth a go-to style in Hollywood.

Contrary to popular belief, many goths are not depressed or obsessed with death, not all wear black, and there is a myriad of substyles. Many goths in a professional environment adapt their dress to what is known as Corporate Goth or Corp Goth, which involves ebony or <u>pinstripe</u> <u>Tailoring</u> (p.195) with subtle spider or skull details; and young adults and pre-teens in their experimental goth phase are referred to as 'Baby Bats'.

<u>COLOURS AND PATTERNS</u>: black, dark purple, blood red, gunmetal

<u>FABRICS</u>: lace, satin, velvet, PVC, leather, chenille

<u>GARMENTS AND ACCESSORIES</u>: corset, maxi skirt, suit, pie-crust collar, platforms, gloves, shirt, top hat, parasol, ruffled cravat, body jewellery, drape jacket

<u>DETAILS</u>: skulls, crucifixes, studs, spikes, bats, spiders, cobwebs, moons, stars, ankh symbols, chains

<u>HAIR AND MAKE-UP</u>: black hair, blunt fringe, ghostly powder, dark lipstick

Hippy

● HIPPIE, PSYCHEDELIA
➡ <u>RETRO</u>, <u>COMBAT</u>, <u>HIPSTER</u>
➕ <u>FESTIVAL</u>, <u>BOHEMIAN</u>, <u>POLITICAL</u>

The hippy movement blossomed in the 1960s and 70s in the wake
of the hipsters and <u>hepcats</u> of the Beat Generation (see <u>Beatnik</u>,
p.214). Arising primarily as a countercultural <u>Political</u> cause (p.260)
in response to America's involvement in the Vietnam War (1955–75),
it rippled across the world as young people rejected conservative
values and the unquestioning ethics of their parents' generation.

Armed with the newly minted contraceptive pill, the hippies
preached messages of peace and free love, and used LSD and
marijuana to expand their consciousness. While Beatniks were
pensive, wore dark clothes and discussed philosophy in smoky
jazz bars, hippies were joyful and listened to rock, wearing a
spectrum of colours, especially purple and indigo, which are said
to relate to the crown and third eye chakras respectively. The
two countercultures had sexual liberation in common, and both
supported group sex, open relationships and homosexuality.

Mileshka in Anna Sui Spring/Summer 2018,
New York Fashion Week, 11 September 2017.

223

Hippy cont.

Allen Ginsberg, who segued from Beat poet to hippy, had won a landmark case at the California State Superior Court in 1957 whereby the judge ruled in favour of his explicit work *Howl*, finding that it was of social importance and not obscene. Ginsberg aligned himself with the work of the Harvard psychology professor Timothy Leary, who had an epiphany about consciousness while under the influence of hallucinogenic mushrooms in Mexico, and famously urged people to 'turn on, tune in, and drop out'. The hippies' experimentation with LSD and other mind-altering substances expressed itself in clothes through swirling, trippy prints in brightly saturated colours.

Hippies despised mass-produced goods and consumer culture, and uniquely streaked tie-dyed fabrics signified their appreciation for African and Asian crafts and culture. Jewellery was also handmade and craft-based, often using crystals, beads, wood and feathers found on their travels as they roamed between music festivals, including the infamous event at Woodstock in upstate New York in 1969 (see also <u>Festival</u>, p.149). Like other <u>Bohemian</u> types (p.217), hippies chose to be clearly identified as 'other' to the mainstream, wearing loose, flowing robes, maxi skirts or harem pants, and romantic blouses, with open-toed sandals and flower garlands in their long, unkempt hair. More mainstream hippies wore fashionable bell-bottom jeans and fringed suede waistcoats, now considered a distinctly <u>Retro</u> aesthetic (p.20).

The hippy icons John Lennon and Yoko Ono epitomized the practice of non-violent action with their famous bed-ins, and made statements against the Vietnam War through dress. Lennon recontextualized army-surplus <u>Combat</u> jackets (p.95), while Ono favoured all-white looks as a message of peace.

The counterculture was particularly attuned to the plight of Native Americans, inspired by their otherness, their inherently tribal way of life in communes and in harmony with nature, and their ritualistic use of cannabis and peyote. Hippies became a helpful ally for Red Power, but, although they were for the most part well intentioned, the appropriation of Indigenous motifs, such as beaded quillwork and war bonnets, was problematic and served only to reduce the diverse cultures of the 574 Indigenous American tribes and First Nation communities of Canada to stereotype.

It wasn't long before the fashion industry took hold of the hippy aesthetic and made it haute. Halston experimented with tie-dye

silk velvet in 1969, and the bold zigzag and wave patterns
of Ottavio and Rosita Missoni's machine knitwear captured the
imagination of the fashion press in the early 1970s. Later the
globetrotting designer Gimmo Etro homed in on paisley –
previously a favourite motif of the Beatles and synonymous with
hippy style – as his house's signature print. Its distinctive curved
teardrop shape, known as *boteh jegheh* ('ancient motif'), which
originated in Persia and decorated the crowns of Iranian kings, is
variously interpreted as a bent cedar tree, symbolizing strength,
and a ripening seed pod, symbolizing life. It was exported on
highly prized Kashmir shawls and later mass-produced in the town
of Paisley in southwestern Scotland, hence its present name.

By the start of the 1970s some hippy factions had become
unbearably Bourgeois (p.202). The next generation was angrier
and edgier than its forebears, and so it was that Punk (p.125)
seeped up from the underground to tear down those messages
of peace and love.

COLOURS AND PATTERNS: white,
tie-dye, purple, red, orange, green,
paisley, spirals

FABRICS: denim, hemp, cotton,
crochet, corduroy

GARMENTS AND ACCESSORIES:
sandals, T-shirt, maxi skirt, blouse,
bell-bottom jeans, floppy hat,
bandanas, tank top, long scarves,
harem pants, longline coat, vest,
waistcoat

DETAILS: flower crowns, fringing,
tassels, ribbons, handmade jewellery,
CND symbols

HAIR AND MAKE-UP: long,
dishevelled hair, no make-up

Hipster

◓ BOBO (BOURGEOIS-BOHÈMES)
◑ RETRO, ROCK & ROLL, BEATNIK
⊕ GORECORE, NAUTICAL, INDIE, KIDCORE, NORMCORE,
BOHEMIAN, HIPPY

In gentrified neighbourhoods across the world, at the turn of the millennium, hipsters were unmissable, congregating outside artisan coffee shops beside their fixed-wheel bikes. They brought with them man buns, moustaches, ripped skinny jeans and patterned vintage shirts worn with colourful braces (suspenders).

A bearded hipster, 8 April 2019.

The original hipsters were the African-American hepcats of the 1940s jazz era, who influenced the 1950s Beat Generation with their laid-back attitude and use of recreational marijuana (see Beatnik, p.214). By the 1960s, the word 'hipster' had been transposed into 'Hippy' (p.223) and came to describe a specific kind of person with a Bohemian lifestyle (p.217).

While the word 'hipster' is often used contemptuously, it is in fact these early adopters of fashion and music who help to set global trends. The hipster movement has significant crossover with the Indie aesthetic (p.131), with a focus on handcrafted, locally sourced consumable products. It was the contemporary hipster who pioneered the trend for second-hand thrift shopping, a habit that lends the subculture a Retro appearance (p.20), extending as far as the use of retro electronics, such as Casio watches.

In the early 2000s the hipster passed through several phases, aligning briefly with Emo (p.129) and Scene before moving on to a phase of ironic trucker hats, beat-up Converse trainers and Kidcore-inspired (p.175) cartoon shirts. Next came a strong mid-century influence, evidenced by thick Buddy Holly-style spectacle frames, chinos, argyle knits and floral tea dresses (see also Rock & Roll, p.110), worn while browsing vinyl at the local record shop.

A common subset of the hipster is the 'fauxhemian', the creative who pursues a bohemian lifestyle while still being of comfortable means. In France, such people are referred to as 'Bobo' (for 'Bourgeois-bohèmes'; see Bourgeoisie, p.202).

From the mid-2010s the hipster became more rugged. The rise of Gorecore (p.88) and the popularity of climbing as a sport meant that urban professionals were bedecked in plaid shirts, hiking boots, cargo shorts and sustainably made anoraks while foraging for organic produce at Whole Foods. They were not to be outdone by the Shipsters (see also Nautical, p.98), with their yellow rubberized macs, rolled-up selvedge denim jeans, cable-knit sweaters, micro beanie hats and penchant for craft beer.

COLOURS AND PATTERNS: tan, plaid, paisley, micro floral prints

FABRICS: organic cotton, denim, shell, bamboo, canvas, corduroy, vegan leather

GARMENTS AND ACCESSORIES: skinny jeans, beanie hat, plaid shirt, braces (suspenders), backpack, V-neck T-shirt, cardigan, blazer, cravat, tracksuit, hiking boots, tea dress, cut-off denim shorts, round glasses, horn-rimmed spectacles, lens-less glasses, shutter shades, trucker hat, loafers, Crocs, espadrilles

DETAILS: rips, rolled up, tattoos, piercings, stretched lobes, mandarin collar, headphones

HAIR: long hair, man bun, beard, moustache

Mod

≈ MODERNIST
→ TEDDY BOYS & TEDDY GIRLS, PUNK, SKINHEAD
+ DOLCE VITA, TAILORING, MINIMALIST

Britain in the years immediately following World War II was
an austere, unglamorous place to grow up as rationing, which
had started in 1940, restricted daily life until 1954. By the time
members of the Baby Boomer generation were in their teens, in
the early 1960s, they were desperate to shake off the oppressive
culture of their parents. Inspired by the Beatniks (p.214) and
similarly fans of modern jazz and soul, while rejecting the pomp
of the Teddy Boys & Teddy Girls (p.115), they wanted to be
unequivocal 'modernists', which became shortened to 'mods'.

As the economy prospered and unemployment in the United
Kingdom reached unprecedented lows of between 1 and 2 per
cent, male mods could indulge their passion for slim-fitting Italian
Tailoring (p.195) in plain dark colours inspired by such movies as
La Dolce Vita (p.168), worn with pale shirts and narrow ties. They
saved money to buy Vespa scooters, which imparted freedom to
roam beyond the routes of public transport. The scooters weren't
in danger of smearing grease over their pristine trousers, and
mods protected their suits further by wearing jackets bought from
army-surplus stores, specifically the Korean War-era United States
Army M51 parka (see Military, p.91), with its smart epaulettes,
alpaca lining and attached hood.

The natural enemies of mods were rockers, who modelled
themselves on American youth culture, listened to Rock & Roll
(p.110), and were distinguished by their Biker (p.67) attire
and motorcycles. They didn't relate to the mods, with their
fastidiousness, sharp suits and progressive approach to
women, and derided their rivals' prized scooters as 'hairdryers'.
The mods reciprocated with hatred for the macho rockers and
their old-fashioned attitudes. Their mutual dislike spilled over
into rioting on the seafront in Margate, Clacton and Brighton
in 1964.

Left to right: Trevor Laird, Toyah Willcox, Phil Davis, Sting, Leslie Ash, Phil Daniels, Gary Shail, Garry Cooper and Mark Wingett in the film *Quadrophenia*, 1979.

Also in 1964, the band the Who was formed in Shepherd's Bush, west London. Their totemic red, white and blue roundel was inspired by the sign used on British Spitfire planes during World War I, to prevent friendly fire (a sign that was itself inspired by the tricolour cockade of French Allied planes, a throwback in turn to the French Revolution). The symbol became diffused into the subculture alongside the band's music. Mod subculture impacted the mainstream in two waves, first during the 1960s with a reputation for violence, and subsequently with a revival in the 1970s. The Who brought to life the Brighton riots of the first wave with the film *Quadrophenia* (1979), based loosely on the band's rock opera of the same name, which was released during the revival. Their sound of the era was picked up during the mod revival and fused with elements of Punk (p.125) by the Jam, fronted by Paul Weller, who earned the alias 'The Modfather'.

Female mods, despite the gender pay gap (the UK's Equal Pay Act wasn't introduced until 1970), were also increasingly autonomous, with their own means, and their liberation was signified by miniskirts, graphic eye make-up and Androgynous (p.270) pixie cuts, inspired by their fashion idol Twiggy (the first

Mod cont.

supermodel), or sharply cut bobs. There was some crossover with Futurism (p.33) in their affection for simplicity and clean lines, although mods were rooted firmly in the present, while futurists looked to the heavens. Little felt more modernist than the abstract painter Piet Mondrian's blocks of primary colour, which in 1965 Yves Saint Laurent transposed into a dress design that is now emblematic of the decade's shift in design aesthetic. It was an important moment in the relationship between art and fashion. Towards the end of the 1960s, the sharp modernist look evanesced into laid-back Hippy (p.223) and Bohemian (p.217) aesthetics, while some hard mods transitioned to Skinheads (p.237).

The mod style has proved durable, and it continues to influence catwalk collections. For Spring/Summer 2013, Louis Vuitton showed an eye-popping black-and-white chequerboard pattern, and at Prada there was a strong 1960s feel for Autumn/ Winter 2011, and in the form-fitting tailoring for Spring/Summer 2023 collection.

COLOURS AND PATTERNS: black, white, cream, sage green, black-and-white houndstooth, black-and-white check, blue-and-white gingham

FABRICS: wool, cotton, suede

GARMENTS AND ACCESSORIES: suit, shirt, narrow tie, parka, polo shirt, trousers, Harrington jacket, Chelsea boots, loafers, desert boots, miniskirt, knee-high boots, go-go boots, sleeveless top, bowling shoes, trench coat

DETAILS: rounded, slim fit, cropped trousers, no turn-ups

HAIR AND MAKE-UP: short hair, Caesar cut, French crop, graphic eyeliner, white eyeshadow, pale lipstick, layers of mascara

Skate

◐ SKATER, SIDEWALK SURFER
● METAL, PUNK, HIP HOP
⊕ ATHLEISURE, INDIE, VARSITY, SURF

When the surfing craze hit California in the 1950s it left its
followers yearning for something to do when the waves were
flat. Their radical solution was sidewalk surfing, as skateboarding
was known initially. Skateboarders were banned from many
public squares owing to the damage they cause through 'grinding'
down ledges and benches, and this gave early skate culture an
element of rebellion.

Style has always been a huge part of the subculture, both
in how the board is ridden and in the clothes worn while doing
so. First and foremost, garments must be functional, and many
professional skaters choose loose-fitting, heavy-duty workwear
trousers by such brands as Dickies or Carhartt, fabricated in heavy
cotton. Layering short-sleeved T-shirts over long-sleeved tops
keeps the body warm while protecting against scrapes in case of
a fall. Footwear is key, and for stability on the board, firm soles are
favoured over running-style trainers. The brand Vans is universally
popular among beginners and professionals alike, initially sold in
high-top styles for extra protection, and later cut away at the ankle
to provide more flexibility for skaters attempting tricks. Board
shorts are designed to function in and out of the water for both
surfing and skating, and are cut to the knee.

Aesthetically, the vibe owes much to its Surfing roots (p.234),
with Hawaiian prints, bold colours, and hoodies or tees branded
with the logo of local, independent skate and surf shops (see Indie,
p.131); it is a mark of the 'poser' to wear labels that are available
in the mall. One such breakthrough brand is *Thrasher* magazine,
which launched in 1981 as a publication merging skate culture with
Punk (p.125) and Metal (p.120), and there are some similarities to
punk in the skaters' DIY approach to knocking together ramps and
rails to perform tricks. The magazine championed a young Tony
Hawk and in 1990 named him its first Skater of the Year; it was later

Skate cont.

appropriated by Instafamous celebrities, much to the chagrin of its editorial team.

The invention of polyurethane wheels by Frank Nasworthy's company Cadillac Wheels in 1972 transformed the appeal of the sport by making boards more responsive and easier to ride. In the 1980s skateboarding spread through youth culture, helped by the movie *Back to the Future* (1985), starring Michael J. Fox as Marty McFly, inspiring a generation to give it a try. In the 1990s Hip Hop (p.142) and skate cultures collided, pushing baggy pants to the limit.

The ultimate high-low collaboration, between French luxury house Louis Vuitton and achingly cool New York skate brand Supreme, brought the subculture into the fashion spotlight with its hotly anticipated Autumn/Winter 2017 collection. It was talked about all the more since in 2000 Louis Vuitton had filed a lawsuit against Supreme, demanding that the latter stop using the iconic 'LV' logo on skate decks and other merchandise. Supreme, which was founded by James Jebbia in 1994, pioneered hype marketing tactics using scarcity of supply to whet consumer interest, releasing products in weekly 'drops', an approach that resulted in queues around the block and money-can't-buy-it publicity.

In 2022 the London label Palace similarly found new hypebeast audiences through collaborations with Y-3 (the streetwear brand by Adidas and Yohji Yamamoto) and the Italian giant Gucci. Palace's designer-founders, Lev Tanju and Gareth Skewis, harked back to the label's British roots with logo-emblazoned shirts inspired by football-kit tops and punk tropes alongside their coveted skatewear essentials, such as calf-high socks – always pulled up – complete with logos.

Skateboarding was born on the sidewalk. As such it was a key influence in the development of streetwear and Athleisure (p.60).

Kim Jones for Louis Vuitton Autumn/Winter 2017–18 Menswear, Paris Fashion Week, 19 January 2017.

COLOURS AND PATTERNS: black, white, graphic prints

FABRICS: denim, canvas, cotton, sweatshirt

GARMENTS AND ACCESSORIES: skate shoes (such as Converse and Vans), T-shirt, calf-high socks, baseball cap, hoody, beanie hat, board shorts, key chains, backpack, sleeveless vest, plaid shirt, rings, baggy trousers, cargo trousers, chain bracelets/ necklaces

DETAILS: logos, short-sleeved T-shirt over long-sleeved top, ripped, drawstrings, reinforced knee panels, slogans, layered silver jewellery, socks pulled up

Surf

- SURFER, KOOK
- ATHLEISURE, SAFARI, ROCK, HIPPY
- CRUISE, BOHEMIAN

Like catching a sweet wave, the feel-good surfer look drops in on summer collections via designer catwalks as an alternative to summer Athleisure wear (p.60). Surfing is more than a subculture; it is a way of life that carries divine significance for the people of Polynesia, who invented it. Wave-riding on planks is clearly depicted in twelfth-century cave paintings from the region, and was first described by white men in 1778, on Captain James Cook's third (and ill-fated) voyage to Polynesia. As the ships *Discovery* and *Resolution* anchored in Hawaii for the first time, Captain Charles Clerke remarked that locals appeared to be in their element on the water.

By the nineteenth century missionaries to the islands had almost eradicated surfing as a cultural practice, but some locals kept it alive. The sport reached global awareness in the twentieth century, owing largely to the prowess of two men: George Freeth, who performed a display in California in 1907 as part of a PR stunt by the Pacific Electric Railroad to promote its coastal line; and Duke Kahanamoku, the statuesque Hawaiian five-times Olympic gold medallist swimmer, who is credited with helping to bring the sport to Australia through an exhibition held in Sydney in 1914. Their athletic physiques, shown off by sleeveless vests and hip-hugging shorts, accessorized with handcrafted bead necklaces, captured the public's imagination.

Hawaii's US statehood in 1959, and the rise of air travel to these newly accessible island paradises, resulted in tourists bringing surfing back to the United States, initially to California. The movie *Gidget* (1959), starring teen queen Sandra Dee, immortalized surf culture on the silver screen, followed by Elvis Presley in *Blue Hawaii* (1961) and the documentary *The Endless Summer* (1965), which fuelled the trend for Hawaiian shirts, colour-blocked swimwear separates and board shorts. These last are longer than conventional swimming shorts, and more akin to casual wear, with pockets and no inner mesh.

The classic Hawaiian or 'Aloha' shirt was first made from kimono fabric by Japanese artisans on the island in the 1930s, and later became big business as a tourist item. Often featuring oversized floral blooms, it has an unstructured camp collar spread wide for cooling (see also Safari, p.105), short sleeves, a handy chest pocket for sunglasses, and (traditionally) coconut-shell buttons. After Japan's attack on Pearl Harbor in 1941, shirt-making went into supplying the war effort, and when peace resumed, prints that were perceived as Japanese – among them cherry blossom and temples – fell out of fashion in favour of local flowers, such as hibiscus.

Paul Smith Spring/Summer 2018 Menswear, Paris Fashion Week, 25 June 2017.

Surf rock, typified by rolling guitar riffs and high reverberation mimicking the sound of waves, had its heyday from 1958 to 1964, and added the youthful sex appeal of Rock & Roll (p.110) to the surfer look. The Beach Boys, who broke through with 'Surfin' U.S.A.' in 1963, added an all-American Ivy League element with relaxed chinos and striped shirts (see Preppy, p.191).

Modern surfer style gained mainstream popularity in the 1990s and 2000s via the film *Point Break* (1991) and such breakthrough surf brands as Quiksilver, Rip Curl and Billabong. Teenagers across the world threw casual jersey hoodies over halter-neck bikini tops, worn with knee-length cut-off denim shorts or baggy combat trousers. Footwear included flip-flops or the ubiquitous sheepskin Uggs for authentic post-beach attire. The look reached its pop-culture zenith in 2002 with the film *Blue Crush*, starring Kate Bosworth, Michelle Rodriguez and Sanoe Lake, which coincided with a surf-themed collection at Chanel.

Neoprene is a key signifier of the surf aesthetic on the runway. The fabric was invented in 1930 by scientists at the chemical

Surf cont.

company DuPont and incorporated into the first design for
a wetsuit – intended for diving and military use – in 1951 by the
physicist Hugh Bradner of the University of California. At the same
time, in a garage in Santa Cruz, the legendary surfer Jack O'Neill
was developing a wetsuit for personal use by cold-water surfers,
opening up miles of previously unsurfable coastline.

Surfing's return as a topic of fashion conversation came via the
Spring/Summer 2018 collections, with sunset-hued Hawaiian shirts
on the catwalks of Paul Smith and Balenciaga menswear, and
tropical prints at Michael Kors, Gucci and No. 21 womenswear.
The trend matured at the Spring/Summer 2019 womenswear
collections with waxed boards and tropical prints at Etro, wetsuit
details and a *Jaws* theme at Calvin Klein, and blue-and-white
tie-dye evoking sea foam at Stella McCartney. The look continued
into Spring/Summer 2022 with more psychedelic tie-dye at
Altuzarra (see also Hippy, p.223), neon rash vest-inspired tops
paired with skirts embellished with scalloped, shell-like paillettes
at Coperni, to distil a sporty mermaid feel, and neoprene scuba
hoods at Nina Ricci, with fishing-net details thrown in.

COLOURS AND PATTERNS: ocean
blue, sky blue, sandy yellow, white,
neon pink, tie-dye, Hawaiian print

FABRICS: neoprene, fishnet, polyester,
nylon, cotton jersey

GARMENTS AND ACCESSORIES:
board shorts, flip-flops, T-shirt, hoody,
rash vest, bikini top, cargo trousers,
bucket hat

DETAILS: zips, drawstrings, shells,
short sleeves, high neck

Skinhead

- SKIN, BOOT BOY, PEANUT, LEMONHEAD
- HERITAGE, AVIATOR, PREPPY, TAILORING, HIPPY, MOD
- PUNK, POLO, ANDROGYNOUS

Towards the end of the 1960s in the United Kingdom a schism of Mod subculture (p.228) divided it into smooth mods with upper-class aspirations, in dapper Tailoring (p.195), and hard mods, proud working-class men. Many of the latter group grafted in industries where long hair was risky, so they shaved their heads. The buzz cut was also a clear rejection of the peace, love and flowing locks of the predominantly middle-class Hippy rebellion (p.223), and, for some, a nod to the clean-cut American astronauts in the news at the time. The skinhead was born.

Skinhead teenager Janet Askham poses with her friends at her home in Huddersfield, West Yorkshire, 6 June 1970.

Of all the aesthetics in this book, skinhead subculture is perhaps the most misunderstood and vilified, having been appropriated by violent white supremacists. Initially the subculture centred on fashion, simply young people who took pride in their appearance, wearing short-sleeved shirts in plain colours or checks, braces (suspenders) and pressed trousers, and incorporating tough utilitarian elements, such as steel-toecap boots or Doc Martens, polished to a high shine. Workwear was key: straight-leg jeans, usually Levi's 501s, rolled up to show off the footwear; denim trucker jackets for casual days; and the British version of a trucker jacket, the Harrington, with its distinctive Fraser tartan lining. American Ivy League style, later known as Preppy (p.191), was a key influence, and the Polo shirt (p.76) was another must-have item.

Skinhead cont.

Britain's changeable weather calls for heavy-duty outerwear, and for skinheads in winter there were three options: the Crombie, the shearling and the donkey jacket. The original Crombie is a single-breasted three-quarter-length topcoat in fine Melton wool, from the Scottish heritage woollen mill-turned-manufacturer Crombie (see <u>Heritage</u>, p.23). It was worn by English figureheads as diverse as prime minister Winston Churchill and gangster twins Ronnie and Reggie Kray; the latter served as unlikely style heroes of the East End of London, where the skinhead subculture bubbled up. Shearling coats were usually made up of panels of tan suede with a natural sheep's-wool inner and piping. The donkey jacket, finally, was created in 1888 as an all-weather garment for construction workers (known as 'navvies', from 'navigation canal') on the Manchester Ship Canal, and named after the steam-powered donkey engine used to clear the channel. This boxy wool coat, usually black, has a leather yoke (PVC on later models) and no lapels, meaning that it can be buttoned up to the neck against inclement weather.

West Indian culture – particularly the street-smart style of the Rude Boy, who came to London from Kingston, Jamaica – influenced mods and skinheads with rakish pork-pie hats and <u>trilbies</u>, cropped trousers, longline coats and tailoring. Black and white working-class youths socialized in the dance halls, and several ska bands of the time brought out tracks referring to skinhead subculture.

It is this appreciation of Black culture that makes the next chapter in the skinhead story all the more surprising. After the crest of <u>Punk</u>'s wave (p.125) broke in the late 1970s, there was a skinhead revival and punk's DIY, bricolage philosophy saw its followers mine previous subcultures for style inspiration. Some punks wore the Nazi swastika for shock value alone, but it spoke to a simmering right-wing faction who blamed immigration for the lack of employment opportunities. The National Front, a neo-fascist political party, actively recruited members from the skinhead community, spreading its message of hate via hooliganism on the football terraces (where the look was televised) into the 1980s, and internationally via White Power rock music. The skinhead community was divided.

Although the subculture was visibly masculine, female skins, known as 'featherwoods' or 'skinbyrds', with their feathered, finely layered, cropped hair and blunt fringes, contributed to the aesthetic. They paired mod-like miniskirts, polished brogues, chunky knitted cardigans and T-shirts or polo shirts with an anti-establishment attitude to rival their male counterparts.

A note of warning to stylists wishing to emulate the bootlaces of archive skinheads and punks: white laces (usually with oxblood leather boots) signified that the wearer was a devotee of White Power, while red laces were a sign that blood had been shed for the movement, or that the wearer was a socialist. Yellow laces, on the other hand, showed that the wearer was anti-racist and a member of S.H.A.R.P. (Skinheads Against Racial Prejudice), while purple signified that the wearer was gay. Green or plaid laces meant neutral, black meant they were traditionalists or punks, and black and white indicated a lover of ska or two-tone. While this code will be lost on most of today's audience, the wrong lace in the wrong place can still be offensive (see also <u>Political</u>, p.260).

<u>COLOURS AND PATTERNS</u>: black, white, red, oxblood, navy blue, black-and-white check, blue gingham

<u>FABRICS</u>: wool, denim, leather, sheepskin, nylon

<u>GARMENTS AND ACCESSORIES</u>: jeans, shirt, Harrington jacket, braces (suspenders), pork-pie hat, Crombie coat, Doc Martens boots, brogues, bomber jacket, donkey jacket, polo shirt, cardigan, denim trucker jacket, shearling coat, trench coat

<u>DETAILS</u>: bleached denim, button-down shirt, rolled-up jeans

<u>HAIR</u>: sideburns, straight-cut fringe, shaved head

La Sape

- SOCIÉTÉ DES AMBIANCEURS ET DES PERSONNES ÉLÉGANTES (SOCIETY OF AMBIANCEURS AND ELEGANT PERSONS), CONGOLESE DANDIES, THE SAPEURS
- AVANT-GARDE, POLITICAL
- TAILORING, DANDY, MAXIMALIST

On the banks of the mighty River Congo, which divides Brazzaville in the Republic of the Congo to the north from Kinshasa in the Democratic Republic of the Congo (DRC) in the south, there is a subculture whose styling prowess far exceeds the posturing of any fashion-week in-crowd. La Société des Ambianceurs et des Personnes Élégantes, known as 'La Sape', is a society for those who are the life and soul of the party. The male *sapeur* and female *sapeuse* are known for their flamboyant threads from luxury designers, often at odds with their surroundings in the city-limit shanty towns. Some saps are street performers who earn a living for their families through mime and dance, while others have 'ordinary' jobs, ranging from the civil service to gardening or driving a taxi.

The origin of the subculture is attributed to a variety of sources. Some say it began in the colonial era, while others attribute it to Congolese soldiers returning from France after World War II, their luggage filled with elegant Parisian suits. Most agree that the style's renaissance in the 1970s was brought about by the Congolese singer Papa Wemba, who used it to make a Political statement (p.260) against the repressive efforts of President Mobutu Sese Seko, who attempted (and failed) to ban the wearing of Western suits in the DRC.

There is a noted split between the creative direction of sapeurs in Brazzaville, who favour French-inspired Tailoring (p.195), and the more Avant-Garde (p.244) style in Kinshasa, with saps wearing pieces by such designers as Yohji Yamamoto, or leaning into Heritage-inspired Scottish kilts and sporrans (p.23). The aesthetic diffused back to the catwalk at Junya Watanabe's Autumn/Winter 2015 menswear collection, as seen in shawl-collar blazers, bowties,

La Sape fans in Libreville, Gabon, 23 April 2014.

rakish trilbies, round spectacles, pristine shirts and impeccably knotted ties. Both err on the side of Maximalist (p.254), and emphasis is placed on accessories: hats, ties, jaunty socks, braces (suspenders), statement sunglasses and polished ebony canes.

Sapeurs are Dandies in the true sense of the word (p.247), defined by Charles Baudelaire as those who elevate aesthetics to a living religion. Such aristocratic refinement, rather than material possessions, is the ultimate goal.

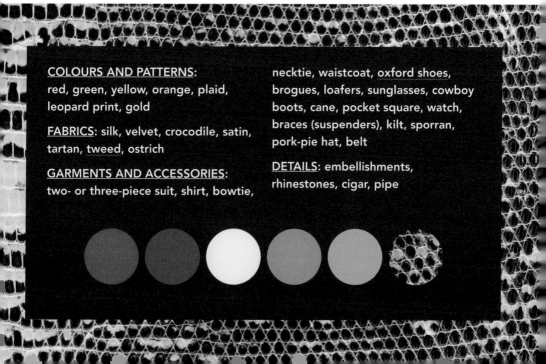

COLOURS AND PATTERNS: red, green, yellow, orange, plaid, leopard print, gold

FABRICS: silk, velvet, crocodile, satin, tartan, tweed, ostrich

GARMENTS AND ACCESSORIES: two- or three-piece suit, shirt, bowtie, necktie, waistcoat, oxford shoes, brogues, loafers, sunglasses, cowboy boots, cane, pocket square, watch, braces (suspenders), kilt, sporran, pork-pie hat, belt

DETAILS: embellishments, rhinestones, cigar, pipe

Statement

While it is true that to some extent all clothing makes a statement about the wearer, some styles speak more loudly than others. Statements range from understated and minimalist to in-your-face and maximalist with wild prints and patterns that can be seen from halfway down the street.

Historically, the dial has swung between periods of minimalism and maximalism. The rococo style, for example, immediately preceded the French Revolution, a bloody event that was a turning point for Western fashion with its showy excesses that highlighted extreme social inequality. After the Revolution came the Great Renunciation of men's clothing, epitomized by the original dandies, such as George 'Beau' Brummell, who streamlined the male silhouette and focused on luxurious fabrics and attention to detail.

Avant-garde styles are conceptual and ahead of the curve in either ideals or technical construction. Lagenlook style takes the same anti-fashion approach and layers easy-to-wear pieces, often in artisanal fabrics. It says, 'I do not follow trends.'

Political statements are designed to be heard, and there are various ways in which clothing can be intentionally political, whether explicitly with slogans, symbolically through certain garments, or with the use of significant colours. Some garments are unintentionally political, such as modest dress, which is described without bias in section 8, Sex & Gender (p.268).

7.

Statements of values and philosophy are stronger than mere subcultures, which is why Romanticism, with its mindset shift towards aestheticism and the celebration of beauty, appears here rather than in section 6, Subcultures & Countercultures (p.212). Having said that, the New Romantic style, which flourished in the 1980s and is a music-based subculture, is included in this section for the sake of clarity. Despite being about 180 years apart, the two are connected by a love of ruffled poet shirts, foppish cravats, dandyish suiting and the occasional use of eyeliner.

Beliefs that we take for granted today are rooted in Romanticism. For example, it was thanks to the artistic and literary works of the emotional Romantics that the previously unheard-of notion of marrying for love, rather than as a social or financial transaction, became common.

Avant-Garde

● EXPERIMENTAL
◐ FUTURISM, GLAM ROCK, PUNK, BOURGEOISIE, CLASSIC, MOD
⊕ LAGENLOOK, ANDROGYNOUS

The term 'avant-garde' comes from the French for 'vanguard', the leading part of an advancing army or navy. In relation to art, fashion and ideas, it refers to work that pushes the boundaries of experimentation in both content and form. Its use in the arts is credited to the French political, social and economic thinker Henri de Saint-Simon. He extolled the value of art and artists, writing in 1825 that the 'magnificent destiny' of the arts was to exercise a positive power over society, propelling forwards humanity's intellectual faculties.

While regular clothes follow the lines of the human form, avant-garde clothes are not bound by such convention. Avant-garde fashion designers create works of art, in which the concept is key, often at the expense of so-called wearability. In 1981 the Japanese designers Rei Kawakubo and Yohji Yamamoto independently showed their first collections in Paris, creating a sense of change among fashion's old guard. Against the backdrop of one of the most lavish decades in history, characterized by glitz, glamour and excess, sat Kawakubo's 'Destroy' collection for her label Comme des Garçons, featuring voluminous black layers (see also Lagenlook, p.250) and artfully ruined knits to evoke a Punk aesthetic (p.125). Her designs eradicated the objectification of the female form, imparting a freeing sense of Androgyny (p.270), although it was not to Bourgeois taste (p.202); some insensitive fashion writers declared it 'Hiroshima Chic' or 'post-atomic'.

Similarly, Yamamoto made a case for every shade of black, declaring it simultaneously modest and arrogant, lazy and easy, and always mysterious. The absence of colour forces the designer to experiment with silhouette and texture for nuance and expression. Garments are laden with meaning, and the Japanese philosophy of *wabi sabi* (from *wabi*, simplicity and anti-materialism, and *sabi*, finding beauty in objects that show signs of wear and decay) can be read

Gareth Pugh Spring/Summer 2007, London Fashion Week, 19 September 2006.

clearly in Yamamoto's designs. He manipulates and warps fabrics
in an aesthetic that is the antithesis of mass-produced, fast fashion.

The Japanese avant-garde movement continued via the
collections of Kansai Yamamoto, whose creations for Glam Rock
(p.122)-era David Bowie in 1973 brought the aesthetic to popular
culture. Issey Miyake, meanwhile, pioneered new methods of
creating permanent pleats in fabric, inspired by the folds of origami.

In the West, the Belgian designer Martin Margiela's house style
reveals deconstructed garments, their inner workings revealed,
with edges seemingly unfinished and pattern paper and pins still in
evidence (see also Minimalist, p.252). Other icons of the avant-
garde include the French designer Thierry Mugler, known for his
galactic glamazons, and the British designer Alexander McQueen,
whose fantastical collections of the 2000s touched on Romantic
(p.263) and Cyberpunk (p.38) themes. Gareth Pugh's sculptural
creations delighted the London Fashion Week press season after
season, albeit at the expense of commerciality. Avant-garde
fashion has a healthy future, and one of the newer admissions

Avant-Garde cont.

to the Parisian Chambre Syndicale de la Haute Couture is Iris van Herpen. This Dutch visionary was one of the first to use 3D printing to construct garments, referring to nature and science in her designs.

There is a history of experimental fashion in Futurism (p.33) and the space-age designs of the 1960s by such designers as Pierre Cardin, André Courrèges and Paco Rabanne, who used new textiles, among them plastic, rubber, foil and chainmail. There were art-led creations before that, such as the Italian designer Elsa Schiaparelli's collaboration with the Spanish Surrealist Salvador Dalí for her unique 'lobster dress' of 1937, featuring a silk-printed lobster, continuing the artist's fascination with the suggestive crustacean. In the mid-1960s Yves Saint Laurent reinterpreted the modernist lines of the Dutch painter Piet Mondrian in dresses (see also Mod, p.228), to critical acclaim.

Thinking outside the box with style does not necessarily mean wearing a box. Avant-garde fashion can be toned down for daywear through minimalism and loose black layers impeccably cut by a fashion designer who approaches their occupation as an art.

COLOURS AND PATTERNS: black, white, off-white, red

FABRICS: cotton, linen, nylon, wool, perspex, chainmail

GARMENTS AND ACCESSORIES: culottes, wide-legged trousers, kimono-style wrap top, cocoon coat, shirt, chunky boots, jacket, trousers, suit, shirt, sleeveless vest, leotard

DETAILS: 3D printing, asymmetrical, pleats, oversized, mandarin collar, deconstructed, ripped, raw edges

Dandy

≈ GENTLEMANLY, QUAINTRELLE (FEMALE)
→ FLAPPER, EQUESTRIAN, MILITARY, MOD, MINIMALIST, ROCOCO,
ANDROGYNOUS
⊕ STEAMPUNK, TEDDY BOYS & TEDDY GIRLS, TAILORING, LA SAPE,
ROMANTIC, CAMP

Dandies are notoriously flamboyant, but in fact George 'Beau' Brummell – universally acknowledged to be the original dandy, who rose to fame during the Regency era in England – streamlined menswear from the grandiose Rococo (p.257) style that preceded it. Brummell was born to a middle-class family, but his father was private secretary to the prime minister Lord North, so he was fortunate enough to be educated in the hallowed halls of Eton College, followed by a year at the University of Oxford. Although not an aristocrat, he inherited a large sum of money after his father's death, and that – along with his charm and wit – helped to establish him in society.

Joshua Kane wears his own designs, photographed at Home House, London, by Bart Pajak, 2022.

A strategic turn in the army as a member of the 10th Royal Hussars allowed Brummell to gain access to and befriend the Prince of Wales, the Prince Regent, later King George IV. After retiring from the military, Brummell took inspiration from his utilitarian Military dress (p.91), designed for horse riding among other physical activities (see Equestrian, p.70), and set the fashion for austere tailored jackets worn with straight-cut trousers. In the Victorian era, this evolved into today's idea of a suit of jacket and trousers (see Tailoring, p.195).

Well known for his quip 'Fashions come and go; bad taste is timeless,' Brummell played his part in the Great Renunciation,

Dandy cont.

when, against the backdrop of the French Revolution, men packed away their peacock finery, silk breeches, wigs and high heels, and adopted a more sober style of dress. He popularized the wearing of one's own natural hair and the trend for taking regular baths. Although he was an enduring menswear icon, his life serves as a cautionary tale. One of the first celebrity influencers, famous for fame alone, he nevertheless fell from grace over a mean comment about the Prince Regent's weight, and after living beyond his means he ended up in a debtor's jail, owing an eye-watering sum of money. He died penniless in 1840 in an asylum in northern France, suffering the mental effects of syphilis.

The nineteenth-century French poet Charles Baudelaire embraced a puritanical, all-black mode of dandyism. For him, dandyism symbolized aristocratic superiority of mind, an aesthetic endeavour whereby the person cultivates the ideas of emotion, beauty and passion in their own person. In that respect, he liked it as a form of Romanticism (p.263). Indeed, the great Romantic writer Lord Byron left later dandies a legacy of frilled poet shirts with balloon sleeves.

There is also a history of Black dandyism, linked inextricably to colonial history. In the Victorian age enslaved Africans were required to dress up, to serve as status symbols for the household, but many added their own flourishes, using clothes as a rare means of self-expression. Style as a subculture continues on the African continent with the Congolese La Sape aesthetic (p.240), which celebrates the art of gentlemanly dress, and 'Swenkas', Zulu working men who compete to see who has the most 'swank'. There is power in dressing well, and as part of the civil-rights movement in the 1960s, Dr Martin Luther King Jr used crisp shirts, neatly knotted ties and impeccably cut suits to underline his image as a leader who intended to be heard and respected by everyone from the people to the president.

The increased emancipation of women in the 1920s brought the Flapper (p.30) and the female dandy, known as a 'quaintrelle', who elevated personal style and pleasure-seeking to an art form. Inspired by the influential and pioneering designer Coco Chanel and her menswear-inspired clothes, via a tuxedo-clad Marlene Dietrich in the 1930s, the female dandy often plays with Androgynous suiting (p.270).

Dandyism and tailoring continue to be linked, although structured separates, such as blazers and trousers, are also acceptable. The devil is in the detail: cravats, ties, cufflinks, scarves, pocket squares, and always a jaunty sock.

The contemporary interpretation of dandyism ranges from perfectly Minimalist (p.2520 to foppish and Camp (p.275). It can be modern and sharp (see Mod, p.228), or reference historical, formal garments, such as Neo-Victorian (p.26) top hats, tailcoats, wing collars, cravats and walking sticks. Given a Retrofuturistic (p.36) edge and tweed three-piece suits, skeleton pocket watches and bowler hats, the look becomes Steampunk (p.42).

The spiritual home of the dandy is Savile Row, a London street of tailors known as the 'Golden Mile'. On it reside such names as Henry Poole & Co., which opened its doors in 1846, Anderson & Sheppard, founded in 1906, and Davies & Son, the oldest independent tailor on the Row, established in 1803. There is new blood in the city, though; a short walk north, in Marylebone, bespoke tailor to the stars Joshua Kane characterizes the attention to detail and luxurious fabrics seen in the heyday of Brummell and Baudelaire.

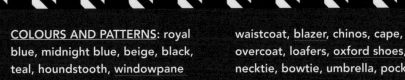

COLOURS AND PATTERNS: royal blue, midnight blue, beige, black, teal, houndstooth, windowpane check, Prince of Wales check, micro dots

FABRICS: wool, velvet, cotton, silk, patent leather

GARMENTS AND ACCESSORIES: three-piece suit, shirt, V-neck jumper, waistcoat, blazer, chinos, cape, overcoat, loafers, oxford shoes, necktie, bowtie, umbrella, pocket square, pocket watch, luxury socks, tiepin, trilby, top hat, flat cap, cane, braces (suspenders), watch, attaché case

DETAILS: ironed and starched shirt, pressed trousers, single-breasted, double-breasted

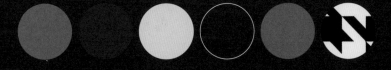

Lagenlook

● LAYERED
◐ NEO-VICTORIANA, STEAMPUNK, COTTAGECORE, HIPPY, AVANT-GARDE
● HYGGE, BOHEMIAN, MAXIMALIST

This less well-known style, from the German for 'layered look', is inherently anti-fashion, with loose garments thrown together in an eclectic way by Bohemians (p.217) and consumers who prioritize comfort. Lagenlook styles are usually unstructured and midi or maxi length. Hyper-feminine layers with ruffles impart a Neo-Victoriana (p.26)
feel that, if deconstructed or distressed, acquires a Steampunk edge (p.42). It's a popular look with art-teacher types, since the typical wearer of Lagenlook enjoys the process of creating a unique combination of colours, textures and lengths, embracing a Maximalist (p.254) approach to styling.

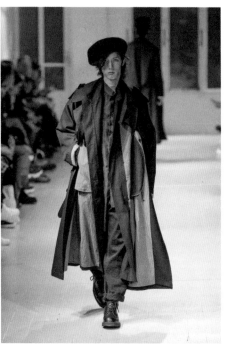

Yohji Yamamoto Autumn/Winter 2020–21 Menswear, Paris Fashion Week, 16 January 2020.

Fabrics are often hand-coloured with natural vegetable dyes and left deliberately crinkled. This connection with the earth crosses over with the environmental aspect of Hippy (p.223) styles, as well as the Japanese woodland aesthetic Mori Kei, ('forest girl'), which emerged from the Harajuku district of Tokyo at the start of the millennium (see other Harajuku styles, such as Kawaii, p.170). Mori Kei bears some similarities to Cottagecore (p.161) in its return to the simple pleasures of baking, gardening and crafting, but also focuses on feelings of cosiness and contentment in the same way as Hygge (p.183).

There have also been Avant-Garde (p.244) proponents of
the layered aesthetic, among them the Japanese designer Rei
Kawakubo, a graduate of fine art and aesthetics rather than
fashion, whose label Comme des Garçons (founded in 1969)
is widely accepted as having reinvented clothing – particularly
womenswear – as art. Kawakubo's aggressively anti-fashion,
form-covering designs eradicated the male gaze, rendering her
a feminist hero even when she refused to identify as one. Many
of her designs are unsized, and for a period she experimented
with removing mirrors in the changing rooms of her stores, to
allow clients to focus on how they felt, rather than how they
looked. She is credited with making black the uniform colour
of urban creatives. Other forward-thinking Japanese designers,
such as Issey Miyake and Yohji Yamamoto, as well as the Belgian
designer Ann Demeulemeester, have developed their own visual
language of multitudinous layers, oversized proportions and
deconstruction. Whether rooted in homespun earthiness or
brutalist and urban, Lagenlook is an aesthetic for creatives of
all ages and body types.

COLOURS AND PATTERNS: black,
white, dusty pink, grey, mustard

FABRICS: linen, cotton, wool, felt

GARMENTS AND ACCESSORIES:
tunic, wide-legged trousers, overcoat,
bloomers, cloche hat, cocoon coat,
harem pants, A-line skirt, caftan,
cloak, cape

DETAILS: layering, asymmetric,
sustainable, oversized, unstructured,
deconstructed, screen-printed,
hand-painted, waterfall, draped,
appliqué, cowl neck, batwing sleeve,
dropped crotch

Minimalist

◑ MINIMALISTIC
➡ <u>GRUNGE</u>, <u>AVANT-GARDE</u>, <u>MAXIMALIST</u>
✚ <u>FUTURISM</u>, <u>CLASSIC</u>, <u>MOD</u>

Minimalist fashion bears some similarities to the minimalist art that emerged in the 1960s and 70s in the work of Frank Stella, Richard Serra, Carl Andre and Sol LeWitt, among others. They came in the wake of the Abstract Expressionism of the 1950s, when artists involved themselves heavily in their work – most famously Jackson Pollock, whose method of 'action painting' even left footprints in the paint as he splattered his canvases. The Minimalists' reaction was to remove all trace of the artist, creating unemotive, anonymous works with no hidden meaning, reduced to elemental simplicity.

Maison Martin Margiela Spring/Summer 2013, Paris Fashion Week, 28 September 2012.

Minimalist fashion eschews riotous prints in favour of a muted greyscale palette, punctuated by neutrals or occasionally block colours. Instead of garments laden with symbols, as in the other styles in this book, they present a neutral lens through which to view the wearer; neither are there obvious labels to hint at the maker. Silhouettes are clean and unadorned, moving the focus to the person. In the words of Stella, 'What you see is what you see.'

Rejecting the <u>Maximalist</u> (p.254) styles of the 1970s and 80s, such <u>Avant-Garde</u> (p.244) Japanese designers as Rei Kawakubo and Yohji Yamamoto created a new playbook, using simplified lines and an all-black palette. Minimalism was an era-defining trend of the 1990s, alongside <u>Grunge</u> (p.134). The Belgian designer Martin Margiela encapsulated it perfectly in his early work, using a palette

of white, purity of form, and garments devoid of logos (even
the inner label was designed to be snipped out). He removed
ego and personality from the brand, referred to his *maison* as 'we'
and shunned interviews. Minimalism diffused across the fashion
industry, appearing in the collections of Helmut Lang and Jil
Sander, and of Calvin Klein, where it remains the house signature.
Later, the British designer Phoebe Philo's tenure at Celine (2008–
18) was marked by a chic, wearable take on the aesthetic. In 2023
Philo's loyal band of followers (known in the press as 'Philophiles')
were pleased to hear that the designer was set to relaunch under
an eponymous brand, with minority backing from the French luxury
powerhouse LVMH.

   A minimalist wardrobe is usually interpreted as a 'capsule'
one, each piece working as a look with one or more of the others.
Clothes become a uniform, simplifying the answer to the daily
question of what to wear. Minimalists are masters of circularity,
investing in high-quality, timeless designs that can be worn from
year to year. In this respect, the style can also be seen as Classic
(p.209). The absence of individuality is a statement in itself.

COLOURS AND PATTERNS: white,
cream, light grey, charcoal, black, silver

FABRICS: crêpe, leather, cotton, wool

GARMENTS AND ACCESSORIES:
trousers, single-breasted suit, single-
breasted blazer, longline coat, cocoon
coat, jumpsuit, skirt, oxford shoes,
white trainers, slip dress, roll neck,
plain T-shirt, culottes, midi skirt

DETAILS: no logos, few or no accessories

MAKE-UP: pared back

Maximalist

◒ LOUD, ECLECTIC
◑ GLAM ROCK, DISCO, LOLITA, MINIMALIST
⊕ KAWAII, DECORA, BOHEMIAN, ROCOCO, ROMANTIC, CAMP

In the same way that Minimalist style (p.252) removes personality, Maximalism is all about the individuality of the wearer. The look is artfully cluttered, and, in truth, anything goes. Some of fashion's more gaudy weapons, such as sequins, lamé, velour, satin, neon fabrics and colourful, large-scale prints, find their place here.

The style pendulum has swung between minimalist and maximalist over time with unfailing certainty. The Flapper (p.30), liberated from World War I and the flu pandemic of 1918, roared through the 1920s in fringing, marabou feathers and sequins, before the Wall Street Crash of 1929 and the global Great Depression ushered in more streamlined, conservative dress. World War II enforced minimalism through the instruction to 'make do and mend', and, at the end of rationing, Dior's New Look and full skirts heralded the beginning of the glamour of the 1950s. Sure enough, the 1960s pivoted to aerodynamic silhouettes inspired by space travel (see Futurism, p.33) and clean, modernist lines (see Mod, p.228). This turned back into the wild, psychedelic trip of the Hippy look (p.223), the short-lived glitz of Glam Rock (p.122) and the sparkle of Disco (p.139).

The 1980s were notoriously over the top, with bouffant hair, power shoulder pads and big jewels. The Italians are experts at maximalist fashion, notably the house of Versace, which led the way with the amped-up glamour of the iconic Medusa logo and the ornate gold 'Barocco' print featuring stylized acanthus leaves, which sits aesthetically between Baroque and Rococo (p.257). The 1990s largely swung back towards minimalism (except at Versace), yet by 2000 conspicuous consumption, rhinestone-encrusted everything, logos and 'It bags' were in vogue. In the Harajuku district of Tokyo many maximalist styles were crystallizing, such as Kawaii (p.170), Decora (p.173) and Lolita (p.177), and 'Harajuku style' has come to mean the extreme Japanese street-style looks of the 1990s and 2000s, photographed by local indie magazines.

Richard Quinn Autumn/Winter 2018, London Fashion Week, 20 February 2018.

Maximalist cont.

Palate-cleansing minimalism returned for a time, but the balance tipped yet again, a circumstance that has been attributed in part to the appointment in 2015 of Alessandro Michele as creative director of Gucci, reviving the brand's ailing street cred. Under Michele, the house code became wildly eclectic, with a cacophony of prints, textures and concepts, and an underlying Romantic sensibility (p.263). Revenue grew exponentially during his time in the role, fuelled in part by the return to socializing at the end of the Covid-19 pandemic. After seven years, during which the maximalist Gucci look had trickled down to the fastest of fast-fashion brands, Michele's exit at the end of 2022 was reportedly linked to a request that he initiate a radical design shift for the house.

Maximalism may at first seem contrary to the shift towards sustainable consumption. However, stylists know that looks can be created by breathing new life into second-hand items sourced from vintage and thrift stores, as well as from such e-commerce apps as Depop, eBay, Vestiaire Collective and Poshmark.

COLOURS AND PATTERNS: leopard print, neon pink, gold, zebra print, oversized florals

FABRICS: sequins, silk, lamé, satin, rubber, PVC, faux fur, heavy knits, velour, velvet, brocade

GARMENTS AND ACCESSORIES: all garments plus extra accessories – hats, handbags, boots, sunglasses, headbands, statement jewellery, spectacles, body jewellery, bangles, hair clips, arm warmers, gloves, rings, chunky trainers, Crocs and other 'ugly' shoes

DETAILS: embroidery, appliqué, corsage, glitter, ribbons, rhinestones, fringing, marabou feathers

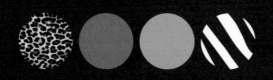

Rococo

● MARIE ANTOINETTE
● <u>PUNK</u>, <u>ROCOCO</u>, <u>CAMP</u>
● <u>PIRATE</u>, <u>LOLITA</u>, <u>MAXIMALIST</u>, <u>ROMANTIC</u>

The decorative style known as Rococo, which emerged in France
in about 1730, has left a lasting impression on fashion collections
nearly 300 years later. Marie Antoinette, the last queen of France,
who was married to King Louis XVI before the couple met their
gruesome end at the guillotine in 1793, is infamous in popular
culture for her penchant for extravagance. This is partly true – her
palace, the Petit Trianon in the grounds of Versailles, underwent
nearly constant interior renovations – and partly false, as is the
comment so often attributed to her, 'Let them eat cake.' This last
statement was probably propaganda, inspired by a phrase that
appeared in the writing of the French philosopher Jean-Jacques
Rousseau while Marie Antoinette was still a child.

It is true that the fashions of the day were some of the most
spectacularly ornate in history, with imposing side <u>panniers</u> holding
up frothy layers of tiered skirts in a wash of pastel hues, decorated
with curved floral motifs and rose corsages. The gowns themselves
were known as 'sack-back dresses' or 'robes à la française',
although they were in fact based on Spanish designs. Later in the
nineteenth century they were referred to as 'Watteau' dresses, after
the French Rococo painter Jean-Antoine Watteau, who featured
them heavily in his portraits of women. A ladder of <u>Romantic</u>
decorative bows (p.263) called an *eschelle* or *échelle* often
adorned the stomacher of the gowns, and *engageantes*, frilled
detachable sleeves of lace, cotton or linen, could be attached
below the elbow-length sleeves that were fashionable at the time.
Tall, powdered wigs, flushed cheeks and a ribbon tied at the throat
completed the look.

Rococo and its playful, feminine aesthetic are part of the
house code at Versace, with its signature acanthus 'Barocco'
print (see also <u>Maximalist</u>, p.254). As its name suggests, it infuses
elements of Baroque, the dark, brooding and often religious

John Galliano for Christian Dior Autumn/Winter 2007–8 Haute Couture, Versailles, 2 July 2007.

style that immediately preceded Rococo as an artistic movement, and that is also a favourite reference of the opulent Italian designers Dolce & Gabbana.

There have been conspicuous examples of Rococo style on the runway. Jeremy Scott's cake-referencing collection for Moschino Autumn/Winter 2020 edged towards deliciously <u>Camp</u> (p.275), while a more high-brow, at times costume-led take on the look was invoked at Christian Dior Autumn/Winter 2000 couture and Autumn/Winter 2007 couture by John Galliano. Master of the flamboyant, the French designer Christian Lacroix offered up Rococo over several collections, including Spring/Summer 1999 couture and Spring/Summer 2008 couture. The godmother of Punk (p.125), Vivienne Westwood, proved how far she had come from the anarchic ripped T-shirts of the 1970s with her Autumn/Winter 1996 collection, featuring asymmetric swirls of silk taffeta and corsetry. The Japanese designer Rei Kawakubo tackled the mood with her Avant-Garde (p.244) interpretation at Comme des Garçons with sculptural pink ruffles for Autumn/Winter 2016.

Even after the French Revolution, the overblown style did not fully fall out of fashion. At the end of the Reign of Terror (1793–4) and its mass executions, an aristocratic subculture called the 'Incroyables' (Incredibles) and its female counterpart, the 'Merveilleuses' (Marvellous Women), organized sumptuous balls, dressed in finery and coloured wigs and affecting effete mannerisms. The style shifted towards neoclassicism, and women wore diaphanous gowns that symbolized their new sense of freedom.

COLOURS AND PATTERNS: white, gold, pastel pink, pastel blue, lavender, dusky rose, cream, dove grey

FABRICS: silk taffeta, silk organza, satin, fur, velvet, brocade, lace, tulle, chenille

GARMENTS AND ACCESSORIES: corset, tiered skirt, panniers, cape, bonnet, long gloves, ribbon choker, petticoats, Louis XV heels

DETAILS: pearls, diamonds, wig, frills, feathers, bows, roses, ribbons, seashells, acanthus leaves, cherubs, *trompe-l'œil*, asymmetry, off-the-shoulder, ruffled sleeve tops, elbow-length sleeves, train

Political

● STATEMENT
● <u>FLAPPER</u>, <u>RAVE</u>, <u>CAMP</u>, <u>MODEST</u>
● <u>MILITARY</u>, <u>COMBAT</u>, <u>PUNK</u>, <u>HIPPY</u>

There are many ways to make a political statement through fashion. The most obvious to spot are slogans scrawled across or printed on plain T-shirts. In the early days of <u>Punk</u> (p.125), Vivienne Westwood and her partner Malcolm McLaren aimed to shock with T-shirts featuring Nazi swastikas. It worked, although later punks moved away from the association with the neo-Nazi far right.

In the 1980s the use of the humble T-shirt as a canvas for political statement was revived by the British designer Katharine Hamnett, whose frank slogan tees in bold sans-serif addressed such topics as 'Choose Life' (anti-drugs and anti-suicide), 'Education, not Missiles', 'Please Stop Killing Whales' and 'Worldwide Nuclear Ban Now'. They resulted in her being named the British Fashion Council's designer of the year. In March 1984 she was invited to meet Prime Minister Margaret Thatcher in Downing Street, where she surprised the politician by wearing a tee protesting against the perceived undemocratic deployment of American nuclear missiles. However, while slogan T-shirts are helpful in spreading a message, even Hamnett warns that they should not make the wearer feel as though they are doing something when they are not.

Symbols are almost as easy to read. The Campaign for Nuclear Disarmament (CND) symbol, known internationally as the 'peace sign', was used prolifically in the garments of the <u>Hippy</u> movement (p.223) in the 1960s to protest against the Vietnam War. It was designed in 1958 by the British graphic artist and pacifist Gerald Holtom, and consisted of the semaphore letters for 'N' ('nuclear') and 'D' ('disarmament'). On a lighter note, the iconic smiley-face symbol is credited to the American illustrator Harvey Ball, who earned $45 for the design for an advertising client in 1963. Its popularity spread and it was trademarked in 1971 by the savvy French newspaperman and marketeer Franklin Loufrani, who saw its potential and licensed it mercilessly while leveraging the 'cool' factors of France's young countercultural hippies. When it was picked up by UK DJs, such as Danny Rampling, for Rave (p.146) posters, it became the unofficial symbol of acid house and, indirectly, the drug ecstasy.

Garments can also be political when used in a specific context. At the end of the 1960s, as the civil-rights movement gained momentum, the Black Panther Party was one of the strongest voices for Black Power. Followers presented a united front in tough black leather jackets, slogan pin badges, black berets to reference the garment's revolutionary and military roots, and anonymizing dark sunglasses. This highly organized uniform was a visual representation of commitment to the mission. Part of the strategy was the monitoring of police patrols, to act as a direct challenge to police brutality. In 2014 the police persecution of Black citizens continued with the murder of Eric Garner, and his dying words, 'I can't breathe,' became a powerful message when the basketball star Kobe Bryant arranged for the Lakers to wear T-shirts carrying the phrase during warm-up and while on the bench.

In some cases, the absence of a garment has caused political controversy. In 2022 Mahsa Amini, a 22-year-old Kurdish woman, died in police custody in Iran after being arrested for infringing hijab rules. Her death was covered by the international press and sparked outrage on social media, igniting a political debate over women's rights to choose what they wear (see Modest, p.284).

Colour can also be used symbolically. In antiquity, the most luxurious colour was purple, since its manufacture involved a Herculean effort: more than 8,000 shells of Mediterranean sea snails from the family Muricidae were required to make just a gram of dyestuff. Purple endured over the centuries as the colour associated with royalty and emperors, notably Alexander the Great, who was famous for his cloak of Tyrian purple. Such was its

Prime Minister Margaret Thatcher greets Katharine Hamnett at 10 Downing Street, 17 March 1984.

Political cont.

imbued meaning that, by the fourth century CE, sumptuary laws passed in Rome dictated that only the emperor could wear the colour, and by the ninth century heirs to a reigning dynasty were said to be 'born in the purple' – a saying that is still used for someone from a high-ranking family. Purple was also used by members of the Suffragette movement, alongside white and green, to signify loyalty and dignity, purity, and hope, respectively.

Colour as a statement extends to the LGBTQI+ Pride rainbow, which was used liberally by the British designer Christopher Bailey in his final Autumn/Winter 2018 collection for Burberry. The show notes explained that it celebrated progress for queer rights and Bailey's own journey from outsider to fashion icon.

In the 2020s there was a shift towards brand activism, an extension of corporate social responsibility whereby traditionally neutral luxury designer brands weighed in on politics. For her debut for Christian Dior in 2017, as the first female creative director in the house's 70-year history, Maria Grazia Chiuri sent a model down the runway wearing a T-shirt emblazoned with 'We Should All Be Feminists', referencing the Nigerian feminist writer Chimamanda Ngozi Adichie's book of that name from 2014.

When a fashion brand makes a political statement that is inauthentic and purely for commercial gain, it is considered 'wokewashing'. For that reason, it is important for stylists to consider with integrity the message being encoded in an outfit.

Romantic

◉ ROMANTICISM, POET
● EQUESTRIAN, TAILORING, DANDY, MINIMALIST
⊕ NEO-VICTORIANA, PRAIRIE, COTTAGECORE, LOLITA, BOHEMIAN,
    MAXIMALIST, ROCOCO

A seismic change in human ideas happened around the time of
the Industrial Revolution (1750–1840), as people moved in droves
from the countryside to the cities. It was the 'Age of Enlightenment',
but urban areas were black from coal soot, noisy engines were
everywhere, science was demystifying the universe and faith in
God was shaken. As a response, the Romantic movement in art
and literature looked nostalgically to the past with paintings of
medieval castles set in dreamy, pristine landscapes. Across Europe,
North America and South America, literature and poetry set trends
with their love-struck protagonists who were willing to die for their
feelings. Early examples are the novel *The Sorrows of Young
Werther* (1774) by the German writer Johann Wolfgang von
Goethe and *Lyrical Ballads* (1798) by the British poets William
Wordsworth and Samuel Taylor Coleridge.

     By the 1820s the aesthetic had trickled down into fashion, as
ladies sought to emulate the heroines of their favourite novels.
The prevalent Minimalist (p.252) neoclassical style, with its simple
column silhouette, Empire line gathered just below the bust, and
classic monochrome palette, gave way to the Maximalist (p.254)
Romantic style, which emphasized a curvy figure. The waist was
accentuated with corsets and sash belts, and wide skirts were
balanced almost equally at the shoulder with gigot sleeves, also
called 'leg-o'-mutton' sleeves in reference to their shape. The
effect was light-hearted and joyful, with bright colours and
naturalistic prints, often festooned with ribbons and bows.

     The deep V-neck of a day dress could be covered for modesty
(or in a draughty room) with a chemisette that gave the impression
of a blouse or undershirt peeping through. By night, décolletage
and off-the-shoulder styles were popular. A small cape called a
pelerine was draped over the shoulders and the back of the neck,

Romantic cont.

a throwback to the garment worn underneath armour
in the fifteenth century, but elevated through the use of such
luxurious fabrics as silk. The popular novels of Sir Walter Scott,
meanwhile, initiated a fad for tartan, and for men, Cossack trousers
were fashionable after Tsar Aleksandr I's trip to Britain in 1814.

The Dandy movement (p.247) had shifted menswear towards
the wearing of Tailoring (p.195), with tailcoats in navy, black, brown
and green, paired with lighter-coloured trousers. There were dress
coats for formalwear, paired with frilled cotton shirts, and morning
coats for more casual occasions, the latter worn with breeches
and boots for riding (see also Equestrian, p.70). Waistcoats were
a layering essential, and helped to enhance the chest, giving the
impression of a muscular physique. Some men resorted to padding
their jackets for the same reason. Elaborate neckwear was the
legacy of the dandies and consisted of either a cravat or a stock
tie – a tall, stiffened band around the neck that helped to keep the
head upright and would provide support in the case of a fall from
a horse. The look was completed with a top hat.

Romanticism is a strong influence in today's fashion collections.
It is invoked everywhere there are breezy, diaphanous fabrics,
prints of flora and fauna, full skirts and ruffled shirts. In London, it
can be seen in the balloon sleeves of Simone Rocha, the delicate
florals at Erdem, and dresses made from clouds of tulle at Molly
Goddard. In Milan, the house of Valentino has made the Romantic
look its signature, even down to its iconic red hue, which –
according to the house's founder, Valentino Garavani – conveys
energy, life, passion and love.

Molly Goddard Autumn/Winter 2019–20 Ready-to-Wear, London Fashion Week, 16 February 2019.

COLOURS AND PATTERNS: pale pink, crimson, magenta, cream, dove grey, lilac, ditzy floral prints, tartan

FABRICS: satin, chiffon, lace, voile, tulle, soft wool, velvet, cashmere, gauze

GARMENTS AND ACCESSORIES: blouse, dress, slip dress, scarves, camisole, wrap, tulip skirt, choker, cameo brooches, pelerine, fluted sleeves, cravat, stock, chemisette, Cossack trousers, dress coat, morning coat, frock coat, waist belt

DETAILS: ruffles, sweetheart necklines, deep V necklines, strapless, heart symbols, loose-fitting, roses, pearls, drop earrings, fine jewellery, peplums, scalloped hems, bows, square neck, basque waist

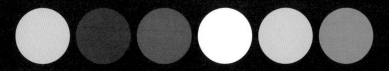

New Romantic

- BLITZ KIDS, NEW DANDIES, ROMANTIC REBELS, PEACOCK PUNK
- GLAM ROCK, PUNK, ROMANTIC, ANDROGYNOUS
- PIRATE, DANDY, MAXIMALIST, ROCOCO

It's 1979, and on Tuesday nights in London's Covent Garden, there is a queue snaking around the block to get into the Blitz Club. It's a place where art-school and aspiring New Wave music talent can embrace glamour in a way that Punk (p.125) didn't offer. On the door is the club promoter Steve Strange, later part of the band Visage. Strange is the gatekeeper, and if you aren't dressed appropriately, you don't get in, as Mick Jagger famously discovered when he was turned away for being too Rock & Roll (p.110).

The Blitz look was inspired by the dazzle of such Glam Rock (p.122) greats as David Bowie, Marc Bolan and Roxy Music, as well as the foppish Romantic style (p.263) of the late eighteenth and early nineteenth century, along with the French subculture of the Incroyables (see Rococo, p.257), 1930s cabaret and a general sense of theatricality. The movement coincided with Vivienne Westwood's 'Pirate' collection (p.102), which was the look used by her partner Malcolm McLaren to restyle Adam Ant into a hussar jacket (see Military, p.91), bicorne hat and breeches. Against a backdrop of hazy synthesizers and electronic beats, it felt progressive, Androgynous (p.270) and non-binary. The trend was for heavily powdered faces, beauty spots, quiffs and pompadour hairstyles inspired by such artists as Boy George of Culture Club, who was known for his high-fashion make-up looks.

Ant and many other bands publicly rejected the label 'New Romantic'. Nevertheless, this was a tidy way for the music and style press (new indie mags The Face and iD sprang up at around the same time) to organize this distinct but short-lived aesthetic from such bands as Duran Duran and Spandau Ballet, who wrote songs to tug at the heartstrings.

Steve Strange and Julia at the Blitz Club, London, 13 February 1980.

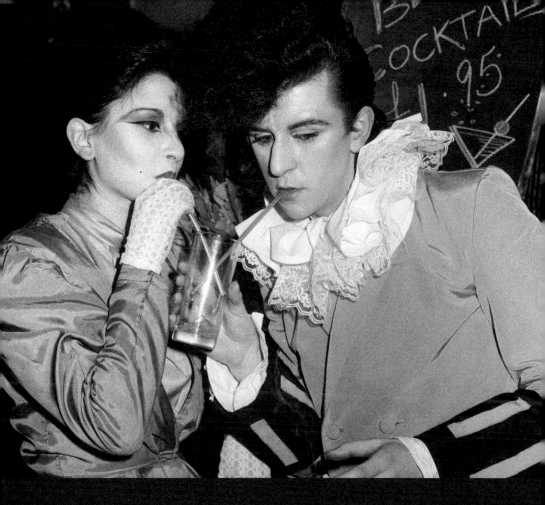

COLOURS AND PATTERNS: black, white, red, tartan, harlequin

FABRICS: satin, velvet, leather, lace, sequins

GARMENTS AND ACCESSORIES: cravat, poet shirt, waistcoat, biker jacket, breeches, pantaloons and stockings, bicorne hat, brooches, hair clips, leather trousers, headbands, statement earrings, pork-pie hat, trilby, bandanas, choker, cape, ruff, Cossack trousers, slouchy ankle boots, long gloves

DETAILS: ruffles, asymmetrical, feathers, embroidery, glitter, gigot sleeves, pearls, rhinestones

HAIR AND MAKE-UP: asymmetrical, side-swept, long fringe, eyeliner, eyeshadow

Sex &

8.

The final stop on this aesthetic tour takes in styles that speak about gender presentation and attitudes towards sex and sexuality. Gender stereotypes have been constructed and deconstructed at several key points in time. As part of the Great Renunciation, which took place after the French Revolution of 1789, men quickly cast aside their high heels and foppish lace. It took more than two centuries for men to be accepted wearing 'women's' clothes again (outside cultural exceptions, such as kilts); women claimed back Tailoring (p.195) far more quickly. Coco Chanel borrowed menswear details for her collections in the early twentieth century, and some Flappers (p.30) favoured the boyish garçonne style. Others, such as the Weimar-era actor Marlene Dietrich, pushed it further, wearing tuxedos and classic men's suits to mixed reactions of shock and admiration.

Androgynous women were the exception to the gender-normative rule, however, and wartime starlets posed suggestively for cards that were pinned to barrack walls and lusted over by lonely soldiers. Back home, taste, grace and feminine style were the foundation of many a respectable woman's wardrobe, from suburban housewives to the First Lady of the United States.

The notion of camp entered public consciousness in the same breath as the Irish poet and personality Oscar Wilde. Queer culture bloomed in the shadows, pushed to the edges of society. In the United Kingdom, the age

Gender

of consent for gay men was equalled to that of heterosexuals only in 2001, with the Criminal Justice and Public Order Act. In the United States, the case of *Lawrence* v. *Texas* in 2003 finally overruled the Supreme Court's judgment on the criminalization of 'sodomy', a judgment that had stood for 17 years. In 2009 drag, which had begun at the very end of the nineteenth century, click-clacked its way from the fringes to the mainstream via reality television. But there are many places in the world where cross-dressing is still taboo.

Technically, all clothes are a form of modest dress, but devout followers of Islam, Christianity and Judaism follow rules about displaying their bodies. Modest wear is an emerging trend among secular consumers, too, as an act of personal expression. Conversely, there are those who exhibit the body consciously, in barely-there slips of fabric. In the most accepting environments, fetish- and bondage-inspired garments in latex and leather are somehow wearable.

Whoever or whatever one desires, gender and sex can be used to paint the colours of self-identity.

Androgynous

⊜ UNISEX, GENDER-FLUID, NON-BINARY
⬤ HERITAGE, GLAM ROCK, CAMP, DRAG, LADYLIKE
⊕ ATHLEISURE, TAILORING, SKATE, ROMANTIC

Androgyny, from the Greek *andros*, 'man', and *gyne*, 'woman', means containing both masculine and feminine elements. In the context of the fashion industry, androgyny essentially comes down to one of three scenarios: a person presenting as gender non-binary; a woman presenting as a man; or a man presenting as a woman.

Of course, what is deemed 'masculine' or 'feminine' in terms of dress is brought about by social conditioning. In many parts of the world the wearing by men of 'skirt'- or 'dress'-type garments is the norm, and part of their Heritage (p.23): for example the *dhoti* in India, the kilt in Scotland and the *kanzu* in parts of Africa. Androgyny is different from Drag (p.278), which is the short-term expression of another gender, usually exaggerated for performative reasons. Cross-dressing is the correct term for wearing clothes that are more commonly worn by another gender.

Styles such as Tailoring (p.195) have long transcended gender, while dresses, halter-neck tops, strapless tops, high heels and lacy blouses are still marketed predominantly to women. Despite this, there is an increasing trend for people to shop outside their prescribed section within a store, and to wear whatever they like. Retailers are catching up, and some offer 'unisex' ranges, although these garments tend to be loose-fitting and boxy, so as to accommodate a variety of body shapes. Athleisure (p.60) can work as ungendered, especially wide track pants, baseball caps, oversized T-shirts and trainers. Similarly, casual androgynous styles can borrow elements from Skate style (p.231) with loose board shorts and hoodies.

For women, an androgynous silhouette employs lines that skim the breasts, waist and hips. The emphasis is on a long, lean profile, and on playing up traditional 'menswear-inspired' pieces, such as suiting in City pinstripes, shirts, ties and brogues. Heavier fabrics, such as wool, tweed and leather, toughen the look. Skin can also

Jean Paul Gaultier Haute Couture, Paris Fashion Week, 7 July 2021.

be used to denote gender traits, and revealing the arms while wearing loose-fitting sleeveless vests can make an outfit feel more masculine.

Conversely, androgynous men emphasize the waist with corsets and waist belts, layering traditionally feminine garments in lighter fabrics, such as lace, satin and sheer organza, as well as chintzy floral prints. Crop tops, off-the-shoulder tops, cut-away details and Romantic blouses (p.263) help to steer the look away from classic menswear. At its most elegant, the look becomes Ladylike (p.281), or, if theatrical, it can veer towards Camp (p.275).

What helps the aesthetic become genderless is partly attributed to the wearer, and to the hair and make-up choices that complete the look. For male-presenting women, short, boyish hairstyles and skin-based make-up looks with strong eyebrows and muted lips help to push the creative direction, while for female-presenting men, growing their hair, embracing romantic curls, doing creative make-up looks and wearing nail polish can create ambiguity for the viewer.

Androgynous cont.

There is a precedent for androgyny on the catwalks through the legacy of such designers as Jean Paul Gaultier, who debuted 'men's skirts' (in reality, kilts) on the runway in 1983, raising eyebrows at the time. The <u>Avant-Garde</u> (p.244) work of such designers as Rei Kawakubo removed gender from the equation altogether. Gender codes have since been explored on the catwalks by several designers, among them the Irish talent Jonathan Anderson, who for his Autumn/Winter 2013 collection presented scalloped-edge shorts and a strapless top, interspersed with more gender-normative pieces.

<u>COLOURS AND PATTERNS</u>: MP (male-presenting): black, grey, <u>pinstripe</u>, <u>chalk stripe</u>; FP (female-presenting): pale pink, peach, lilac

<u>FABRICS</u>: MP: wool, leather, <u>tweed</u>; FP: lace, satin, organza, silk, lamé, marabou feathers

<u>GARMENTS AND ACCESSORIES</u>: MP: suit, waistcoat, <u>blazer</u>, chinos, trousers, <u>oxford shoes</u>, brogues, braces (suspenders), shirt, top hat, pork-pie/<u>newsboy</u>/baker-boy/trucker hat, tank top, board shorts, hoody, sweatshirt, combat boots, Converse; FP: dress, skirt, crop top, halter-neck top, high-waisted tight trousers, corset

<u>DETAILS</u>: MP: straight cut, oversized, tailored; FP: hourglass figure, pearls, ruffles, pussy bow

<u>HAIR AND MAKE-UP</u>: MP: short hair, muted make-up, strong eyebrows; FP: long hair, curls, nail polish

Garçonne

● TOMBOY
◐ AVIATOR, TAILORING
⊕ FLAPPER, ATHLEISURE

The word 'garçonne' is derived from the French *garçon*, 'boy', with a feminine ending. It is usually translated into English as 'tomboy', although this quaint word, conjuring images of rough-and-tumble play and tree climbing, does not adequately reflect its sophisticated origins.

After centuries of rib-crushing steel- and whalebone-reinforced corsets, new clothing styles liberated the women of the 1920s. The garçonne is technically an extension of the Flapper style (p.30), and refers specifically to the straight-cut, dropped-waist dress with a hemline that swished around the knees, a garment made fashionable by such designers as Coco Chanel. Magazines celebrated a slim, boyish figure and flappers cut their hair short and slicked it down into an 'Eton crop', as worn by the American dancer Josephine Baker, to show to advantage the elegant curve of sleek cloche hats.

For the first time, women in the media spotlight were allowed to present an alternative view of their gender, in practical trousers and jackets, such as the pilot Amelia Earhart (see also Aviator, p.63), who first crossed the Atlantic in 1928 as a passenger in an aeroplane. Earhart completed the mission solo in 1932, but disappeared while flying in 1937. Her fellow aviator Ruth Elder had failed in her attempt to cross the ocean by plane in 1927, but returned to a hero's welcome and went on to star

Marlene Dietrich in the film *Morocco*, 1930.

273

Garçonne cont.

in the popular films *Moran of the Marines* (1928) and *The Winged Horseman* (1929).

Garçonne was also the title of a progressive Weimar-era lesbian publication, and in general, at this time, Germany underwent a significant cultural shift. The actor Marlene Dietrich epitomized the look in suits, shirts and neckties for daywear, and famously in her tuxedo and top hat in the film *Morocco* (1930; see Tailoring, p.195). She is an enduring style icon of the era, being initiated into Berlin's cabaret scene and its hedonistic nightlife before ascending to Hollywood stardom.

COLOURS AND PATTERNS: black, silver, mahogany, white, geometric

FABRICS: cotton, wool, jersey, artificial silk

GARMENTS AND ACCESSORIES: tie, neck scarf, high-waisted trousers, hat, dress, strings of pearls, straight-cut dress, cloche hat, stockings, suit

DETAILS: pleats, dropped waist

HAIR AND MAKE-UP: side-swept bob, Eton crop, Marcel wave, plum-red lips

Camp

≈ N/A
→ NEO-VICTORIANA, NAUTICAL, BOURGEOISIE, ANDROGYNOUS
⊕ KIDCORE, DANDY, MAXIMALIST, ROCOCO, ROMANTIC, NEW ROMANTIC, DRAG, PIN-UP

Camp is a deliciously abstract concept. Many have attempted to define it, notably the American writer and philosopher Susan Sontag in her brief essay 'Notes on "Camp"' (1964). The essay inspired the theme for the Costume Institute's exhibition 'Camp: Notes on Fashion' at the Metropolitan Museum of Art in New York City in 2019, and a wider discussion of camp within the fashion sector.

According to Sontag, 'camp' is a seriousness that fails, a taste for the Androgynous (p.270), a flair for the unnatural and the exaggerated, and ambitions of greatness that go too far. She distinguished between deliberate camp, which is conscious, and

Lady Gaga and Brandon Maxwell attend the Met Gala celebrating the opening of the exhibition 'Camp: Notes on Fashion', New York, 6 May 2019.

Camp cont.

naive camp, which is unconscious. To add to this definition, the Drag queen Ru Paul (p.278) said eloquently in an interview that camp is seeing the facade of life, and being in on the joke. The word was first used as a verb in the French writer Molière's play *The Deceits of Scapin* (1671), to describe actions and gestures of exaggerated emphasis: 'Camp about on one leg. Put your hand on your hip. Wear a furious look. Strut about like a drama king.'

By the mid-nineteenth century the word was being used as an adjective within the queer community. In 1870 two Victorian men, Ernest Boulton and Frederick Park (better known to their friends by their aliases, Stella and Fanny), dressed as women, were arrested and charged with 'the abominable crime of buggery'. Fanny lamented to a friend in a letter that their '"campish" undertakings were not at present meeting with the success which they deserve'. It was difficult for the prosecution to prove that the pair had gone beyond the lesser misdemeanour of 'personating a woman', however, and after a second trial they were found not guilty.

Sontag dedicated her essay to Oscar Wilde, and it was via this Irish poet that the word came to be associated with a person. Wilde was a leader of the Aesthetic Movement (see Neo-Victoriana, p.26), and Sontag considered that camp, at its core, was a kind of aestheticism. It went beyond usual aesthetic notions of art, beauty and materiality to encompass 'the degree of artifice, of stylization'. Wilde quipped with his usual wit in *Phrases and Philosophies for the Use of the Young* (1894) that 'The first duty in life is to be as artificial as possible. What the second duty is no one has as yet discovered.' Followers of the movement adopted the gaudy sunflower as their symbol.

The visual style is necessarily associated with gay culture, but not always. Camp is a model on the catwalk of Jean Paul Gaultier, dressed as a wanton sailor (see Nautical, p.98). It is extravagant and showy, and in that respect works well with Rococo styles (p.257). It is flowery and emotive, and sometimes draws on Romantic symbolism (p.263). Sontag described it as middle-class pretentiousness, and in that sense it is Bourgeois (p.202). One logo is not camp. A whole fabric of repeated designer logos is camp. This style refuses to grow up, and so has some crossover with Kidcore (p.175). It is wildly theatrical, and there is common ground with costume and Cosplay (p.158).

COLOURS AND PATTERNS: magenta, orange, lime green, lilac, gold, zebra, Pride rainbow, repeated logos

FABRICS: tulle, satin, polyester, faux fur, PVC, lamé, velvet, sequins, plastic-coated, patent leather

GARMENTS AND ACCESSORIES: top hat, gown, dress, platform shoes, cloak, bell-bottomed trousers, fascinator, shoulder pads, statement earrings, tiara, bracelets

DETAILS: feathers, rhinestones, ruffles, fringing, appliqué, slogans, train, Peter Pan collar

Drag

◉ DRAG QUEEN, DRAG KING
➡ CARNIVAL, COSPLAY, ANDROGYNOUS
➕ MAXIMALIST, ROMANTIC, CAMP

The etymology of the word 'drag' has been attributed to several
sources. Some say it's an acronym for 'dressed as a girl'; others
attribute it to nineteenth-century theatre slang, from the feeling
of long skirts trailing on the floor; or it could hark back to dressing
in 'grand rag' at masked balls (see Carnival, p.152).

Drag usually takes the form of a man impersonating a woman
for performative reasons (the 'drag queen'), although it can
be a woman impersonating a man (the 'drag king'), and, very
occasionally, a woman exaggerating her feminine attributes in drag
(the so-called bio queen). Drag is not about questioning gender
identity, but rather a means of self-expression available to all sexes
and genders. That said, most drag queens have historically been
cisgender gay men, and drag is an integral part of gay culture.

The early days of drag were dangerous. The first person to be
documented as a drag queen was William Dorsey Swann, who was
born into slavery in the United States and in adult life was known to
his friends as 'the Queen'. In 1896 he was arrested and imprisoned
for throwing a drag ball, and he is said to be the first American to
pursue legal action to defend the rights of the queer community to
gather. In the 1920s and 30s in Harlem, New York, ballroom culture
started at a meeting spot called Hamilton Lodge, attracting media
curiosity. An article in the *New York Age* in 1926 reported that men
'in their gorgeous evening gowns, wigs, and powdered faces were
hard to distinguish from many of the women'. The newspaper also
mentioned that this was an inclusive, multiracial crowd.

The exaggeration of female attributes is distilled into some
Androgynous tricks (p.270), with men who present as women
accentuating the waist with a corset to achieve an hourglass figure.
For drag, there may be the additional help of padding for breasts,
hips and buttocks, always with wigs and dramatic fake eyelashes.
Clothing is designed to be ultra-feminine, so dresses – especially

Sugar attends the MTV premiere screening of *RuPaul's Drag Race* season 15, New York, 5 January 2023.

Drag cont.

gowns with long, trailing skirts and cinched waists – high heels and Romantic details (p.263), such as corsets and lacing, are popular.

Given that drag acts are performers, fabrics follow the direction of stagewear. Sequins and shiny fabrics, such as PVC, catch the light; polyester fabrics are reasonably priced for home sewing; and layers of tulle add volume and softness.

Drag contains many different subsets. 'High drag' is the most Maximalist (p.254), and 'comedy queens' incorporate elements of Camp (p.275). Androgynous drag emphasizes male and female elements, such as a full skirt and corset with a bare male chest, or presents a glamorous non-binary appearance. Some drag performers impersonate famous music artists, such as Madonna, Cher and Tina Turner, and here there is some crossover with Cosplay (p.158).

Drag culture entered the mainstream with the success of the reality television show *Ru Paul's Drag Race*, which after first airing in the United States in 2009 brought sequins, glitter, high jinks and even higher heels into living rooms across the world.

COLOURS AND PATTERNS: pink, leopard print, gold, red, purple, silver, black

FABRICS: polyester, sequins, lamé, tulle, spandex

GARMENTS AND ACCESSORIES: dress, jumpsuit, platform shoes, prosthetic breasts, corset, padding for breasts and buttocks, leotard, kimono-style wrap, leggings, bracelets, choker, necklaces, earrings

DETAILS: hourglass figure, cleavage

HAIR AND MAKE-UP: wig, false eyelashes and false beard for drag kings; exaggerated make-up using foundation, powder, blusher, mascara, highlighter and glitter

Ladylike

≋ POLISHED
→ NAUTICAL, BEATNIK, MODEST
⊕ SLOANE, BCBG, CLASSIC, ROMANTIC

What defines a lady? In style it has come to mean elegance, refinement and soft femininity. The ladylike look reigned in the 1950s and 60s, epitomized by First Lady Jacqueline Kennedy with her endless array of chic shift dresses and boxy two-piece skirt suits, accessorized with white gloves and demure pillbox hats (many of them made by the colourful designer Halston, who was, perhaps unexpectedly, later known for his contribution to the Disco style, p.139).

Jacqueline Kennedy, June 1955.

Key factors in this style are that the outfit looks planned, being styled with consideration, then worn for the rest of the day with easy nonchalance. There are some similarities to Classic (p.209) in that the ladylike look endures as a timeless style that is never out of fashion, and is always a safe bet for a high-class occasion. The palette is understated, containing warm neutrals, such as camel, navy and flesh-toned nudes, cream, and Romantic (p.263) dusky shades of rose and desaturated pastels. There may be judicious accents of leopard print on bags, hats and pointed-toe kitten heels.

The flattering, collarbone-grazing boat-neck shape is associated with this style. It was used on *marinière* shirts by the French Navy in 1858 (see Nautical, p.98), adopted for everyday dress in the 1920s, and made fashionable by Coco Chanel in the 1930s. It was also associated with Beatnik (p.214) style in the 1950s and 60s, when taken in a different direction.

The lady is never vulgar and never flashes excessive skin, so cap or elbow-length sleeves and skirts that sit at or below the knee are appropriate. For evening occasions, though, an off-the-shoulder gown is the lady's secret weapon, offset with diamonds or other fine jewels. It is hard to discuss ladylike dress without mentioning class, and there is some crossover with the aristocratic intentions of the Sloane (p.205) and BCBG (p.207) in the wearing of cardigans, pearls and sensible shoes, always clutching an expensive yet low-key, structured handbag.

The male version of ladylike is 'gentlemanly'. This is usually synonymous with Dandy (p.247) in its meticulous attention to detail.

Grace Kelly, 1950s.

COLOURS AND PATTERNS: beige, navy, duck-egg blue, dusky pink, camel

FABRICS: lace, silk, cashmere, cotton, wool

GARMENTS AND ACCESSORIES: twinset, pencil skirt, circle skirt, ballet pumps, elbow-length gloves, cat-eye sunglasses, oversized sunglasses, pillbox hat, gown, pussy-bow blouse, white cotton shirt, shift dress, coat, trench coat

DETAILS: knee length, midi length, round neck, pointed toes, pearls, ribbons, long sleeves, boat neck

Modest

- N/A
- BODY-CONSCIOUS, PIN-UP, FETISH
- HERITAGE, NEO-VICTORIANA, ATHLEISURE, LAGENLOOK, LADYLIKE

Modest dress is a lens through which most of the styles in this book can be viewed, except those that are diametrically opposite and emphasize sexuality, such as Pin-Up (p.290) and Fetish (p.293). Whether religious, spiritual or as an element of self-expression, modesty is not a universal concept, but varies among countries, religions and cultures.

Abrahamic faiths, such as Christianity, Judaism and Islam, prescribe the covering of certain areas of the body, such as the hair of women, since this is considered potent. It is also deemed proper to cover the knees, elbows, necks and décolletage, and to steer clear of anything overly Body-Conscious (p.287).

Muslim women may wear such styles as the *hijab* (Arabic for 'barrier' or 'partition'), a scarf or shawl worn on the head, neck and shoulders, and sometimes over the chest. The popular *abaya* ('cloak') is a robe-like dress, often black, and similar to a kaftan. It can be worn with a *niqab*, a veil that covers the face but leaves the eye area uncovered. The niqab is often confused with the *burqa*, which is the most concealing and is a one-piece garment that covers the entire body, with a mesh veil over the face, more commonly seen in Afghanistan. The *jilbab*, mentioned in the Qur'an, is a floor-grazing outer garment worn with an undershirt and other modest clothing.

Devout Muslim men pay attention to modesty, too. Examples include the *thawb* (alternatively called *thobe*, *dishdasha* or *jalabiyyah* in different parts of the Middle East), an ankle-length robe with long, wide sleeves, usually worn over the sarong-like *izaar* or *lungi*, perhaps with a *kufi* prayer hat. Additionally, the *thobe* is part of the traditional Heritage dress (p.23) of Palestinian women, and is often intricately embroidered.

From the mid-2010s onwards Muslim models were represented increasingly on the runways of global fashion weeks, with such names

DASKA 2022.

as the Somali-American model Halima Aden breaking through and being referred to as 'supermodels'. Aden made her debut at New York Fashion Week in 2017, and two years later became the first person to wear a hijab on the cover of the magazine *Sports Illustrated*. After achieving her goal of visibility for hijab-wearing models, Aden quit the fashion industry in 2020, speaking out against the way her hijab had been fetishized and how the last two years of her career had caused her 'internal conflict'.

Modesty in Islam is about more than just clothing; it embodies the associated character traits of decorum and discretion, a tradition shared by Jewish culture and known as *tzniut*, referred

Modest cont.

to in the Torah. Orthodox married women shroud their hair when outside the home, and conceal their arms and legs with loose clothing. For men, similarly loose-fitting trousers and shirts may be paired with a head covering, such as a *kippah* or *yarmulke*.

More pious times in the West, such as the Victorian age (see Neo-Victoriana, p.26), have left their legacy on modest dress in pie-crust collars and bishop sleeves. Back then, even a flash of the ankle was deemed improper, and calf-length boots were a practical option, seen poking out from underneath full skirts.

Modest fashion entered global marketing consciousness around the turn of the millennium, and since then ready-to-wear fashion designers, channelling their own needs and experiences, have created high-fashion interpretations that accentuate loose, longline silhouettes with luxurious folds of silk and satin. Modest fashion has also become a trend across social media among secular consumers, as a reaction to the increasingly sexualized designs popularized by fast-fashion brands.

Modest dress remains a politically charged arena for discussion (see also Political, p.260). Those against it argue that it oppresses women, while those who are for it (including many women) argue that it empowers them. The point of contention is freedom of choice.

COLOURS AND PATTERNS: any

FABRICS: silk, satin, cotton jersey, polyester

GARMENTS AND ACCESSORIES: dress, abaya, hijab, jilbab, roll neck, trousers, burkini, cape, cloak, gloves, tights, kaftan, shawl, tunic top

DETAILS: long-sleeves, maxi length

Body-Conscious

≈ BODYCON
➡ <u>AVIATOR</u>, <u>CLASSIC ROCK</u>, <u>ANDROGYNOUS</u>
➕ <u>ATHLEISURE</u>, <u>RAVE</u>, <u>FESTIVAL</u>, <u>MINIMALIST</u>, <u>PIN-UP</u>

The bicycle is the surprising culprit when it comes to the introduction of form-fitting clothes, as pro-emancipation women in the late nineteenth century traded skirts for bloomers so that they could ride more easily astride. Garments that revealed more than they concealed entered the style lexicon in the 1920s with the <u>Flapper</u> (p.30) and her playful approach to hemlines, and shorter skirts were an outward sign of liberation.

By the 1940s and 50s, with the rise of <u>Pin-Up</u> girls (p.290) and the golden age of Hollywood, it was seduction that dictated how tight or short a woman's dress was cut, and the body-conscious style was immortalized on screen by such luminaries as Ava Gardner and Marilyn Monroe. The so-called wiggle dress, also known as a 'pencil dress' or 'sheath dress', has a hem narrower than the hips, which accentuates the wobble of the wearer's derrière as they take short steps. Monroe wore a floor-length flesh-coloured sheath gown encrusted with crystals to sing 'Happy Birthday' to President John F. Kennedy at Madison Square Garden on 19 May 1962. Dubbed 'the naked dress', it drew an audible gasp from the crowd as Monroe slipped off her white fur coat to reveal the glittering second-skin creation by the French costume designer Jean Louis, based on a sketch by the American designer Bob Mackie. The 'naked dress' is still a popular red-carpet choice for those brazen enough to wear it. Such dresses either are sheer, providing a window on to the body underneath (knickers required for decency, bra optional), or employ *trompe-l'œil* to trick the viewer into thinking the wearer is naked when, in fact, they are fully covered.

Textiles evolved to include figure-hugging ribbed jerseys, machine knits or those with a high percentage of elastane (such as Lycra or spandex), which skim the body's contours. Such synthetic fibres are hard to recycle at the end of the garment's life, but they are commonly used in sportswear for their aerodynamic and

Body-Conscious cont.

compression effects. As such, the bodycon style pairs well with such Athleisure (p.60) garments as cycling shorts and leggings. Clothes that allow freedom of movement can be inspired by dance, with leotards and unitards also suitable for clubs (see Rave, p.146) and Festival wear (p.149). The catsuit is a tight-fitting jumpsuit (see also Aviator, p.63). It became popular in the 1960s through the medium of television, with American chanteuse Eartha Kitt slinking across celluloid as the Catwoman in the decade's *Batman* series, and the English actor Diana Rigg becoming a cult figure as Emma Peel, spy extraordinaire and partner of John Steed in *The Avengers*.

The French designer Hervé Léger was famous for his signature bandage dresses, which wrapped around the form and pushed body parts in, up and out, as required. The look defined an era, and the dresses were ubiquitous on red carpets in the 1990s.

Alexander McQueen famously sent ultra-low-rise 'bumsters' down the runway for his Spring/Summer 1994 'Nihilism' collection, and again for his Autumn/Winter 1995 'Highland Rape' collection, revealing what can only be described as buttock cleavage when viewed from behind. The designer later clarified that it was in fact the area at the base of the spine that he was framing. Either way, it set the trend for the waistband height of the mid-2000s. Millennials will remember Paris Hilton, Christina Aguilera, Gwen Stefani, the band Destiny's Child et al. and their uniform of cropped tank tops and jeans sitting so low on the hips that a bikini wax was required.

Male bodycon involves skintight jeans (with or without rips), a 'muscle' T-shirt that shows off the physique, or a shirt unbuttoned to reveal acres of the chest in the manner of a Classic Rock star (p.118). As gender fluidity became normalized in fashion marketing, Androgynous styles (p.270), such as tight-fitting tops with cut-outs and cropped midriffs, gained traction among Gen-Z men.

David Koma Spring/Summer 2022.

Bodycon dressing can be high or low fashion. At its zenith are the creations of the late Tunisian designer Azzedine Alaïa, named the 'King of Cling' by the fashion press for his sculptural take on the female form and celebrated by such powerful women as Grace Jones and Michelle Obama. Maison Alaïa continues his legacy, elevating women into goddesses through sinuous draping. To be sure to stay on the right side of high fashion, stylists for magazine editorial shoots often pair a sleek bodycon dress made from thick, supportive material with a Minimalist 1990s aesthetic (p.252) and pared-back jewellery and accessories, while the make-up artist ensures that any skin on show is buffed, moisturized and ready for the camera.

COLOURS AND PATTERNS: any

FABRICS: crêpe bandage, jersey, machine knits, elastane, velour, chiffon, sheer fabrics

GARMENTS AND ACCESSORIES: camisole, catsuit, bandage dress, pencil skirt, vest, high heels, thigh-high boots, corset, slip dress, cycling shorts, micro-miniskirt, leggings, hot pants

DETAILS: zips, camisole straps, cut-away, asymmetric, cropped, halter-neck, plunge neckline, thigh splits, rips, laser-cut, bumsters, low-rise, low back, fishtail

Pin-Up

● BOMBSHELL, CHEESECAKE
● LOUNGE
● RETRO, COWBOY, NAUTICAL, ROCKABILLY

The idealized female form has been the subject of the male gaze for millennia. In art this arguably dates back to Sandro Botticelli and his *The Birth of Venus* (1485–6), in which the goddess of love emerges like a rare pearl from the ocean, standing on a giant scallop shell. At the time it represented a scandalous departure from conservative Christian iconography.

Although we most commonly associate the pin-up girl with the morale-boosting illustrated cards that soldiers pinned to the walls of their barracks during World War II, similarly coquettish figures were drawn for World War I recruitment posters. They, in turn, were preceded by the pen-and-ink drawings of Charles Dana Gibson, whose comely hourglass heroines, dubbed 'Gibson Girls', graced the pages of *Life* magazine for 20 years from 1895.

In 1930 the Polish-born, Los Angeles-based animator and director Max Fleischer created the first animated on-screen sex symbol with Betty Boop. She was dressed in a black strapless gown, an early incarnation in pop culture of the 'Little Black Dress' (see Classic, p.209). Her suggestive winks, dancing and risqué outfit were toned down to appease prudish censors after the Motion Picture Production Code of 1934, dubbed the 'Hays Code', which was in effect until 1968. Less well known is the fact that Fleischer's character was based on the African-American jazz singer Esther Jones.

Classic 1940s pin-up posters featured ladies caught in various states of accidental undress while performing such mundane tasks as cooking, cleaning, painting fences and walking dogs. Usually, the edge of a full, knee-length circle skirt is caught by a door/ breeze/playful pup to reveal petticoats and shapely legs in stockings, suspenders and high heels. They were drawn from life models by such artists as Earl Moran, Gil Elvgren and Alberto Vargas, and were heavy on Americana, with the winsome ladies

Ava Gardner, c. 1946.

often dressed as titillating cowgirls (see <u>Cowboy</u>, p.79) or sailors (see <u>Nautical</u>, p.98). Peasant blouses or baby-doll dresses slipped carelessly off the wearer's shoulder.

By the 1950s the eroticism had been dialled up, and more obvious states of déshabillé were normalized with a sheer negligee, a type of gauzy dressing gown (see also <u>Lounge</u>, p.179), over brassieres and knickers. Photography as a medium overtook illustration, and aspiring starlets made their names posing for semi-nude shots. Jayne Mansfield, the archetypal blonde bombshell in competition with Marilyn Monroe, gained notoriety wearing a scarlet bikini and posing suggestively on the cover of the newly launched *Playboy* magazine in 1954. While a two-piece swimsuit

Pin-Up cont.

with high briefs was relatively commonplace, the more skimpy
bikini was deemed a particularly scandalous garment and
contravened the Hays Code, which deemed the ribs acceptable
but the navel not. (As a side note, Mansfield was far from the
'dumb blonde' that she often played; she spoke five languages
and had a reported IQ of 162.)

The bikini itself was created by the French designer Louis
Réard, who named it after Bikini Atoll in the Pacific Ocean. The
first atomic bomb test was carried out on these idyllic sands on
1 July 1946, with 22 subsequent detonations. Réard's chosen name
well described the nuclear reaction of the public, as the showgirl
Micheline Bernardini (no 'respectable' fashion model would take
the job) posed for photographs at the bikini's launch that same
year, holding a matchbox to demonstrate how small the garment
could be folded. It gained notoriety in 1951 at the inaugural Miss
World competition, held in the United Kingdom, which included
a bikini contest and was won by Sweden's Kiki Håkansson.

COLOURS AND PATTERNS: red,
white, blue, black, polka dot, leopard
print, stars and stripes

FABRICS: wool, rayon, cotton, denim

GARMENTS AND ACCESSORIES:
halter-neck top, pencil skirt, kitten
heels, cardigan, sheath dress, circle
skirt, waist belt, cat-eye frames,
stilettos, wide-legged trousers,
bikini, high-waisted briefs, one-
piece swimsuit, capri pants, swing
dress, fishnet stockings, headscarf,
gloves, pleated miniskirt, negligee,
petticoats, cone bra, strapless bra,
peasant blouse, strapless dress, high-
waisted shorts, tied-front shirt

DETAILS: sweetheart neckline, halter-
neck, fishtail hem, bows, high waist

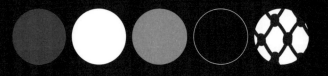

Fetish

● BDSM, BONDAGE, KINK
➡ NAUTICAL, CLASSIC, NEW ROMANTIC, PIN-UP
✛ CYBERPUNK, METAL, PUNK, AVANT-GARDE, BODY-CONSCIOUS

At the most disruptive end of the style spectrum lies clothing inspired by humans' 'kinks'. There is a diverse menu of fetishes, and bondage falls under BDSM, which encompasses bondage and discipline, dominance and submission, and sadomasochism. Bondage means restraint, and in fashion design this is interpreted as straps and harnesses that squeeze and highlight the flesh underneath, such as the luxe dress versions created by Gianni Versace for his Autumn/Winter 1992 'Miss S&M' collection. This bondage-lite symbolism is repeated as a house signature and was reworked by his sister Donatella Versace for Spring/Summer 2022.

Fetishes can include a perverse attraction to latex, a glossy fabric that moulds to the skin. Latex is a naturally derived rubber from the sap of more than 20,000 plant species and is often confused with PVC (polyvinyl chloride), also called vinyl, which is synthetic. Latex is expensive and sustainable, while PVC is cheap and cannot be broken down at the end of its life; both are vegan, however. Waterproofing fabrics with natural rubber was practised by the Aztecs and came into mainstream fashion through the Scottish inventor Charles Macintosh, who launched his famous raincoat in 1824 (see also Nautical, p.98). It wasn't long before a community of rubber lovers sprang up to celebrate the erotic charms of this textile, referring to it as 'macking'. Couture latex can be surprisingly wearable, and the modern Pin-Up (p.290) dresses and skirts by Atsuko Kudo and William Wilde are useful styling pieces to layer with other fabric textures.

It was the Punk subculture (p.125) that first got its teeth into fetishwear, largely through Vivienne Westwood and Malcolm McLaren's store SEX, which opened in 1974 in London. It stocked latex and studded leather garments, such as chaps, zipped trousers, straitjacket-inspired outerwear and corsets, the last reappropriated as a symbol of feminine power rather than subjugation.

Fetish cont.

Richard Quinn Autumn/Winter 2020, London Fashion Week.

The use of latex, bodysuits and/or gimp masks is familiar from Avant-Garde designer runways (p.244). It reared its head in Thierry Mugler's futuristic creations, notably for his Autumn/Winter 1995 couture show. In 2013 the mysterious designer Martin Margiela reinvented the Classic (see p.209) blue-jeans-and-white-tee combination in latex, paired with masks. There was oil-slick-black eveningwear at Moschino by Jeremy Scott for Autumn/Winter 2018 and among Olivier Rousteing's designs for Balmain Autumn/Winter 2019, and offerings from Anthony Vaccarello for Saint Laurent Autumn/Winter 2020 and John Galliano for Christian Dior Autumn/Winter 2003 ready-to-wear.

Provocateur Demna Gvasalia is a regular purveyor of the bodysuit and gimp mask, and his Spring/Summer 2019 collection (before he left Vetements), according to the show notes, was a comment on his terrifying escape from war-torn Georgia in 1993. He revisited the full bodysuit at Balenciaga in 2022, complete with attached gloves, this time minus the mask and in a more accessible stretch fabric that wouldn't look out of place in a dancer's wardrobe (see Body-Conscious, p.287). He rebooted it for a show on Wall

Street, New York, in the spring of 2023. Across the pond, the British designer Richard Quinn is known for juxtaposing skintight bodysuits and full-face masks with chintzy floral dresses and statement coats, and his Autumn/Winter 2022 show closed with the Drag star (p.278) Violet Chachki parading her similarly latex-clad pet gimp on a leash.

An commonly cited source of inspiration for fetishwear is the savagely creative 1980s performance artist and New Romantic (p.266) club kid Leigh Bowery, who was born on the outskirts of Melbourne and made his name in London. Described by Boy George of Culture Club as 'modern art on legs', Bowery gained notoriety as a muse of the artist Lucian Freud, and regularly wore his disturbing masks and suits to such favourite Soho clubs as Heaven and Taboo.

While most consumers leave fetishwear in the bedroom (or dungeon), there are some high-fashion occasions when it is permissible to take it out in public, such as red carpets, fashion weeks, Halloween, or particularly fashion-forward cocktail bars and nightclubs. Just don't forget a safe word.

COLOURS AND PATTERNS:
black, silver

FABRICS: leather, latex, nylon, PVC, patent leather

GARMENTS AND ACCESSORIES:
dress, miniskirt, leggings, gloves, collar, choker, body harness, bodysuit, balaclava, mask, catsuit, trench coat, corset, thigh-high boots, platforms, stilettos, chaps, hood

DETAILS: chains, straps, harnesses, whips, ropes, gags, lacing, padlocks, metal hardware, piercings

Glossary

adire A tie-dyed cloth using indigo to create striking blue-and-white patterns. Traditionally made by Yoruba women of Yorubaland, which encompasses parts of Nigeria, Benin and Togo in West Africa.

alpargatas The Spanish term for rope-soled casual shoes with a canvas upper. In French, the same shoes are called *espadrilles*.

aso-oke A premium cloth handwoven by expert clothmakers of the Yoruba people (see also *adire*). Often striped in bright colours and worn for special occasions to identify family groups.

basque waist A form-fitting bodice that extends past the waist, often with a V-shaped point at the front. The shape originated in the dress of the Basque Country in northern Spain, and was popular during the Victorian era.

bicorne hat A two-cornered hat, famously associated with Napoleon but also introduced by the British Royal Navy in 1827 as part of the dress uniform.

bishop sleeve A full-length sleeve that is more fitted at the top, becoming roomier between elbow and wrist, and gathered into a cuff.

blazer A stand-alone jacket (rather than part of a suit) originally designed in bright colours to identify university rowing teams.

blockchain The technology behind cryptocurrencies, such as bitcoin. It is a public ledger that uses a network of powerful computers to validate transactions with irrefutable certainty.

boater A round hat made of straw, initially worn by Venetian gondoliers. Commonly seen during the summer at outdoor events, such as rowing regattas and tennis tournaments.

bogolan An earth-toned handwoven cloth (also known as 'mud-cloth') and an important symbol of Malian culture. It is dyed using tree leaves and fermented clay that is high in iron, which reacts with the dye to produce the colour black.

boina hat A soft hat from the Basque region of Spain, made from wool or wool felt and originally worn by shepherds. Shaped like a beret, although some have a slight peak.

bolero hat A wide-brimmed, flat-topped hat first worn by Gauchos (p.82) in Argentina and Uruguay.

bolo tie A thin tie made from corded leather with an ornamental clasp and tips. The Native American Hopi, Navajo, Pueblo and Zuni peoples have been silversmithing the decorative clasps since the mid-twentieth century.

bombachas Comfortable, loose-fitting trousers with a tapered hem, worn tucked into boots by Gauchos (p.82) on horseback or with *alpargatas* for walking.

Borsalino hat Headgear made by Borsalino, the oldest Italian luxury hat manufacturer (est. 1857).

Boston A 1950s men's haircut in which the hair is cut straight across the nape of the neck, without tapering.

bouclé From the French for 'loops'. A fabric with a soft, textured appearance, usually made from wool.

bustle A padded undergarment that came into fashion in about 1870 and was worn to add structure and fullness to ladies' skirts. Also known as a 'dress-improver', or in French as a *tournure*.

camp collar A wide, skin-exposing spread collar that allows the wearer to keep cool in hot climates.

chalk stripe An evenly spaced stripe on a plain background that looks as though it is drawn from chalk. Wider than a pinstripe.

Chelsea boot A leather ankle boot with an elasticated panel. Based on the design of a short style of horse-riding boot and named for its popularity in the 1960s with London Mods (p.228), who gravitated towards Chelsea.

chemisette A sleeveless slip of fine cotton and lace that gave the appearance of a blouse when worn under low-cut dresses for modesty, without the bulk of sleeves. A key accessory during the Regency era.

chukka boots Hardwearing low-cut boots usually in tan or brown leather or suede, with a round toe, a thin sole, and two or three eyelets. Thought to originate in India, named after the seven-minute period of play in Polo (p.76) called a *chukka*.

circle skirt A skirt with a basic pattern cut from a circle of cloth, with a central hole for the waist. The full circle, half or quarter of the circle can be used to create varying degrees of fullness in the skirt.

circular economy A model of production and consumption whereby markets aim to eliminate waste and pollution and maximize the use of raw materials through recycling, repairing, refurbishing and sharing.

Cossack trousers Trousers that are full at the thigh, taper towards the foot and have a strap that ties under the instep. They became fashionable in Britain in 1814 after Tsar Aleksandr I visited London, accompanied by his entourage of Cossack soldiers.

cryptocurrency A decentralized digital currency not operated by the banking system and that uses cryptography to encrypt transactions.

dashiki A brightly coloured pull-on tunic top, often with a patterned V-shape at the neck. Originally from West Africa, it spread to African Americans in the 1960s as part of the civil rights and Black Panther movements to celebrate African identity.

deerstalker A cloth hat with bills to the front and rear, and ear flaps, famously associated with the fictional detective Sherlock Holmes.

duster coat A long, loose, lightweight coat originally designed to be thrown on over clothes to protect them when riding down dusty trails.

faja A fabric sash tied as a belt, originally worn by Spanish and Latin-American men and women. Central and South American versions often incorporate local Indigenous designs.

fedora A soft, medium-brimmed hat with a medium crown, usually in felt, creased lengthways with two pinches at the front.

frogging Decorative braiding closures with a knotted button, often used on Military (p.91) coats.

fungible token A fungible token, like real-world currency, is considered identical and dividable. Bitcoin is a fungible cryptocurrency. Compare non-fungible token.

Gen-X An abbreviation of Generation X: people born between 1965 and 1980.

Gen-Z An abbreviation of Generation Z, also known as 'zoomers': people born roughly between 1997 and 2012, after the millennial generation.

go-go boot A boot originally designed by André Courrèges in 1964 and characterized by its square toe, block heel and mid-calf height. Usually shiny and made of vinyl or patent leather.

gyaru A Japanese fashion subculture defined by conspicuous consumption, where girls dress as if they are at high school. *Gyaru* is Japanese for 'gal'.

Harrington jacket A lightweight showerproof jacket with a plaid lining. Named after the character Rodney Harrington (played by Ryan O'Neal) in the 1960s US soap opera *Peyton Place*.

hepcat Originally Flapper-era (p.30) jazz slang for someone stylish; the term grew in popularity in the 1940s and 50s and came to signify members of the unconventional Beat Generation.

herringbone A geometric pattern found in tweed fabrics; also known as 'broken twill weave'. Resembles a fish skeleton, with vertical interlocking chevrons.

hypebeast An enthusiastic follower of the latest streetwear trends, especially trainers/sneakers.

ikat A fabric that is dyed before weaving, from the Malay-Indonesian word *mengikat*, to 'tie' the threads.

isicholo A traditional African crown hat traditionally worn by married Zulu women of South Africa, based on an earlier hairstyle.

jodhpurs Tightly fitted full-length trousers with suede knee patches for horse riding. Named after the historic capital of the Kingdom of Marwar, now in the state of Rajasthan in northern India.

K-pop South Korean popular music that originated in the mid-twentieth century. Linked to the development of idol culture in the 1990s, before resurging as a global trend around 2018 with such international breakthrough bands as BTS and Blackpink. The music itself spans several genres.

kente cloth A brightly patterned cloth woven from strips of fabric, originating from the Asante people of the Akan kingdom, in present-day Ghana. Many of the patterns are symbolic and are connected to local proverbs or families. Originally commissioned by royalty and now worn by community leaders and on special occasions.

kepi hat A structured flat-top cap with a straight visor originally used by the French Army and police, replacing the more cumbersome shako. Also used by both sides fighting the American Civil War.

kitenge A multipurpose African cloth with intricate patterns achieved through wax-resist dyeing.

kogal An English-sounding adaptation of Japanese *kogyaru*, itself a contraction of *kōkōsei gyaru* ('high-school gal'). Refers to a style of dress that emerged from Kawaii (p.170).

kutte jacket (battle jacket) A denim or leather jacket with sleeves cut off, covered with DIY patches and slogans, studs, chains and spikes, traditionally pledging allegiance to a band or biker gang.

letterman jacket A Varsity (p.193) jacket, originally awarded to athletes selected for university sports teams in the United States.

Louis XV heel A curved medium-height heel with a narrow waist and a splayed foot inset under the shoe.

Madras check A lightweight cotton plaid design, often brightly coloured, named after a city (now Chennai) in southeastern India.

mandarin collar A stiff standing collar, straight or curved at the front, with a gap or overlapping. Used in China since the Ming Dynasty (1368–1644), but given its Western name, 'mandarin', later by the Portuguese, from *mandarim* ('counsellor'), as the Europeans first described the Chinese officials who wore it. Sometimes fastened with *pankou* knots, the Chinese term for frogging.

Mary Jane shoes Simple low-heeled shoes with a round toe and a strap or 'bar' across the top of the foot. Named after a comic strip about Buster Brown and his sister Mary Jane, which first appeared in the *New York Herald* in 1902.

metaverse An iteration of the internet conceived as a universal immersive virtual world. It is virtual, but not virtual reality unless immersive tech is used, such as virtual- and augmented-reality headsets.

millennial People born between 1981 and 1996.

Newmarket stripe A golden-yellow fabric with red-and-black stripes, originally used for blankets to keep racehorses warm and named after the famous racecourse in Suffolk, eastern England.

newsboy cap (baker-boy cap) A roomy soft cap, usually made from panels, with a hard peak visor. Can be differentiated from other types of flat cap by the button on the top.

non-fungible token A unique digital asset that cannot be replicated. Compare fungible token.

oxford shirt A shirt with a button-down collar, inspired by Polo (p.76) players' habit of pinning down their lapels to stop them from flapping. Made from oxford cloth, a heavy, durable, naturally breathable fabric woven in Scottish mills. More versatile than a dress shirt, it can be styled formally with a tie and/or jacket, or casually with a T-shirt or jumper.

oxford shoe (Balmoral shoe) In a true oxford shoe, the lacing is closed and the shoelace eyelets stitched down to the vamp (midsection). It can be plain leather or two-tone. Originated in Ireland and Scotland; students at Oxford University later adopted the design as a practical option for the short walk or bicycle ride to lectures.

pannier (hoop) A structured undergarment historically made from metal, whalebone or cane and worn under a skirt to create a wide-hipped silhouette. Popular in the eighteenth century and seen in Rococo fashions (p.257).

Peter Pan collar An exaggerated flat, rounded collar that owes its name to a version worn by the actor Maude Adams in the Broadway version of *Peter and Wendy* in 1905.

pie-crust collar A standing, ruffled collar resembling the pinched crust around the edge of a pie. Popular on shirts in the Victorian and Edwardian eras; came back into fashion in the 1980s.

pinstripe A very thin stripe reminiscent of pinheads. Compare the wider chalk stripe.

poet shirt A loose-fitting shirt with bishop sleeves, often with frills at neckline and cuffs.

pompadour A hairstyle in which the hair is swept up and back, with volume at the crown to create a sleek finish. (In contrast, a quiff is brushed forwards.) Popular for men in the 1950s.

Prince of Wales check Based on Glen plaid check. Updated by the Prince of Wales (later briefly Edward VIII) to include colourful overchecks in bold colours (see windowpane check), setting trends in high society.

scene A subset of the Emo (p.129) subculture that focuses on style rather than music.

shako hat A structured stovepipe-shaped Military (p.91) cap with a hard peak, usually with a metallic badge on the front, and sometimes topped with a plume of feathers known as a 'hackle' or pompom.

shawl collar (shawl lapel) A curved fold-over collar. Often seen on cardigans; more structured satin versions appear on tuxedos and smoking jackets.

sombrero A wide-brimmed, high-crowned sun hat that fastens under the chin, made from felt or straw. Originated in the fifteenth century, named after the Spanish word *sombra* ('shade'), and became popular in North and South America with cattle herders, preceding the Cowboy (p.79) hat.

Stetson An American heritage hat brand founded in 1865 by John B. Stetson, said to be the inventor of the Cowboy (p.79) hat.

Tilley hat Headgear by Tilley, a Canadian company (est. 1980) known for its expedition headwear.

Transhumanism The philosophical concept that humanity can evolve as a race, beyond mortality and morphology, using technology.

trilby hat A soft hat, similar to a fedora but with a narrower brim. Popular in the 1960s as higher hats fell out of favour, being inconvenient to drive in.

tweed A twill-woven wool textile that originated in Scotland, where it proved warm and weather-resistant. Can be plain or striped, checked (with small checks), with large squares (windowpane check), houndstooth and its smaller puppytooth variation, and plaid. Gun check is the same as houndstooth but in natural colours, to serve as camouflage for hunters, and may feature an overcheck or over-plaid, in which case it may be called 'estate' or 'gamekeepers' check.

twill A durable weave characterized by its diagonal appearance, often with a dark front surface and a paler back. Yarns of different colours can be used to achieve patterns.

twinset A matching jumper and cardigan that are worn together.

ukara Blue-and-white-patterned cotton cloth from parts of Nigeria and Cameroon, resist-dyed in indigo using raffia sewn on to the fabric.

windowpane check An oversized square check formed by perpendicular pinstripes. A windowpane check on top of another check or pattern is known as an overcheck (see tweed).

winklepicker A long, sharply pointed toe named after the sticks used to prise periwinkles (a popular snack at the English seaside) out of their shells. It can be seen on shoes and boots.

Picture Credits

Index

Page numbers in *italic* refer to the illustrations.

301

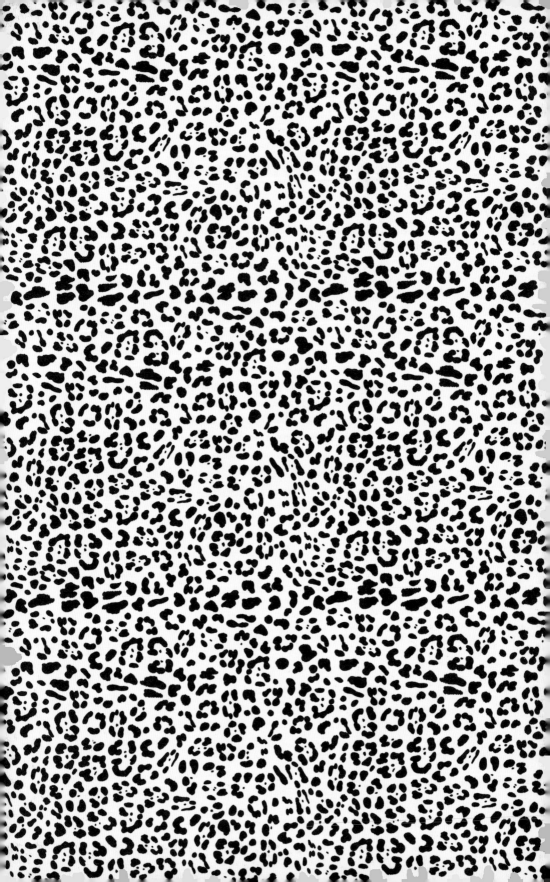